THIS IS NEW JERSEY

THIS IS
NEW JERSEY

FOURTH EDITION

JOHN T. CUNNINGHAM

RUTGERS UNIVERSITY PRESS

New Brunswick, New Jersey

Cunningham, John T.
    This is New Jersey / John T. Cunningham. — 4th ed.
        p.   cm.
    Includes index.
    ISBN 0-8135-2140-8 (cloth) — ISBN 0-8135-2141-6 (pbk.)
    1. New Jersey—History, Local.   2. New Jersey—Description and
travel.   I. Title.
F134.C86   1994
974.9—dc20   94-25942
                                              CIP

for Jay and Ruth

CONTENTS

PREFACE
Accidental Historian

New Jersey became a full-time vocation—and avocation—for me in 1952, at a time when as a young journalist I had little interest in the state and no enthusiasm for New Jersey history. My goals did not include either the writing of books or becoming an historian. Then, in the spring of 1952, Lloyd Felmly, editor of the *Newark Sunday News*, freed me from my desk in the city room to travel throughout New Jersey to write brief histories of each of the state's twenty-one counties. It was bold venture by the *News*: no New Jersey writer before had been presented that challenge and that opportunity. I could go wherever I wished, take all the time I needed, write as I wanted. It became a dream assignment that dramatically transformed me and changed my life forever. I wandered across the state, through hardwood forests in the northwest and deep into the mysterious Pine Barrens of the south. I found local historians with vast knowledge of their heaths and local historical society libraries, where priceless treasures awed me.

As the articles began appearing in the *Sunday News*, Rutgers University Press asked me to consider the materials as the basis for a book. The articles required little editing; historians who read them for the Press vouched for their accuracy; some praised the readability. The only major change was grouping the counties by region rather than alphabetically as they had appeared in the *News*. In the autumn of 1953 my "Cavalcade of Counties" (the *Sunday News*'s title) became the handsome first edition of *This Is New Jersey*. The book appeared in bookstore windows in mid-November, just in time for the Christmas market. Within two weeks *This Is New Jersey* went back on press for a second printing.

Overnight I had become an author, in demand at author luncheons and, to my considerable surprise, at annual meetings of historical societies in every county. I also had become a historian, not by degrees but by a commitment to accuracy and a journalistic intent to write with readability and reliability.

Life swept me along in a lively current. Rutgers Press published three more of my books, *Made in New Jersey, Garden State*, and *The New Jersey Shore*. New Jersey Bell Telephone Company made a celebrated movie based on *This Is New Jersey* and, fortunately for me (and for sales of the book), used the title. Nearly eight million people saw the film over a fifteen-year period.

One of those who saw the movie was George Long, a senior editor of *National Geographic* magazine, who acquired my book and then assigned me to write the *Geographic*'s cover article, "I'm from New Jersey," for the January 1960 issue.

The first edition of *This Is New Jersey* went through five printings before rapid changes sweeping the state forced a second edition in 1968 and the third edition in 1978.

Consider what has happened in New Jersey since I began my explorations. Neither the New Jersey Turnpike nor the Garden State Parkway had been completed in 1952. A trip from Newark to Cape May required at least four-and-a-half to five hours—far longer on a hot July Saturday. Route 9, two lanes much of the way, was the only "major" road from heavily populated northern New Jersey to the Jersey Shore.

New Jersey then had more than 25,000 farms, including several in Essex County and even a few in Hudson. Holstein milk cows abounded on the slopes of Warren and Sussex counties; Sussex boasted that it had more cows than people. Nearly twenty million Leghorn chickens laid close to three billion eggs annually, mainly in Hunterdon, Ocean, and Cumberland counties. Today, most of the milk cows are gone; chickens are a fading memory. Two-thirds of the 1952 farms disappeared by 1990.

Government largess in the so-called "G.I. Bill of Rights" enabled World War II veterans the opportunity to own homes guaranteed by the United States government. By 1952 developers were transforming pastures and vegetable fields into homes in wide arcs around major cities. Most of the new homes housed veterans.

Cities rode high in 1952, filled with commerce, entertainment, notable stores, and economic vigor. Every New Jersey city, from Camden to Newark, from Jersey City to Trenton, had at least one fine hotel. Every city nurtured scores of industries; Newark had more than one thousand. Business and industry had not yet begun to desert cities for modern "campuses" in the hinterlands. That would come soon enough. New Jersey became the most urban and most densely populated state in the nation by 1970. Urbanization continues outward along the Parkway, the Turnpike, and the Interstates, turning erstwhile pasturelands into cities without downtowns, unless malls can be called today's downtowns.

But the state is NOT all concrete, not all urban sprawl. It is a fascination of contradictions: the huge county parks adjacent to Newark; the heralded environmental struggles that saved the Great Swamp and much of the Pine Barrens; the eternal appeal of the Jersey Shore and the eerie nighttime quiet in the Kittatinny Mountains. I know New Jersey, in all hours of the day and night, in all seasons of the year, in all the centuries of its history. I am fully, peacefully at home in my own state.

My only regret is that most of my original local tutors who gave me the basis for knowing New Jersey are deceased but it gives me pleasure to know that three of them, Arlene Reasoner Sayre Newby, Richard P. McCormick, and Roger McDonough remain friends, for they showered me with kindness and knowledge as a way of sharing New Jersey with me. I am grateful.

This edition is enhanced by the first appearance of Walter Choroszewski in *This Is New Jersey*. A noted, gracious photographer of a New Jersey whose beauty he celebrates, Walter is a good friend. His work appears more than one hundred times in this book, including all of the representations in the color section.

JOHN T. CUNNINGHAM

Florham Park, New Jersey
Autumn, 1994

THIS IS NEW JERSEY

THE SPIRIT OF NEW JERSEY

You watch the moon cut a silver path across Lake Hopatcong or you climb Sunrise Mountain in Stokes State Forest to look at sun-bathed Kittatinny Valley. You watch cattle picking at grass on rocky slopes in northwest Jersey or you stop to see a maple tree tapped for syrup at Newfoundland.

. . . and television comedians get roars of laughter merely by mentioning "Joisey."

You wake up in a Bridgeton hotel on a beautiful August morning, and the delightful aroma of spices seeping through the window tells you forcibly that it's catsup time again in South Jersey.

. . . and all over America people think New Jersey smells like the Secaucus meadows.

The wind whistles through stunted trees as you shuffle across the sand beneath old Barnegat Lighthouse, and dark clouds scudding overhead foretell an impending October seaside storm, one of nature's most impelling spectacles.

. . . and millions of people think the Jersey Shore is just a long boardwalk or acres of burning skin.

You look at dozens of two-hundred-year-old houses in old Salem or you see the charm of the old churches at Tennent, Shrewsbury, and Middletown. You sit on the fishing docks along the canals in Sea Isle City or you watch the oyster fleet come in at Bivalve.

. . . and wonder why all roads lead to New England.

Climbing the water tower in the Batsto Mansion to look out over hundreds of square miles of almost unbroken pinelands, you contrast this vast wilderness with the Essex County view off Eagle Rock, where the eye encompasses the most densely settled section of America.

. . . and you're glad you are in New Jersey.

The words above were written by me in 1953. They remain valid forty years later except that the "aroma of spices" in Bridgeton (and even the hotel) is gone, the cattle are diminishing, and the oyster fleet is stilled. Despite the addition of three million people and traffic-generating superhighways, it is still easy to find serenity and beauty. The more New Jersey changes, the more it remains the same. Familiarity with New Jersey breeds respect, because here there is diversity, here there is contrast. There are windmills by the Millstone River, factories by the Passaic; rugged grandeur in the Palisades, handsome hills in Somerset; vegetables in the fields of South Jersey; traffic intertwining in Middlesex; wild orchids in the Burlington pinelands; millions of pieces of scientific glassware made in Cumberland; and the frenetic casinos in Atlantic City.

New Jersey is a paradox. Its location astride the main transportation routes of the East has made it both tremendously vital and relatively unadmired. The rising sun throws New York's shadow over the state, the setting sun bathes New Jersey in the shade of Philadelphia. Caught between these two great cities, New Jersey has been thought of largely as a path—or, as Benjamin Franklin wrote, "like a barrel tapped at both ends."

Away from that Philadelphia–New York path, there is intriguing variance, so much that it makes knowing New Jersey difficult for all but dedicated admirers. Statistics can prepare the way to knowing the state, although they can't reveal the charm. New Jersey is small, as everyone knows—forty-sixth in size in the country, so small that if all states were the size of New Jersey, the American flag would have 470 rather than 50 stars. Yet within this small space live about 7.5 million people, most of them so jammed in the "city belt" between Hudson County and Camden that 65 percent of the state's acreage is still either farmland or forestland. That belies the enduring legend that New Jersey is "one long strip of Megalopolis concrete."

A Garden State? Well, yes and no.

Yes, to the extent that its eight thousand farms have an annual gross income of close to $350 million and a national standing of first in value of gross farm income per acre. No, to the extent that New Jersey's industries rank seventh in value of manufactured goods, ranging from jewelry to chemicals to books and from beer to space instruments to cosmetics and medicine.

All work and no play then? Hardly. The lakelands in North Jersey and the famed beaches and Atlantic City casinos in South Jersey add up to an industry estimated to account for more than $8 billion annually. That is "play" fit to make cash registers jingle.

But statistics do not engender pride or deepen the sense of heritage. That requires the focusing of attention on the home lots, on the twenty-one counties that comprise New Jersey. The result transcends mere provincialism, because here are found all the elements that have combined to change a seventeenth-century wilderness into the United States in little more than three and one-half centuries.

The Dutch, Swedes, and Finns first settled New Jersey in the 1630s, but they found no difficulty in living with their English conquerors who took over in 1664. Dutch, Swedes, Finns, English, Irish, Scots, in turn, found room for Germans who came before the Revolution to farm the fields of Hunterdon, to work in Salem County glassworks, and to man the Passaic County iron mines. Black slaves labored in New Jersey since colonial days, in the fields of Bergen County Dutchmen and in the parlors of academics in Princeton and Newark.

Later, in the nineteenth century, masses of Irish immigrants who fled potato famines in the Old Country came to build the state's railroads and dig the canals. Germans who fled political persecution in the 1840s breathed freely in New Jersey. The state found room for Italians who arrived soon after the Civil War to help create such oases as Vineland and Hammonton in the arid South Jersey pinelands. Then, in the 1880s and 1890s, as immigrant ships brought in "the tired, the poor" from all of Europe, the growing industries of New Jersey absorbed hundreds of thousands of them. The Hungarians, the Poles, the Swiss, the Russians, the French, the Czechoslovakians, the Lithuanians, and the Scandinavians came to add their virtues to the melting pot. New Jersey's three centuries of growth have taken vitality from the varied people who came within its boundaries, including the blacks, Puerto Ricans, Asian Americans, and others now struggling for their rightful share of America.

This state's geographical diversity offered some reminder of the homeland to all these newcomers. Nature has split the state into three varied areas: the mountain country, the central hill and valley country, and the coastal plains of South Jersey.

In the mountain country, the rich iron mines—plus fast-running streams and seemingly unlimited forests—attracted the ironmakers to Morris, Passaic, Warren, Sussex, and Hunterdon. Farmers broke the hilly ground and struggled for a living, until they found that dairy cattle brought dividends greater than anything that could be grown in the fields. Estates of the wealthy were clustered on the mountains, and, when railroads came, the North Jersey commuter was born. Today the cattle and iron and homemakers have been joined by vacationists who know and appreciate the lakes in the highlands.

Nevertheless, the most vital portion of New Jersey is the central strip—that fifteen-mile–wide corridor linking New York and Philadelphia. This is the "city belt," and, with the exception of Atlantic City, every heavily populated city in the state is in this corridor. This is the heart of New Jersey industry, the homeland of the commuting population whose very life revolves about New York and Philadelphia. Through this corridor stretch the busiest highways in the world, linked at either end with the docks and piers that give and take in world markets.

Finally there is southern New Jersey, itself a study in sharp divergence. These are the components of South Jersey: a thin strip of beachfront running 127 miles from Cape May to Sandy Hook, where surf and sand combine to make a seaside playground for the nation; a vast area of pines and scrub oak trees, where mere man generally has met only bewildering frustration and economic collapse; and finally a wide belt of verdant, prolific soil spread in an arc west of the pines, where the Delaware River bends.

Atlantic City is probably the nation's best-known vacation resort. Cape May and Long Branch had national fame by Civil War days, while Asbury Park grew rapidly since its founding right after the Civil War. Such quiet towns as Sea Bright, Bay Head, Surf City, Avalon, and Stone Harbor have their devotees. Old Cape May retains its Victorian splendor, to the delight of many. The Jersey Shore is known to countless millions of people, most of whom have not the slightest interest in anything else in the Garden State.

New Jersey deserves the name Garden State because of the rich strip of soil that starts in Monmouth County and circles southwestward down through the lower parts of Middlesex and Mercer counties, through the western part of Burlington and on into Camden, Gloucester, Salem, and Cumberland counties. Most of the state's vegetables and fruits are grown in this garden strip.

New Jersey's strategic geographical placement has shaped its history. The state's leading role in the Revolution evolved because troops of both sides marched and countermarched across the state to threaten or to defend the vital ports of New York and Philadelphia. General Washington and his main army spent more than one-quarter of the war on New Jersey soil. Major battles at Trenton, Princeton, Red Bank, Monmouth, and Springfield and nearly two hundred minor engagements took place between the Hudson and the Delaware. Three times Washington took to the New Jersey hills for winter headquarters, twice in Morristown and once in Somerville. South Jersey food and North Jersey iron supplied the troops throughout the war. Bloody footprints in the snow and starvation in wretched quarters were as much a mark of Morris County's Jockey Hollow as of Valley Forge. New Jersey's "summer soldiers," "sunshine patriots," and outright Tories contrasted with the state's doughty minutemen and daring seashore privateers in their contributions to the infant nation.

As the nation grew, it divided on the issue of slavery; New Jersey was caught in the middle. The Quakers of South Jersey had long opposed slavery, with Mount Holly's John Woolman a vigorous advocate of emancipation in the eighteenth century. Warren County's Benjamin Lundy won recognition early in the nineteenth century as the leader of the abolitionists. Slavery haters strung out from Salem to Hoboken helped fleeing blacks escape their pursuers via the Underground Railroad across the state.

However, the tailors and shoemakers of Newark and the snuff-makers of Middlesex County opposed the war, fearing loss of their huge Southern markets. One-quarter of the state lay below the Mason-Dixon line, or at least below where it would have been if extended eastward to the Atlantic. Cape May, where Southern aristocrats long had gathered, knew Southern sympathy. Half of Princeton University's student body came from the South—and half of the Princeton men who were killed wore gray uniforms.

Copperhead sentiment couldn't eclipse the fact that the state's first volunteers came from New Jersey's Warren County, or that Cumberland County supplied a greater number of volunteers in proportion to its size than any other county in the North. The first fully uniformed troops to reach Washington were from the Garden State. New Jersey did its share, particularly after war contracts proved to be every bit as lucrative as the lost Southern trade.

Postwar industry boomed in the state. Railroads reached almost every part of New Jersey by 1870, and by 1900 the state had the greatest concentration of railroad track in the country. The Hudson County waterfront was transformed from mud flats to busy piers. Factories arose beside the tracks—in Jersey City, Hoboken, Bayonne, Harrison, Kearny, Newark, Elizabeth, New Brunswick, and southward to Trenton and Camden.

Iron mines in the Morris hills and zinc mines in Sussex prospered. Phillipsburg grew from hamlet to city, thanks to railroads and the Morris Canal that was finished across state from Jersey City to Phillipsburg in the 1830s. Paterson workers first built locomotives and then spun silk. Trenton found that pottery and iron could be combined to make a stable economy. Camden's economic star rose on soup, shipbuilding, steel pens, and Victrolas (record players). Thomas A. Edison perfected the incandescent lamp in Menlo Park. The movie industry started and grew in New Jersey, beginning in Edison's West Orange laboratories and spreading to the Palisades, where the earliest movie companies filmed thrillers at Fort Lee. New Jersey was abustle everywhere, always in the stream of industrial progress, often far ahead of the current.

Strikingly enough, despite this industrial growth, New Jersey didn't move from rural to urban status until the census of 1880, when 54 percent of the population was adjudged urban. That same census also saw New Jersey's population top the million mark for the first time. Yet, in 1900, when the population soared to 1,883,669 (70 percent urban) farms also reached a new high in number—34,650.

Since then, farm acreage has been cut by three-quarters, but farm output soared spectacularly as New Jersey farmers moved well out in front of the nation's agriculturists in increasing the rate of milk production per cow, egg production per hen, and yield per acre for many crops.

The state's most spectacular increase for years was in egg production, until depressed markets cut output drastically in the late 1950s. Dairy farmers moved ahead, too, only to be checked when developers began competing for pastureland in the 1950s. Seabrook Farms in Cumberland County helped stimulate a big jump in vegetable production for quick freezing. Tomatoes, string beans, asparagus, peppers, onions, peas, and cabbage all continue to be important South Jersey crops.

The garden patches of North Jersey yielded as the railroads rolled over the mountains to Morristown, down the plains to Somerville and across the meadows to Paterson and Hackensack; people began to move into the country. Still, it took the automobile to force New Jersey to absorb more than five million people since 1900. Nowhere has the increase been more startling than in once-bucolic Bergen County, where the population has rocketed. The 1900 total of 78,441 now is more than 825,000. Completion of the George Washington Bridge in 1931 had much to do with the increase, but the fact is that Bergen grew 75 percent in population between 1900 and 1910, another 53 percent from 1910 to 1920, and still another 73 percent from 1920 to 1930.

Such residential increases as those in Bergen—and in Morris, Essex, Union, Passaic, Middlesex, and Somerset—have solidified North Jersey's reputation as a "dormitory for New York." Similar increases in population in Camden, Burlington, and Gloucester counties also have made a "dormitory" for Philadelphia. Today, however, New York and Philadelphia do not hold nearly the economic grip they once enjoyed. Since World War II,

hundreds of new factories have been built in counties that were nearly rural in the 1930s.

Completion of the Garden State Parkway and the New Jersey Turnpike in the 1950s also recast the state's structure. They cross in Middlesex County, and the population boom there has been unceasing. Monmouth and Ocean counties have both sprouted rapidly beside the Parkway. The Turnpike, for its part, is bringing rapid increase to counties along its way, and people are following Interstates 78 and 80 out to former farm regions.

So, New Jersey has variety, even if that fact escapes most visitors. Putting the headlines aside, one way to grasp quickly the variety is to contrast and compare the component parts, the twenty-one counties of the state. Run down them alphabetically.

Compare Atlantic County's recreation industry and small year-around population with the teeming population and concentrated industry of Bergen. Put Burlington's farmlands and pinelands against Camden's growth in the shadow of Philadelphia, then contrast both of them with the quietude of old Cape May, where it is said that there are more descendants of *Mayflower* passengers than there are in Plymouth, Massachusetts. Certainly there are more Victorian houses in Cape May than anywhere else in New Jersey.

Take tidewater Cumberland, with its fine farms, and contrast it with Essex, where airport, seaport, factories, malls, insurance houses, and financial vitality mingle with the pleasant homes in the Orange Mountains. Cumberland and Essex differ, but not nearly so much as old Gloucester, the "Garden Patch of Philadelphia," and Hudson, the longtime railroad terminus of the state. Hunterdon, 60 percent rural, has a farm atmosphere radically different from Gloucester's—and Hunterdon's pleasant hills are somewhat more attractive than Hudson's waterfront (in most opinions, at least).

The "M" counties—Middlesex, Mercer, Monmouth, and Morris—might well be called the "heritage" counties, because within them is found a major portion of the state's Revolutionary War importance. The M's include historically important Princeton and Rutgers universities. Middlesex and Mercer combine to make up the tiny thirty-two–mile waistline across the state's center. Much of New Jersey's history has been shaped along this waistline, of course, because of its transportation vitality. The iron of Morris helped influence New Jersey manufacture, the marl beds of Monmouth influenced statewide agriculture. The state capital at Trenton has made Mercer County a logical center, while Middlesex has always been the center of transportation.

Ocean County, still keyed to the sea, is far different from factory-minded Passaic. Salem's lush fields and quiet dignity compare favorably with both the estate country in the Somerset hills and the dairy farms on the rocky Sussex mountain slopes. Through these three counties can be glimpsed a picture of New Jersey's differing topography—ranging from the flat swampy Salem lowlands where muskrats live, through hills leveling into valleys in Somerset, and on up to New Jersey's highest spot in Sussex County.

Finally, place Union's heavy industry and convenient commuting towns against Warren's beautiful hill scenery, where only Phillipsburg is industrial. Should any-one think that Warren has all the scenery to the disadvantage of Union, however, let him drive through Union County's Watchung Reservation. Beauty is never far away.

Somehow New Jersey escapes the words that praise it (and, fortunately, most of the words that damn it). The reason is that New Jersey is more than people, more than geography, more than history, more than industry, more than agriculture.

It is a flotilla of sailboats on a North Jersey lake, a picnic in a state forest. It is the old streets of Cape May, the modernity of the New Jersey Turnpike. It is the red and gold touched on North Jersey maple leaves in the fall, the appeal of Atlantic City's casinos year-round. It is the George Washington Bridge and the wooden covered bridge at Sergeantsville.

Jersey is old, Jersey is new. It struggles to be all things to all people, and both fails and succeeds. It is factory and farm; it is High Point and Cape May.

Diversity—that's the spirit of New Jersey.

Sussex County's finest view, and possibly the best in New Jersey, is from Sunrise Mountain near Culver Lake. Visitors see a panorama of farms and lakes from this viewing area on the noted Appalachian Trail. (*Walter Choroszewski*)

THE HILL COUNTRY

In New Jersey we call them mountains, although we know that in Colorado or Utah—or even New Hampshire—they might be considered mere mounds. But visitors agree that these midget mountains, or rolling hills, have a rugged handsomeness all their own.

The Hill Country sets the topographic pattern for New Jersey, starting at the very northern tip on High Point and rolling southeastward from the Kittatinny Mountains through a series of declining highlands to the plains below the Watchung Mountains.

This is the Hill Country, where streams dash downward to the sea and give to the land the richness to sustain abundant dairy farms and great estates; where cool blue lakes offer relief from the summer sun; where the quiet of the forests is the unobtrusive background for a waterfall tumbling a hundred feet through a clearing in the trees.

This is the Hill Country, where iron abounds in the highlands, and zinc and lime add variety to the riches of the lands; where the Falls of the Passaic at Paterson, cascading from a rocky precipice, gave America's heavy industry its birth; where modern laboratories and research buildings fit harmoniously into the neatness of residential life.

This is the Hill Country, where Washington three times brought his weary Revolutionists to rest and to rearm. This is a land of heritage, of industrial beginnings, a land of vacationists and homemakers, a land of beauty and opportunity.

This is the Hill Country; this is our scenic best.

Sussex County's handsome Greek Revival courthouse has dominated the center of Newton ever since it was built in 1847 to replace an earlier courthouse on the same site. It features six tall Doric columns, a severely plain pediment atop the columns, and sturdy stone steps that conform to the steep hillside on which the building rests. This well-preserved seat of government has been modified only slightly in its long life.

SUSSEX

CREAM ON TOP

Sussex County, at the very top of New Jersey, obviously has no monopoly on natural beauty, but it can boast of a major share of mountain scenery, lakes, and sprawling parklands. Sussex has the highest point in New Jersey and a share in Lake Hopatcong, the state's biggest lake. Scenically, Sussex is the cream of New Jersey. Literally the county has a high cream content, too; Sussex has long been one of the state's prime milk-producing counties.

Rich dairyland potential and mountain scenery were not the attractions that lured the first Dutchmen down the valley from what is now Kingston, New York, in the 1640s. Had agriculture been on their minds those Hollanders probably would have ignored Sussex. Rolling, rocky country, so unlike their flat, wet homeland, did not interest colonial Dutch farmers.

Those Hollanders were not farmers; they sought gold in the tree-covered mountains, and by 1650 had followed the valley down to the rocky mountain slope just north of the Delaware Water Gap. There they found copper ore, possibly as early as 1640, definitely by 1657. They took the ore back along the mountains to be loaded at Esopus (now Kingston), New York, for shipment to Holland for smelting. As they went north they developed the first road in the United States, a 140-mile thoroughfare linking the copper mine with Esopus.

Much to the relief of the Dutch diggers, no Indian

trouble developed, even though Lenape Indians had inhabited these tree-covered Kittatinny Mountains for nearly 10,000 years. The Lenape believed in peaceful coexistence in pursuing their simple life as the state's first farmers.

Excepting several notable archaeological digs, the Indian presence is best known in the numerous Lenape names that dot the county: Kittatinny, Pochuck, Papakating, and Wawayanda as examples. One strong "Indian" name, Lake Mohawk, is fictional as far as New Jersey is concerned. No Mohawks ever lived in Sussex County. Lake Mohawk was created in 1926 by damming the Wallkill River.

Other Dutch settlers and French Huguenots from Esopus followed the Old Mine Road southward. Some remained in the valley to plant crops along the Delaware River. Others climbed over the Kittatinny Mountains to settle along the flat, marshy "Drowned Lands" where the sluggish Wallkill River overflowed its banks near the New York border.

A few English, Irish, and Scottish immigrants came overland from New York soon after 1700 to settle the Kittatinny slopes, which they called the "Blue" Mountains. One New Yorker, Colonel Thomas De Kay, exchanged sixty acres of land in lower Manhattan for twelve hundred acres along Hamburg Mountain—considered a rather neat bargain in 1724. Germans came up from

Philadelphia in the 1740s, led by John Peter Bernhardt and Caspar Shafer, and settled along the Tockhokkonetkong River (now known by the less jaw-cracking name of Paulins Kill).

So while some in New York knew of the lands on either slope of the Blue Mountains, Philadelphia leaders heard to their astonishment in 1730 that people lived in that wilderness—and without getting English permission at that! Up the Delaware River journeyed Nicholas Scull, famed English surveyor, and John Lukens, chain bearer, to investigate. Sure enough, there on the fertile lands of the Delaware they found Hollanders thoroughly at home. Samuel Dupui, their leader, welcomed Scull and Lukens (who marveled at the orchards—"greater

than any in Philadelphia"). Dupui told Scull of the Old Mine Road, used by then to take Delaware Valley wheat and cider to Kingston and to bring in supplies. The Philadelphia-oriented Scull asked Samuel why he didn't use the Delaware River to get to market. Dupui replied simply that he didn't know to where the river ran.

Scarcely six hundred people lived in the county region in 1750, when settlers first started to grumble about going all the way to Morristown for court. The area had no towns, not even any plantations, and in general the vast acreage had little economic importance. Morris County did not regret losing the area when the legislature created Sussex County on June 8, 1753.

Leaders of the new county met on November 20,

Long known as "the icebox of New Jersey," Sussex County each year experiences low temperatures and deep snows. Temperatures in the county have dipped as low as 32 degrees below zero. (*Walter Choroszewski*)

1753, to grant tavern licenses and to fix fees for liquor and dry food for animals. This reflected a major economic interest of the day, since for many decades the Sussex County tavernkeeper's position meant a big boost in the climb to economic and political status.

In the following spring, county fathers levied taxes of £100 annually, two-thirds of which went to pay bounties for the killing of wolves and panthers. The remaining money went to build a "log gaol," a lockup so flimsy that the sheriff complained he couldn't keep prisoners in. For their part, prisoners said they wouldn't stay in the jail if the sheriff couldn't keep the sheep out.

Sussex courts returned temporarily to Morristown in 1757, driven there by savage Indian uprisings along the Delaware Valley. Indians who had long brooded over the loss of their territory in the valley struck back at white settlers in 1755. Alarmed New Jersey officials appropriated £10,000 in December 1755 to build stone forts along the Delaware River.

The most noted of the Indian slayings took place near Swartswood Lake where, in May 1756, Anthony Swartwout, his wife, and a daughter were killed, and two young children were taken as Indian captives. Other tomahawkings prompted Governor Jonathan Belcher to offer rewards for male Indians over fifteen years of age, dead or alive. Tom Quick, an Indian killer of repute (or disrepute, depending on what kind of humane yardstick is used for measurement), boasted of single-handedly killing scores of Indians.

Fortunately, wiser heads on both sides succeeded in ending the killings in 1758 by persuading the Indians to relinquish peacefully their territorial claims. Tom Quick also desisted, but legend says that when he died of smallpox, Indians dug up his remains, cut them into small pieces and distributed them as souvenirs—thus spreading smallpox and permitting Quick to kill even more Indians after death. The end of the bloody Indian struggle focused attention on another battle, the war over the New York–New Jersey border line, which raged with more or less heat for fifty years after it started in 1719. Many beatings and shootings ensued before bistate action fixed the border in 1772 at its present line. By the joint agreement, New Jersey lost 210,000 acres to New York State.

Jonathan Hampton of Essex County, a man of some

This engraving from James Moody's book shows him freeing prisoners from Newtown jail.

influence in Trenton, moved a place called New Town into prominence in 1761 when he persuaded the legislature to authorize a county courthouse and jail a half-mile from Henry Hairlocker's house. Not coincidentally, Hampton owned the proposed site. Surveyors chained off the half-mile and found the suggested location in the middle of a stream. A bit of chain stretching moved the site halfway up the hill to the south. Ever since, Newton folk have wished the surveyors had really stretched the chains and gone all the way to the hilltop, where the courthouse logically belongs.

A substantial stone courthouse was built in 1765 on a plot of ground conveyed to the county by Hampton for five shillings. No one questioned Hampton's public-spiritedness, but few missed the fact, either, that his adjacent lands quickly increased in value.

Days of scarcity and struggle marked Sussex from 1760 to 1775, but in the latter year the freeholders found the rebellious courage to face up to the Crown with the announcement that Sussex County no longer would pay the salaries of any royal judge. The Revolutionary War passed mountainous Sussex County by, except for supplies that flowed from field and forge—and except for James (Bonnell) Moody, a local Tory who was one of the best-known of all British spies. Moody hid out in a cave located between Big and Little Muckshaw ponds, near Springdale, from where he sallied out to contact British sympathizers.

The price on Moody's head rose sharply in May 1780, when he led six men into Newton to free the prisoners in the jail. "Poor Jemmy," the jailer, "trembled like a leaf"

Cranberry Lake, created in the 1830s to provide water for the Morris Canal, has long been a favored resort. This view looks toward what is called the "Old Lake."

and handed over the keys. Moody threw open the doors, gave three lusty cheers for the king—and tradition declares the cheers and the Indian war whoops of Moody's men frightened Newton people so badly that all of them fled the town. Moody fled, too, and most historians agree that the American army never caught up with him.

Sussex County's economic position sagged during the Revolution, and a 1781 state assessment against it of £8,038 to help pay for the war staggered the county. The economic struggles of these Jersey frontier settlers so absorbed them that they scarcely noticed an influx of major landholders from 1780 to 1810. Robert Ogden became Sparta's first permanent settler in 1778 and the Ogden family of Newark worked the rich mines in Sparta Mountain. Others came to acquire great estates—Lewis Morris, Thomas Lawrence, and John Rutherford, to mention a few.

Census figures in both 1800 and 1810 showed Sussex County second only to Essex County in population. The building of turnpikes between 1804 and 1815 helped boost the county and, after stages began to run in 1808, newcomers filtered in by way of Sparta and Morristown. The influx of new residents lifted county population to 32,754 in 1820, making Sussex first in the state in people. True enough, Sussex then included all of today's Warren County—but second-ranked Essex then also included all of modern Union County and the Paterson area of Passaic County.

Most of Sussex County's prosperity and population centered well south of Newton, however, and that region began to stir discontentedly in 1815. The defeat of an 1819 legislative act to permit the alternating of courts between Oxford and Newton hastened a split; constant pressure finally caused the legislature to cut Warren County away from Sussex in 1824. Sussex County population dropped to 20,346 in 1830 and remained almost stationary throughout most of the nineteenth century.

Even with Warren County gone and a subsequent reduction in number of taverns, temperance leaders in the 1830s shook their heads in despair. An early chronicler tells of the consumption of "liquid poison," which increased "until, like the great deluge, it seemed to flood the land." Lovers of spirits seemed especially numerous in the vicinity of Swartswood Lake, where three towns within a few miles of one another were known far and wide as "Gin Point," "Brandy Hook," and "Rum Corner."

William Rankin, who founded a notable private school at Deckertown (Sussex) in 1833, felt that education was the answer to drinking and lawlessness. Indeed, he advertised in 1834 that after only a year of his school in Deckertown the village "now contains a goodly portion of pious and moral citizens." Be that as it may, the fact remains that Rankin's school within twenty years turned out nearly five hundred graduates who went on to become schoolteachers elsewhere.

Rankin's school vied continuously for county educational leadership with a school that Edward Stiles opened in 1833 at nearby Mount Retirement. In 1844 Rankin had seventy-six students, Stiles seventy-four—all private scholars. Sussex County looked unkindly on free education; as late as 1853 a town meeting in Newton rejected the idea of raising money for free schools.

Interestingly enough, therefore, is the fact that Daniel Haines of Hamburg, who served as governor of New Jersey in 1843–1844 and 1848–1851, led a bitter fight to improve the state's educational system, particularly the free schools. His success in paving the way for New Jersey's first teacher training (or "normal") school at Trenton in 1855, plus his previous leadership in the adoption of the new 1844 State Constitution, made his administrations outstanding.

Completion of the Morris Canal just south of Sussex County boomed the iron mines at Andover in the 1840s and gave new life to forges, such as those at Stanhope, Waterloo, and Franklin Furnace. Yet, of all the ore digging, that at Franklin was most vital, because there Dr. Samuel Fowler, a distinguished local physician, became the first to appreciate the value of the zinc ore in the Sussex hills.

Dr. Fowler, whose medical practice spread over five counties, moved from Hamburg to "The Plains" in 1810. He built mills, shops, and dwellings, and called the village Franklin. Soon he recognized the presence of zinc and interested other mineralogists in an ore that he called Franklinite.

Among other things, Dr. Fowler perfected a process in about 1830 for making a bluish-white zinc oxide powder to use as a paint base. He naturally took great pride in 1838 when the federal government used Franklin zinc in making the nation's first standard set of brass weights and measures. His death in 1844 opened the mines to others, and when two companies were organized in 1848 and 1849 to exploit the mines, a fifty-year legal battle over ore rights started.

Nevertheless, an experimental plant at Newark started to use Franklin zinc in 1852 to make zinc oxide. Shortly after the Civil War the manufacture of metallic zinc began in Newark, with the "Horse Head" and "Bertha" brands of Franklin slab zinc quickly becoming recognized as the acknowledged world zinc standards. The Franklin mines became the foremost zinc enterprise in the nation and held that leadership for nearly a century.

The nature of Sussex agriculture underwent a radical change after the Sussex Railroad rolled into Newton in 1854. First of all, Newton became the center of farm trade. Wagons that once hauled Sussex County farm produce to Chester in Orange County, New York, now headed for the railroad depot in Newton. The butter wagons that had gone overland twice weekly to Chester stopped running.

Woodcut of Deckertown, as Sussex was known 150 years ago. (*Barber and Howe*)

Western competition virtually killed markets for Sussex County beef, pork, corn, and flour, but the ability of the railroads to get milk to big-city outlets changed the cattlemen's emphasis from beef to dairy herds. The county's first milk trains to Newark and New York started in 1863 from Newton and, as other railroads laid tracks over the county, milk depots sprang up everywhere. Railroads employed milk agents to roam the countryside, seeking new shippers. Dairying became the county's prime industry before the end of the Civil War.

Sussex County paused for the war, of course, although there were plenty of people who didn't find the pause refreshing. In fact, many of the county's young men joined the "Skedaddle Army" that marched off to Canada, in May 1862, to avoid the draft. In March 1863, a Southern-minded assailant fired a bullet at the Reverend G. W. Lloyd, pastor of Branchville Presbyterian Church and an outspoken Union advocate. Fortunately the bullet missed its mark.

Defections of the Copperheads did not hide the fact that Sussex County had a full-sized war hero in Hugh Judson Kilpatrick of Deckertown, who as a West Point cadet asked permission to leave the academy to join the troops in the field in 1861. He entered service as a lieutenant, fought throughout the war, and wound up as a major general. Some years later, in 1878, he induced the Grand Army of the Republic to hold its annual encampment at Deckertown (Sussex)—with the result that forty thousand people turned out (about twice the total population of the county) and literally ground the surrounding fields into dust.

Dairymen, making up for time lost during the war years, overproduced so much in the 1870s that the glutted market crashed in 1879. City wholesalers fixed the price of milk so low that Sussex farmers revolted in 1880 and established the Milk Producers' Association under the leadership of Senator Thomas Lawrence of Hamburg. The Dairymen's League succeeded the association in 1907 and proved its power with a tempestuous fourteen-day strike in 1916—when farmers overturned milk wagons, battled with nonconformists in their own ranks, and finally won their fight with the wholesalers.

Iron mining had a brief upsurge after the Scranton interests of Pennsylvania built a huge blast furnace in 1872 at Franklin Furnace. Then Thomas Edison bought the iron mining rights at Ogden mines in 1891 to test his theories of electromagnetic separation of iron from unwanted elements in the ore. The tests were not commercially successful, and after sinking $2.5 million into the pits, Edison abandoned his efforts in 1898. Iron faded, but lime kilns in Hardyston Township prospered after 1875.

Much small local industry thrived in the 1880s and 1890s, such as Virgil Crisman's mill at Branchville, which in the late days of the nineteenth century produced a buckwheat flour that became so well known that it was a household word as far away as the Western states. A shoe factory and a silk mill moved into Newton, and the town of Sussex had a woolen mill and a big plow factory (where the much-respected "Sussex" and "Wantage" plows were manufactured). Generally speaking, industry was a local proposition, on a make-it-for-the-neighbors scale, not far removed from the days of the village smithy.

Zinc continued to dominate the industrial picture, and joy was felt in Franklin when borings in 1891 and 1892 showed rich zinc deposits eight hundred to twelve hundred feet down. When the shafts had been sunk to one thousand feet, water flooded in. The mineowners persistently pumped out water—eight hundred gallons a minute, twenty-four hours a day, for a full year—before man beat the elements and sank the shaft the rest of the way.

The richness of the new zinc deposits made it imperative to settle long-standing legal difficulties over ore

Franklin Furnace in 1855, when the State Geologist noted its emerging importance as a zinc source. (*State Geologist's Report*, 1855)

Although the encroachments of "civilization" have spread across parts of Sussex County, enough farms and open parklands remain to present a decidedly green impression. (*Walter Choroszewski*)

rights, and that settlement came in 1897 when the New Jersey Zinc Company acquired stock of three other companies with plants in New Jersey, Virginia, Pennsylvania, and Wisconsin. The company built a zinc refining plant at Palmerton, Pennsylvania, to use ever-greater quantities of zinc ore. Franklin's prosperity seemed forever assured.

While dairymen and zinc men headed toward new riches, Sussex County began to realize its vacationland possibilities at the turn of the century. Vacationists had come to Sussex as early as 1840—to Sparta, to Newton, to Culver's Lake, to Swartswood Lake, and to the west shores of Lake Hopatcong. Fishermen knew the attractions of the county's streams and hunters loved its woods. These pioneer vacationists really had to love the

outdoors, since the uncertain travel made a trip arduous. When they arrived, they slept either in tents or in primitive boardinghouses.

It took the automobile to popularize the Sussex lakeland, with the biggest spurt taking place after World War I. By then the state also had fully recognized the natural virtues of Sussex. It began to acquire acreage for the Stokes State Forest in 1907. That forest now spreads across 13,000 acres on the slopes of Kittatinny Mountain. Colonel and Mrs. Anthony R. Kuser of Bernardsville gave New Jersey 11,000 acres for a state park in 1923, including High Point—1,803 feet above sea level, highest spot in New Jersey. The familiar shaft atop High Point, 220 feet high, was dedicated there in June 1930 as a monument to veterans of all wars.

Sussex farming entered a new era in 1912 with the coming of young H. W. Gilbertson as New Jersey's first agricultural agent, stimulating scientific farming. Increasingly, improved methods built farming into an $11.5 million enterprise in Sussex by 1950, with about 75 percent of that figure derived from dairying. Sussex County leaders were proud to say that cows outnumbered people (and cattle did have top rank until the census of 1950, when people took a slight lead). Sussex in the 1950 census had only 34,423 people living within its borders—65 per square mile—both figures then being the lowest in the state. If the price of milk had stayed up, the county's human beings wouldn't have minded being outnumbered by cows forever. Dairylands, combined with mountain playgrounds and lakeside vacationlands, would have sustained a pleasant, bucolic pattern of living. It was not to be.

All is not serene in Sussex County. Competition from foreign zinc mines during the 1950s created dire economic woes for Franklin and nearby Ogdensburg, where another of the zinc company's mines had offered hope that the Sussex County ore still might be profitably exploited. The hope was not fulfilled; zinc is fading into memory. People in the Franklin area take pride that geologists and "rock hounds" claim that more varieties of minerals can be found at Franklin than anywhere else in the world—but such distinction offers no economic comfort. Mineral museums in Franklin preserve part of the heritage.

Dairy farmers have long been concerned that increased costs of production, marketing, higher land taxes, and intense competition from cheaper out-of-state sources may make it nearly impossible for county dairymen to stay in business. Additionally, people have found other uses for the pasturelands.

Thanks to Interstate Highway 80, opened in the 1970s, and the widening of old Route 15 into a modern four-lane highway in the 1980s, Sussex County is in the midst of a continuing land boom. Between 1950 and 1990 population rose fourfold, from 34,423 in the "more cows than people days" of 1950 to the 1990 "away with cows" figure of 130,943.

Lest there be concern that the natural beauty is being engulfed by home and industrial development, fear not.

High Point, at 1,803 feet the highest point in the state, caps the long range of the Kittatinny Mountains.

The county has only three areas of rapid population growth, Hopatcong, Sparta, and Vernon, and even that "rapidity" is in question. Vernon Township, the leading growth center, had 21,211 people in 1990, far from enough to term it urban sprawl.

Interestingly, each of the three "growth centers" as recently as 1960 owed their initial popularity to recreation rather than fast transportation. Hopatcong began its "boom" conversion of aging summer cottages into year-round homes during World War II. Sparta developed as a home area centered on Lake Mohawk. Vernon's sleepy valley has attracted new settlers because of its ski slopes. For one brief time, the Vernon area even had a Playboy Club, the most rural setting for human bunnies in the nation.

The major pressure for land has come from the U.S. government. In the 1960s, the Corps of Engineers, ever ready to dam a river or fill a swamp, proposed the so-called Tocks Island project to control floods on the Delaware River and to store water. Hoping to sweeten public reaction, the Corps proposed a huge new surrounding recreational area to be known as the Delaware Water Gap National Recreational Area.

Conservationists erupted in anger. They scuttled the dam but the recreation area remains, fortunately now controlled by the less-threatening Park Service. Many people moved from the area after the government bought their homes. Thus far, most of the park-spurred activity is in Warren County near Delaware Water Gap.

Real estate speculators own much of the land along or near Interstate 80, anticipating a burgeoning tomorrow. Increasing numbers of Sussex County commuters speed eastward to jobs each morning, then return at night. This is one side of a controversial coin. Thoughtful residents shudder at what might happen if the recreational area is ever fully developed, luring visitors northward on the narrow Old Mine Road. They recognize that the sad bureaucratic solution undoubtedly would be to widen the historic road into four lanes.

State parklands are widespread in the Kittatinny Mountains. Magnificent hardwood forests sweep outward from High Point monument. The rugged Appalachian Trail snakes southward on the high ridges of the mountain as part of the daunting path that links Georgia and Maine. Visitors find picnicking, camping, and trout

Ski areas at Great Gorge and Vernon Valley are among leading winter sports regions in northern Sussex County.

streams aplenty. State-owned park acreage has been most recently swelled by the acquisition of large tracts surrounding Wawayanda Lake in the county's northeastern hills.

Thousands of skiers each winter enjoy the slopes at Great Gorge and Vernon Valley, the ski resorts closest to the metropolitan New York area. Human ingenuity supplies artificial precipitation to cover the slopes when nature has been less than generous. Residents in the valley between the Kittatinny Mountains and the Delaware River take perverse pride of their rough winters. It is not uncommon for their thermometers to dip as low as thirty-two degrees—below zero.

Continue to look to Sussex County for natural beauty and the unpredictability of natural life. Much of the county is as wooded and handsome as it was three centuries ago. Indeed, some acreage in the parks is more isolated than ever. Sussex streams and lakes continue to sparkle and forests offer tranquillity. After more than three centuries of human occupation, this is still New Jersey's scenic best, off the beaten track; a place where bobcats yowl on the Kittatinny Mountain and were visitors find rest or stimulation, depending on their needs.

Three years after Warren County was separated from Sussex in 1824, the county opened its red-brick courthouse. Additions and alterations gradually altered the appearance in the nineteenth century, and in 1950–60 the roofline was extended forward from the cupola. Four pillars were added for colonial appearance, but the basic architectural pattern remained intact. The clock in the old cupola must be wound by hand weekly.

WARREN

RURAL DESTINY

Only by a wide stretch of the imagination is it possible to visualize great industries spread all along the Delaware River from south of Phillipsburg to north of Belvidere; yet it might have been. Viewed solely from the standpoint of the natural power of the streams pouring out of the Warren County hills to the Delaware River, it should have been.

Tick off the names of those streams—the Paulins Kill, the Pequest, the Pohatcong, the Musconetcong—whose waters have for countless centuries cascaded into the Delaware River. The mighty Delaware itself ground out the awesome gap through Kittatinny Mountain, and at Foul Rift the Delaware drops sixteen feet in less than a quarter mile. Such water power, in the hands of an Alexander Hamilton, whose vision helped create Paterson, would have meant another industrial center on the banks of the Delaware.

But disputed land titles held the region back in the early nineteenth century, when great industrial expansion began everywhere else. No Alexander Hamilton came forward to visualize the use of water power (as he did at Paterson), and Warren County remained essentially rural through the years.

Not that Warren got off to a slow start; as early as the 1650s, Dutchmen from Esopus (Kingston, New York) started to dig copper out of the Kittatinny Mountain, just north of the Delaware Water Gap at Pahaquarry. They built the Old Mine Road northward along the river valley and laboriously hauled copper to the Hudson River, when with only moderate effort they might have floated it down the Delaware on rafts.

There were no markets downriver when copper began heading for Esopus. Philadelphia didn't come into existence until 1682, and when the English took over all of New Jersey in 1664, the Dutch just stopped digging copper and settled down to farming. Nevertheless, the Dutch exhibited only mild curiosity in the Delaware River or where it ran; for seventy-five years their attention was focused upon the Old Mine Road to Esopus.

William Penn saw the power possibilities at Foul Rift, but he never developed the five thousand–acre tract he bought there in 1716. Warren's prosperity was not to be tied either to Esopus on the Hudson or Philadelphia on the Delaware. In 1726, settlement of Warren County began in earnest when George Green and John Axford came overland from Long Island. Tradition says they climbed a tree, and from their vantage point agreed that Green should settle at the pond that is now Mountain Lake and Axford should build his cabin at what is now Oxford. Dividing a wilderness can be so simple.

Others followed—Abram Van Campen bought 1,666 acres on the mountain above Delaware Water Gap in

The old Oxford Furnace, erected in 1742, has fallen into ruins. The building has been stabilized at a considerably diminished size from the time when it stopped producing ironware in 1882. (*Walter Choroszewski*)

1732; Lodewick Titman bought land near the Gap in 1737; Harmon Shipman settled on Scotts Mountain in 1740; settlers built a log church at Mansfield (now Washington) in 1741; and that same year Aaron Depui established his famous store in John Axford's town.

Such modest colonization merely set the scene for the arrival in 1742 of Jonathan Robeson, Philadelphia financier, to build an iron furnace at Oxford. Robeson shipped his first ore on March 9, 1743, hauling it over-land to a wharf just below Foul Rift on the Delaware and floating it in boats downstream to Philadelphia. Oxford immediately became important; people from thirty miles around shopped at Depui's store. Robeson's iron-works required great manpower to turn out two to three tons of ore a day—men to dig the iron, men to cut the timber needed to make charcoal, men to feed four hundred bushels of charcoal into the furnace for every ton of iron produced. Workers had to be brought to the wilderness.

Control of the booming iron enterprise slipped from Robeson's hands in 1754, when the Shippens of Philadelphia, Dr. William and his brother Joseph, acquired full control. The Shippens built an elaborate stone house near the furnace in 1754, and Oxford became a social center where wealthy Philadelphians frequented the gay parties and the exciting annual fox hunts in the fall—with "Gentleman Joe" Shippen ever in the fore. One visitor was Miss Peggy Shippen, of Philadelphia, niece of the two Oxford Shippens. Later she gained considerable notoriety as Benedict Arnold's wife.

Other small settlements emerged, such as Greenwich-on-the-Delaware, which Robert Patterson established in 1750 at the point where the Pequest River met the Delaware. Helm's Mills had enough settlers in 1760 to make it worth while for Judge Samuel Hackett to call them together for a barrel of good spirits at the local tavern. As they imbibed, tradition says that the judge suggested that Hackett's Town might be a better name for the village than Helm's Mills—and the barrel-emptiers agreed.

Early farmers found it so difficult to till the rugged mountain slopes that severe food shortages occurred between 1753 and 1763, but Moravians from Bethlehem, Pennsylvania, saw the potential of the land and bought a thousand acres in 1769. They first called their settlement Greenland, honoring Samuel Green, who had invited them to the area and had asked very nominal pay for his land. In 1775, when the community became permanent, the Moravians changed the name to Hope. They put up enduring stone buildings, including a seemingly indestructible mill. They built for the ages. The Moravians gave up their experiment with this model village in 1808 and returned to Bethlehem, but their sturdy buildings and the lovely town name of Hope have lasted.

The first man to visualize the tremendous industrial potential of the Pequest River was Major Robert Hoops, who bought Patterson's river holdings in 1769 and used Pequest power to turn mill wheels. Hoops officially called the settlement Mercer, but as early as 1777 he referred to it in letters as Belvidere.

Hoops sent grain down the Delaware to Philadelphia in Durham boats, flat-bottomed craft that went downstream readily enough, but had to be poled laboriously upstream. He built a slaughterhouse just in time to be of tremendous service to General Washington's army during the bitter winter months in Morristown. At times every available wagon for miles around was requisitioned to carry Belvidere grain and meat to Morristown.

Oxford iron also helped the Continental cause

greatly, although historians disagree on whether the Shippens favored the Crown or the Cause. They probably leaned to Great Britain, although, during the British occupation in 1777, they left Philadelphia for Oxford.

Many Tories fled from other parts of the state to the Montana region of Scotts Mountain, but to its patriotic credit the county contributed Brigadier General William Maxwell of Greenwich, commander of all New Jersey regular troops for most of the war. It also contributed Mrs. Margaret Vliet Warne, who lived in what is now Broadway. Peggy (as the countryside knew her) took over when the doctors of the county went off to service. She traveled on horseback with her nostrums packed in saddlebags, and continued her duties as an obstetrician and midwife well into the nineteenth century. Peggy also gave birth to ten children of her own even as she helped much of young Warren into the world.

When Robert Hoops lost his fortune in the postwar depression, he left Belvidere in the 1790s to found the town of Olean, New York. Before he departed, Hoops sold a large tract south of the Pequest to the celebrated Robert Morris. Morris gave the tract to his son-in-law and daughter, Charles and Mary Morris Croxall, in a deed that restricted title to the Croxalls and their heirs for all time. That hampering provision held up the development of Belvidere for nearly thirty years (and perhaps could have forever). It took an act of the legislature to set aside the deed in 1818.

Simultaneously, fledgling Phillipsburg suffered from competition with the young town of Easton directly across the river in Pennsylvania. Founded in about 1735, Phillipsburg grew slowly, but in 1790 it was bigger than Easton. Then the heirs of William Penn stepped in and inaugurated a series of land manipulations deliberately designed to stop development in Phillipsburg. As a result, land values declined so much by 1793 that Jacob Reese and Philip Seager bought the entire ninety-two—acre town of Phillipsburg for $530.

Phillipsburg was so insignificant that the charter for the Washington Turnpike in 1806 called for the pike to be built from Morristown to a point "opposite to Easton." Actually, the principal reason for the pike was the mineral springs atop Schooley's Mountain, where those wealthy enough to spend the summer being sick

Thanks to the Morris Canal, Phillipsburg emerged as a leading Warren County town in the 1840s. (*Barber and Howe*)

gathered to relieve their aches and pains. Wagons and carriages from the turnpike rolled right through Phillipsburg and over the covered wooden bridge to Easton. That bridge, built in 1805 from the proceeds of a lottery, lasted ninety years.

The early years of the nineteenth century brought varying fortunes. First, the old Oxford Furnace closed down in 1809 after timber supplies gave out. Down the valley, Colonel William McCullough built the brick Washington House in Mansfield in 1811, and as the village prospered it took the name of Washington, after the tavern. John Rutherford's great estate surrounded the grain mill in Allamuchy, where Rutherford had come in 1778.

So prosperous had the area become, in fact, that residents pushed for freedom from Sussex County, to which they had been tied since that county's establishment in 1753. Finally, on November 20, 1824, the legislature created a new county and named it for General Joseph Warren, the Massachusetts Revolutionary War hero who was killed at the Battle of Bunker Hill.

Among the new county's 18,000 residents at the time were many men and women of note, but none of greater proportions than Miss Catharine Learch, born in 1816 in Greenwich. Her mother died a few days after Catharine's birth and her father said he raised the baby "mit der spoon." He did such a remarkable job that Catharine grew up to weigh 764 pounds, with a waistline of nine feet, six inches. She married William Schooley of

Greenwich and moved to Ohio, then later toured America as possibly the fattest woman in all history.

Belvidere prospered after county voters chose it in 1825 as the county seat over Hope and Washington, in a decision reinforced by Garret D. Wall's gift of a thousand dollars and a plot of ground for county buildings. Wall also gave land for the county park that is still the heart of Belvidere. He provided that this green be "always kept and continued open as a public square, walk or promenade for the free, common, and uninterrupted use of the citizens of the County of Warren forever." Belvidere land values jumped in 1826, with one corner lot bringing the "extravagant" price of thirty-six hundred dollars.

No such good times pervaded Phillipsburg, even after the Morris Canal stretched across the state to Newark in 1832 with Phillipsburg as the western port. Scarcely a new house went up in the village, and industrial activity continued to center in Oxford, where William Henry rekindled the old furnace in 1831, in anticipation

One of the many dams along the Pequest River that tumbles rapidly toward Belvidere, headed for the Delaware River.

24

Interstate Highway 78, shown here in a picturesque intersection near Bloomsbury, brings increasing numbers of new residents to Warren County.

of a boom that he felt must follow the canal as it flowed along the Musconetcong River valley by way of Saxton's Falls, Hackettstown, Port Murray, Port Colden, and Washington.

A new hot-blast process was originated in England in 1828, and, at Oxford in 1834, Henry used it for the first time in America. He refined the English blast so much that he raised temperatures to 500 degrees (compared with a maximum of 220 degrees in England). His blast revolutionized the iron industry everywhere; output at Oxford shot up 40 percent; costs dropped 40 percent.

George W. and Seldon T. Scranton bought the Oxford property in 1839, and a few years later left to join William Henry in bringing boom times to Scranton, in the mountains of Pennsylvania. Despite the departure of these leading ironmasters, Oxford bloomed as an iron center and in the 1850s made huge quantities of railroad car wheels. Those railroad car wheels symbolized a new day for all Warren County, first because of the vigor several railroads eventually brought Phillipsburg, and secondly because of John I. Blair.

Phillipsburg in 1848 had only forty-seven dwellings, but by 1852 it had attracted J. R. Templin's small iron and brass foundry and the furnaces of the Trenton Iron Company. The latter were tremendous for the day: three furnaces continuously smelted iron for the company's rolling and casting mills in Trenton.

Later the same year, the Jersey Central Railroad

Onions, lettuce, celery, and other salad greens grow profusely in the rich black soil of Great Meadows, where commercial growers have harvested crops for nearly a century. (*Walter Choroszewski*)

rolled into Phillipsburg and by 1855 the Belvidere-Delaware and the Lehigh Valley railroads also had entered town, making Phillipsburg the railroad gateway to the West. Its importance was further augmented in 1865 when the Morris & Essex Railroad finally fought its way across North Jersey from Dover and through to Phillipsburg by way of Hackettstown and Washington.

These were the days when the spread of railroads brought power on a national scale to a famed, if modest, Warren County son named John I. Blair, whose life spanned almost the entire nineteenth century. He was born at Foul Rift in 1802 and died in Blairstown in 1899. In between, he became a highly successful merchant at Gravel Hill (which changed its name from Buttz's Ridge

to Blairstown in 1839), founded Blair Academy in 1848, became a railroad builder and financier active throughout the United States, and amassed a fortune estimated at $70 million. Despite his tremendous successes, he lived quietly at his home in Blairstown for almost eighty years and never lost his warm affection for the mountain slopes of Warren.

Although the railroads thrived and helped Warren County to grow, there were many in the western part of the county who doubted that railroads could replace the Delaware River as a means of transportation. Flat-bottomed Durham boats disappeared soon after the Morris Canal started, but the inception of steamboating stirred men along the Delaware. One noble effort ended tragically on March 6, 1860, in the attempt to run the steamer *Alfred Thomas* from Easton to Belvidere. Just as the ship slipped out into the river from Easton on her maiden trip she suddenly blew up, killing twelve persons, including two of her owners. That ended steamboating north of Phillipsburg.

Local tragedy faded into the greater tragedy of the Civil War, and a Warren County man, Benjamin Lundy, can be recognized as the man who first systematically fanned the flames of discord over slavery. Lundy, born and raised in Quaker Settlement near Allamuchy, probably never saw a slave until he left his father's Warren farm in 1808 at the age of nineteen to visit Wheeling, (West) Virginia. There he witnessed the brutal herding of bewildered blacks into so-called "stockyards." His revulsion led to the founding of the American Abolition Society. Horace Greeley later called Benjamin Lundy "the first man to devote his life to the slaves," and it was Lundy who converted William Lloyd Garrison to the cause of abolitionism. As a Quaker, Lundy abhorred war, but his pen and his never-ceasing lectures against slavery did much to speed the open break with the South.

Fittingly enough, Warren County claimed that it supplied the nation's first volunteers after President Lincoln called for men on April 15, 1861, three days after Southern guns pounded Fort Sumter. Captain Edward Campbell of Belvidere rallied seven officers and fifty men about him and marched them into Trenton on April 18, much to the astonishment of unprepared authorities there.

Industry moved ahead in Warren County after the war, particularly in Phillipsburg. Warren Foundry, established in 1856, grew rapidly. The Andover Iron Company succeeded the Trenton Iron Company and built two additional furnaces in 1868. Stove works, a boilerworks, a rolling mill, and a sheet iron company followed in the 1870s. Phillipsburg toiled as it expanded. Coal, iron, and railroads gave it an industrial supremacy that even the power of the river gave no other part of the county.

Oxford continued to be a bigger iron story than ever, particularly after the Oxford Iron Company took over in 1863 and built a new furnace, with a capacity of 12,000

tons annually. A new nail factory making 240,000 kegs of nails a year, a foundry, and a rolling mill kept men busy digging iron ore from the nearby hills.

John Riegel and five partners invested $27,000 to start an extensive paper mill along the Musconetcong River at Finesville in 1862. Hackettstown found prosperity in the manufacture of wagons and carriages, an industry dating from the factory that Jacob Day had built in 1815. By 1880 the town had ten carriage factories.

The village of Judge Hackett also catered to the carriage set that visited Schooley's Mountain, and in 1867 the village heard with satisfaction that the Newark Methodist Conference had chosen Hackettstown as the site for Centenary Collegiate Institute (now Centenary College). The institute finally started classes for 183 students in 1874 in a new five-story brick building. It was coeducational until 1909, became a two-year women's college in 1910, and has been a four-year, coeducational institution since 1988.

Culture also had much to do with the prominence Washington attained in the last half of the nineteenth century as the nation's organ-making center. The industry dated back to 1850 when John A. Smith started to make melodeons in Washington. Ten years later Robert Hornbacker made the first parlor organ.

Daniel F. Beatty made the organ industry important. Starting with a capital of one dollar, Beatty by 1880 owned a five-story Washington factory capable of turning out 500 organs a month. He sold these throughout the world via hard-selling advertisements. Fire leveled his factory in September 1881, but within eight months Beatty had rebuilt it bigger than ever. The first month after the new factory opened, his men made 1,003 organs. Two years later Beatty failed. His rebuilding apparently had been too costly.

Other Washingtonians made organs, too—Star Parlor Organ Company, H. W. Allegar, and Cornish & Company among them. Cornish, which at first specialized in large church organs, led the town in organ making in 1900. By World War I the demand for home organs declined, largely because Thomas A. Edison's phonograph had made parlor singing old-fashioned. Organ making became a thing of the past in Washington during the First World War, when the companies found themselves unable to collect on hundreds of organs placed in Europe on credit.

If Edison had anything to do with the lessened demand for organs, he partially made up for it in 1899 when he opened a huge cement plant at New Village, close to Alpha, where the Vulcanite Portland Cement Company had opened a plant in 1894. The Warren plants made nearly four million barrels of cement annually before they began to decline in the 1920s. Edison's plant closed just before World War II.

Oxford's iron industry collapsed in the 1920s, organs left Washington, carriages left Hackettstown—and despite its water power Belvidere never attracted much industry. Phillipsburg strengthened its industrial leader-ship after the Ingersoll-Rand Company decided to move its compressed air and hydraulic machinery plant across the river from Easton in 1904. Silk mills, too, played a part in Phillipsburg's growth.

All this time agriculture developed slowly. The 1870s saw thousands of acres of rich muckland in the "Great Meadows" reclaimed after an extended drainage program. At the turn of the century celery and lettuce growers began in earnest to utilize the fertile black soil of this glacial-age lake bed. Cattle breeders began developing herds of milk cows in the 1880s and 1890s, particularly after dairying proved so profitable on the hilly farms in neighboring Sussex and Hunterdon counties.

Actually, agriculture's role in Warren County has had

Huge trout in outside storage tanks are merely one of the attractions at state-run Pequest Trout Hatchery and Natural Resource Educational Center near Great Meadows in Warren County. (*Walter Choroszewski*)

Moving relentlessly through countless centuries of time, the Delaware River carved out the Delaware Water Gap, 1,100 feet deep, 900 feet wide at water level, and 4,500 feet across at the top. (*Walter Choroszewski*)

no spectacular spurts, yet much of the county is still in farmland, and still more sports thick forests. Only Phillipsburg, with about 15.7 thousand people in the 1990 census, and several excellent industries, can claim to be urban. The rest of Warren's population is widely scattered, Washington and Hackettstown being the only other towns with more than six thousand residents.

Washington has the look of a town with a population much greater than 6,400 since its stores cater to a very wide shopping area. Hackettstown's well-preserved old Main Street and its collegiate tone make favorable impressions upon visitors.

Belvidere has a handsomeness all its own. Few towns in New Jersey—or anywhere else—can match the at-

mosphere that surrounds the serene old county park in Belvidere. The red-brick courthouse, expanded through the years to its present size and shape, dominates the square, but the old homes and the well-kept churches lend memorable dignity to this county seat. It looks more like a typical 1890s small town than a county seat. Its population, slightly less than three thousand, reinforces that impression.

The mystery of what thwarted great industrial development in Belvidere persists, particularly after recognizing that the Pequest River falls fifty feet in its last mile dash through Belvidere into the Delaware. In addition, the Delaware River drops twenty-two feet within a mile and a half of Belvidere. That water power was never fully

This stone grist mill, built in 1768, is a memento of the years from 1768 to 1804, when Moravians inhabited Hope. (*Irving Tuttle*)

used, and in the electric age is unlikely ever to be used.

Modern visitors, or at least those who care about natural beauty, can be pleased that cascading waters did not attract the huge industries that might have made the riverbank another Pittsburgh or Bethlehem. That alternative is almost unthinkable in comparison with today's Warren County.

Think of no shaded square in Belvidere or a county without Hope, Harmony, and Tranquility, three towns whose names speak for themselves. Think of no ruggedly charming Scotts Mountain or no Sunfish Pond.

Think of no speckled trout rising in the Pequest, Paulinskill, or Musconetcong rivers. Think of considering the Delaware Water Gap as merely a rocky nuisance to industry.

Take away the cattle grazing on the sloping fields, the quaintness of Blairstown, the bustling small-town character of Washington, and Oxford's tall stone iron furnace that tells of a distant past. Surely all would be gone from the perimeters of a mighty industrial region. Perhaps many would prefer great factories clanging on the banks of the Delaware. There can be good arguments in favor of a theoretical industrial colossus, but none is as convincing to the senses as a trout rising to strike in the rushing water of the secluded Pequest or the peacefulness of pristine Sunfish Pond atop the Kittatinny Mountains near Delaware Water Gap.

Still, the threat of drastic change hung over the county in the late 1960s and early 1970s when the Army Corps of Engineers promised (or threatened, depending on viewpoint) to back a huge reservoir up behind a mighty dam at Tock's Island close to the Water Gap. Determined conservationists from Warren County and far beyond took on the Corps in a classic battle for nature. The Lenape Indians who lived in the valley and mountains north of the Gap called the area Minnisink —meaning "the waters have gone" (presumably referring to a spreading prehistoric lake north of the Gap). The meaning is as much alive as ever; the reservoir waters are gone, too, at least for now.

Certain change will come because of Interstate Route 80, completed across the county north of Hackettstown, Allamuchy, and Hope. Every intersection has been sought out by land speculators who are certain that a population boom is riding the highway west. Those who think in terms of "the economy" see both the road and a big reservoir as blessings. Those moved by Warren County's charms shudder at what two decades might bring if there is no political vigilance or protection.

Forgive those who cherish Warren's handsome slopes for hoping that symbolically, and actually, there also will always be room for Hope, Harmony, and Tranquility in Warren County. Forgive those who are stirred by the fact that Pahaquarry, which had only about three residents per square mile in 1950, had only *one* resident for the same square miles in 1990. Pahaquarry, where the county began, now claims only twenty residents.

New Jersey's most famed courthouse has been in place since 1828 in Flemington, Hunterdon County's seat. Bruno Richard Hauptmann was found guilty here in 1935 on the charge of kidnapping the Lindbergh baby, in a trial reported around the world. The courthouse has been changed very little: the four Doric columns, the white-painted brick walls, and the cupola are typical of the nineteenth-century Greek revival.

HUNTERDON

LAND OF PLENTY

Every day throughout the first six weeks of 1935 the eyes of the world focused squarely on Hunterdon County—yet the world saw it not. The eyes skipped lightly over the broad farmlands and paused only briefly in Flemington to take in the exterior of the handsome old county courthouse. Within, on the second floor, a grim Bronx carpenter finally stopped the eyes.

Wintry winds swept Flemington on January 2, 1935, when Bruno Richard Hauptmann sat down to face eight men and four women on the Hunterdon County jury that had to determine whether he was guilty of the kidnapping and murder of the infant Charles A. Lindbergh, Jr. A regiment of writers, radio announcers, photographers, and communications men descended on the county seat to make certain the world got every detail.

As quickly and as noisily as it came, the regiment stampeded out of town right after the foreman of the jury rose on February 13 to declare Hauptmann guilty, sending him to his death in the electric chair. The moving fingers, having writ, moved on—and left behind only mixed memories and a mountain of empty beer bottles, crumpled sandwich wrappings, penciled note paper, and stained coffee cartons.

To its eternal credit, Hunterdon quickly regained contentment in the pleasant rural status that some of the sophisticated press visitors had deplored in dispatches to big-city papers. But, as the editor of a local paper gently pointed out to those visiting critics, Flemington had never aspired to be more than a country town, no matter what the sophisticates thought. Chance, the very same kind of chance that made little Dayton, Tennessee, notorious for the Scopes "monkey" trial, dropped one of the most spectacular court trials in modern history into Hunterdon's lap.

The chance came from the irregular jagged border line set up in the Sourland Mountains when Mercer County was cut away from Hunterdon in 1838. The Lindbergh estate straddled the border line, but the house from which the baby was kidnaped lay on the Hunterdon side. So, Hunterdon, rather than Mercer, was designated for its forty days of agony, of drama, of pride, of frustration. The trial would have been spectacular anywhere; in Flemington it was overwhelming.

Those few flamboyant days of 1935 were in painful contrast to the placidity which had marked the area ever since the early 1700s when the first settlers drifted up from Burlington, over the rocky slopes of the Sourland Mountains and down into what is now Hunterdon County. They came singly, in pairs, in small groups, mostly without definite colonization aims, but with awareness that the sloping hills were as fertile as they were beautiful.

Linked by covered bridge to New Hope, Lambertville was a busy, smoky riverfront town in the 1860s. (*Barber and Howe*)

Two colonial provinces, East New Jersey and West New Jersey, joined hands over Hunterdon, an immense catchall when it gained county status by splitting from Burlington in 1714. Named for Governor Robert Hunter, most popular of New Jersey's colonial governors, Hunterdon extended from Assunpink Creek in the south part of Trenton north to the New York border. It included most of what are now Mercer, Morris, Sussex, and Warren counties. The last three separated from Hunterdon in 1739 as a loosely defined chunk called Morris County. A full century later (1838) Hunterdon and Mercer divided along a jagged arbitrary line through the Sourlands, a line so erratic that it prompted latter-day wags to wonder if the surveyors hadn't been sampling Hunterdon's splendid apple brandy.

This land of plenty had room for all; long before the Revolution, English, Irish, Scottish, German, Dutch, and French settlers came to Hunterdon, took one look and decided to remain. Thus Hunterdon became one of the state's first genuine "melting pots," where nationality met nationality without prejudice, and creed met creed without rancor.

The soil richly rewarded those who didn't mind calloused hands and tired bodies. Swiftly rushing streams watered the red, shaly earth and provided power for numerous gristmills and sawmills. Every natural feature predestined Hunterdon County's well-being to rise and fall in direct relation to the fortunes of its farmers.

Travelers headed over Indian paths crisscrossing Hunterdon and pushed the region into an important secondary role—that of giving assistance to wayfarers. John Ringo, who built a log hut in 1720 at the junction of two cross-county trails, soon found himself entertaining strangers. John's hut grew into the widely known Ringo's Tavern, a pleasant place to stop before venturing on to the busy Delaware River ferry that Emanuel Coryell established in 1732 at what is now Lambertville.

Up the South Branch of the Raritan River came the Dutch, following as ever the fertile banks of a broad stream. Germans, heading overland from Philadelphia to New York, spread throughout most of the county before concentrating in the northeastern section now known as Tewksbury Township. So many had arrived there by 1750 that the area became German Valley and their principal settlement New Germantown (changed to Oldwick when World War I engendered bitter anti-German feeling).

An Irishman, Samuel Fleming, gave the county seat its name in 1756 by building his "castle" (a small, trim white structure, castlelike only in contrast with other houses in the area). Almost a decade before, John Philip Kase and understanding old Indian Chief Tuccamirgin had come to real estate terms in the village, but villagers were more lastingly impressed by Fleming's domicile.

Another young Irishman, Robert Taylor, arrived in the county in 1758 at the age of sixteen and taught school for a while before becoming bookkeeper for the Union Iron Works in the deep valley at what is now High Bridge. William Turner and Joseph Allen had built the works in 1742, near the site of a much older Union Forge, and when young Taylor joined the firm, Turner and Allen were surreptitiously operating an iron slitting mill in defiance of British orders. Taylor became works manager at the age of thirty-two and by the time of the American Revolution had full control. He was the first of five generations of Taylors to direct the operation, which in 1912 became the Taylor-Wharton Iron & Steel Company.

Taylor turned diligently to making ammunition for Washington's armies, but except for the Union Iron Works and the food production of Hunterdon's farms, the war touched the county mainly at the ferry slips. Part of General Washington's badly weakened army crossed over Coryell's Ferry after the gloomy November 1776 retreat across New Jersey. The following year some of the British prisoners captured after General Burgoyne's defeat at Saratoga crossed the Delaware, at what is now Frenchtown, on the way to prison camp.

Captain Daniel Bray of Kingwood played a vital, if little heralded role in Washington's crossing of the Delaware on Christmas Day, 1776, for the momentous strike on Trenton. Before he crossed to Pennsylvania, Washington instructed Bray to gather all boats for many miles up and down the Delaware River. Bray did the job, thereby thwarting British pursuers and also setting up the river fleet necessary for the subsequent attack on Trenton.

Washington's army, in Pennsylvania for the dreadful winter of 1777–78, broke camp at Valley Forge and surged back across the Delaware in June 1778, headed east to begin the cross-state pursuit of the British that was climaxed by the Battle of Monmouth. Washington stopped briefly in Coryell's Ferry at the home of Richard Holcombe. There Mrs. Holcombe, with understandable curiosity, asked Washington where he was headed. "Madam, can you keep a secret?" the General asked. "Why, yes!" responded the eager Mrs. Holcombe. "Well," said Washington, "so can I!" Next day the army climbed through the Sourland hills to the east and started after the British.

Flemington became the county seat in 1785, after farmers argued that Trenton (then still in Hunterdon) was much too far away. That same year Thomas Lowrey, Samuel Fleming's son-in-law, bought extensively along the Delaware River, at what are now Milford and Frenchtown. Lowrey sold 968 of his upriver acres to Paul Henry Mallet-Prevost, who had fled the French Revolution in 1792, just one neck ahead of the guillotine. Mallet-Prevost stunned "Old Quicksilver" Lowrey (who loved his interest on mortgages) by paying cash. The land became known as French's Town, because no one ever bothered to learn that Prevost was really Swiss, not French.

Hunterdon County felt the economic pinch of the Revolution badly, so much that it was not able to build a courthouse until 1791. The tremendous effort of the Union Iron Works in supplying munitions for the American cause all but closed the only early industry in the county, mainly because the roaring furnaces had burned up all available timber on surrounding slopes.

Creeks and streams dashing out of the mountains proved both a godsend and a troublesome matter; the former because of the impetus they gave to rising farm prosperity and the latter because they seriously hampered travel, particularly during spring floods. As early as 1795, county freeholders began levying taxes to bridge inland creeks. The spanning of the Delaware, however, was left to private stock companies, two of which built bridges across the river at Coryell's Ferry and Center Bridge (Stockton) between 1812 and 1814. Through the years, rampaging waters constantly smashed the wooden Delaware River bridges (particularly in 1841, 1862, and 1903) before steel framework fended off the fury of the river.

Coryell's Ferry as a place name ended with the coming of the bridge, and even the name disappeared in 1812 when Senator John Lambert secured a post office and changed the village title to Lambert's Ville. Descendants of Emanuel Coryell heatedly rejected the new name ("more likely Lambert's villainy," they declared) but they complained in vain. The name change was scarcely of widespread interest, for Lambertville had less than a dozen houses at the time, although it boasted of some prosperity as the terminal point for lumber rafts floated down from the upper Delaware.

The riverfront village had expanded enough by 1828 to challenge Flemington's right to the county seat after the original courthouse burned that year. Flemington's fitness satisfied the legislature, however, and later in 1828 the county built the two-story Greek revival courthouse in which the Hauptmann drama took place 107 years later. Flemington had a good case—boasting the Fulper Pottery Company (one of the nation's first potteries) as a leading industry and pridefully pointing out that many residents set out trees. Just to prove progress, a local citizen laid the town's first sidewalk in 1833.

The entertainment of visitors continued to be a leading Hunterdon business: in Flemington at Fleming's Castle; at Centerville, halfway point on the Swift-Sure stage route between New York and Philadelphia, and at

New Jersey's last covered bridge at Sergeantsville was severely damaged by a heavy truck in 1960 but has been rebuilt. A new steel span handles eastbound automobile traffic. (*Walter Choroszewski*)

Larison's Corner, where the old inn lured sporting men bent on gambling or cockfighting.

In the northern part of the county the New Jersey Turnpike, started in 1806 to link Phillipsburg and New Brunswick, led to the building of many new inns and to the revived popularity of old taverns. The sparkling white walls of the Whitehouse Tavern attracted many overland passengers, but others preferred the inn on "Jugtown" Mountain or the Brick Tavern at Perryville. The latter became a gathering place for scores of cattle and sheep drovers on their way to New Brunswick by way of the pike. Needless to say, the fastidious avoided Perryville and went on to Hunt's Mills (Clinton) to stay in the hotel near the old gristmill beside the waterfall.

Most of the taverns naturally featured Hunterdon apple brandy, made from home-grown apples. The county's extensive nineteenth-century apple orchards dated back to early deeds requiring every land buyer to plant one apple tree for each acre of ground purchased. Cider millers found that Hunterdon County cider readily ripened into smooth apple brandy.

The taste for Hunterdon "apple" spread; soon wagonloads of the brandy rolled to Trenton and Philadelphia for sale at twenty-five cents a gallon. Union Township became especially known for its brandy with ten distilleries spread along Spruce Run and Mulhockaway Creek.

The Belvidere-Delaware and the Jersey Central railroads gave the county an economic lift in the 1850s. Lambertville boomed as a locomotive and railroad car manufacturing center, then added an iron mill, an India rubber works, and paper, cotton, and rope plants. Junction (now Hampton) was founded in anticipation of the junction of the Jersey Central and the Delaware, Lackawanna & Western Railroad in 1856, and for their foresight the founders gained extensive railroad shops.

Above all, the Jersey Central gave High Bridge both an economic shot in the arm and a new name, the latter for the extensive bridge the railroad built high over the valley. Taylor's Forge revived when the Jersey Central brought in anthracite to feed its long-hungry furnaces. Business at Taylor's increased threefold within two years

and the upsurge of the forge led to intensified iron ore mining in and near the Musconetcong Mountains—at High Bridge, Cokesbury, Asbury, Jugtown, and Glen Gardner. The West End Mine at Jugtown continued until 1888; it produced a million tons of ore in its last decade of existence.

Many a man digging Hunterdon iron ore wished he were in California with James Marshall, Lambertville local-boy-turned-famous. Marshall, who had drifted westward from Lambertville in 1834, started the 1848 gold rush when he accidentally discovered gold nuggets while digging a raceway for a sawmill at Sutter's Mill (Coloma), California. Gold did Marshall no good; he enjoyed few comforts before he died alone and

Once heavily industrialized, Lambertville has increasingly become a pleasant tourist destination of period homes, small shops, and excellent restaurants. (*Walter Choroszewski*)

Hunterdon's rolling hills abound with farms such as this near Rosemont. (*Irving Tuttle*)

unhonored in a California county hospital. A sample of California gold, furnished by Marshall, was placed in the cornerstone of Lambertville Baptist Church in 1868.

Meanwhile, on farms close to Flemington, several mining companies unleashed dreams of fortunes to be made from local ore. Their lure was copper, whose digging provided a spectacular craze that lasted from 1836 to 1865, when the last of the copper mines closed. Hugh Capner, who sold his farm to a copper company in 1837, was said to be the only honest man to make money from the copper rush ("honest" being a necessary qualification because a stock-jobbing outfit used the mine near Copper Hill to perpetrate a huge swindle).

The real Hunterdon County fortunes lay for the taking in the fields and pasturelands, and for 150 years the ripe lands gave and gave and gave. Farmers took and took and took, with the result that farming ran into sad days throughout most of the last half of the nineteenth century.

Railroad competition hurt, because Hunterdon beef, pork, wheat, and wool couldn't compete with lower-priced Western products. The taste for Hunterdon apple brandy diminished by the time of the Civil War; apple orchards wasted on the hillsides. Above all, the fabulously rich soil finally was exhausted from years of poor husbandry. What happened is partially illustrated by county population. After rolling steadily upward to 40,758 in 1865, population began an unchecked slide that dropped the total to 32,885 in 1920. Hunterdon showed its first population gain in 65 years in 1930 and did not go above 40,000 again until the late 1940s.

Peaches at first seemed a rosy way to prosperity. Farmers became enthusiastic about the fruit after Joseph K. Potts of Franklin Township and Dr. George H. Larison of Sergeantsville started large orchards in the 1850s. Eventually two million trees covered the county in 1890, the year when bad weather caused the peach crop to fail completely. Worse, the 1891, 1892, and 1893 crops were so tremendous that the bottom dropped out of the glutted market. Finally, the deadly San Jose scale ate into the orchards in the middle 1890s. In dismay and disgust, farmers took their axes to the peach orchards and chopped down more than one million trees between 1895 and 1909. Today Hunterdon has few peach orchards.

Hunterdon farm values reached a low point in 1900. Yet, even as agriculture floundered through its most bitter days, the foundations of today's farmland prosperity were laid in the last part of the nineteenth century. Farmers started then to raise dairy cattle instead of beef cattle and began growing chickens commercially. Railroad shipments of milk to the cities started modestly in the 1870s and grew quickly after the Lehigh Valley Railroad built through the county's heartland. Establishment of local creameries in the 1880s gave additional impetus to the Hunterdon dairy business.

Introduction of the portable incubator spurred the county's poultry business in the 1880s. Many objected to incubators, expressing concern over what being mothered by a hunk of tin would do to a baby chick. Others believed incubated chicks would forever smell and taste of kerosene. When a few of the less squeamish found the incubators profitable, even the most scrupulous readily revised their thinking—and Kerr's Hatchery in Frenchtown gained national fame by producing between five and six million chicks annually.

As dairy cattle spread over the hillsides and chickens peeped from beneath incubators, Hunterdon's farm prosperity edged upward; property values doubled within the first decade of the twentieth century. Not that the county sped out of the economic woods. Indeed, Hunterdon's fiscal picture never looked blacker than after the county borrowed $315,000 between 1910 and 1915 to resurface its archaic roads. Unfortunately, the resurfacing proved as fleeting as the bonds proved enduring. Bitter farmers slogging over rutted roads in the early 1920s complained that the county had built "one-year roads on thirty-year bonds."

By 1930 the county debt rose to $1.5 million and the roads were worse than ever. The darkness was blackest, but just ahead was economic dawn.

Some of the "city folk" who had bought small Hunterdon farms in the 1920s began to get the hang of the land

by 1930. That year, for the first time in more than six decades, the county census showed an increase over the previous ten-year mark. Then, county freeholders voted in 1930 to issue no more bonds. Finally, and possibly most important at the time, the Flemington Auction Market started.

Hunterdon farmers, long used to accepting for their products whatever they could get, showed little enthusiasm for the auction at first. More than twelve hundred chicken farmers were contacted; only forty sent eggs to the first sale held in a Main Street basement in August 1930. A leading auctioneer predicted that the venture would be a certain failure, and refused to sell the eighty cases of eggs that local farmers offered on the first day.

Within a year, however, the cooperative venture proved sound. In 1931 the group began to auction live poultry and in 1936 added livestock auctions. By 1950, auction sales were in the neighborhood of $8.5 million annually. The auction market saw its activity decline in the early 1960s, thanks to a statewide drop in poultry products, but it was a continuing factor in improving agricultural conditions, because it taught farmers to know prices and to know breeding and marketing techniques.

Clinton Historical Museum occupies one of two much-photographed old mills at Clinton's dam across the Raritan River. (*Anne Oakes Studio*)

The cooperative auction market led to other noted Hunterdon cooperative agricultural ventures. In 1939 the Hunterdon County Board of Agriculture established near Clinton the first cooperative artificial cattle breeding unit in the United States. The New Jersey Poultry and Egg Co-operative Marketing Association, a statewide farmers' cooperative, chose Flemington in 1946 as its central point for packaging state-certified eggs.

Working together, Hunterdon County farmers made their own prosperity, but much of the county's prosperous condition just after World War II must be traced to a tax windfall between 1937 and 1945, when more than 170 large corporations from all over the nation set up "offices" in Flemington as a subterfuge to take advantage of low local taxes. Standard Oil started the parade in 1937 by "moving in" from Linden. More than $275 million in ratables followed—and, while the corporations existed in the borough mainly in filing cabinets or as long lists of names on office doors, local tax rates dropped dramatically.

The state acted in 1945 to end collection of such intangible corporation taxes by Flemington (or any other municipality), but that eight years of economic dreamland saw Hunterdon emerge happily, its roads in good shape, its budget firm, and its bonded indebtedness reduced to zero. The tax rate has jumped since, of course, but the county has fewer tax worries than most of its neighbors.

The Hunterdon hills these days shelter a relatively new type of settler, the wealthy or artistic exurbanites who have bought some of the handsome old stone houses and beautiful rolling acres. A few commuters have also entered the county, and enough of them became businessman-weekend farmer combinations that the county agricultural agent kept his office open Saturdays.

Such slow increases in population mask a story of intensive internal change, much of it generated by the people who moved in after World War II. In 1945 the county still had thirty-two one-room schoolhouses, and its many scattered high schools were small, poorly equipped, and understaffed. Hunterdon won no honors for the quality of education offered its young, sentiment over little red schoolhouses notwithstanding.

The school situation changed dramatically after 1948, when a crash building program was begun. Within four years all the one-room schoolhouses, plus five other rural schools, were abandoned, with classes combined in modern consolidated elementary schools. Since then four new regional high schools have been built, serving every part of the county. Cooperation has become the way of education, and, in an allied sense, the way of health. Countywide volunteer subscriptions have built and enlarged a multimillion-dollar medical center on a rise north of Flemington.

More than anything, Hunterdon has been jolted out of any inclination to dwell on the past by the bountiful water within its boundaries or on its border. First there were floods. Torrential rains brought by hurricanes Connie and Diane in August 1955 dumped 10.45 inches of rain on Flemington. An even greater downpour inundated the Delaware Valley to the north.

The placid Delaware became a raging terror, engulfing both riverbanks as it roared toward the sea. Floodwaters crested at more than two feet above the "all-time highs" recorded in the 1903 floods. Six hundred families were made homeless in Hunterdon County; damage in the county was estimated at more than $4 million. Lambertville lost $500,000 in its mud-filled streets and buildings, and the Riegel Paper Company suffered losses of more than $1 million. Floodwaters collapsed the Byram-Point Pleasant Bridge, but the bridges at Lambertville. Frenchtown, Milford, and Riegelsville stood firm.

Ironically, as the flood waters rampaged through the valley, state legislators were debating the need for reservoirs, two of them slated for Hunderdon County's Spruce Run and Round Valley. Spruce Run's waters now fill the long fingers of many coves northwest of Clinton. Round Valley Reservoir occupies a huge natural bowl south of Lebanon. Both offer a variety of recreational activities in addition to storing water, a pioneering use of reservoirs as multi-use facilities.

Hunterdon is on the edge of turbulence. Highway builders have gouged at the hills in the northern part of the county, first making Route 22 wider and safer, then slicing through Interstate Route 78. Interchanges and highway bridges soar over and dip under one another at

Swirling waters of the Delaware River inundated Stockton after hurricanes Connie and Diane struck in 1955. (*Hunterdon County Democrat*)

Clinton to sadden lovers of quietude and to delight those who see poured concrete as proof of civilization.

Long streams of traffic head toward the sun, and work, each morning, then return at night into the setting sun. Often the traffic slows to a halt in ominous foreboding of what the future can hold. That's a negative view. More in keeping with Hunterdon traditions is the likelihood that population growth in the foreseeable future will come close to Interstate 78, leaving the rest of the county open and green. Only three areas have shown significant growth—Readington and Raritan townships and Clinton. Readington and Clinton abut the interstate. Raritan is wrapped completely around Flemington. Raritan has about 16,000 persons, Readington 13,500, and Clinton 12,000, not densities likely to push the three to metropolitan status in the next twenty-five years—if ever. The rest of the county ranges from reassuring small-town to widespread rural.

Hunterdon County's inhabitants still find as much tranquillity as there is anywhere in New Jersey. Visitors are charmed—by the greenness of the dairy farms, by the blueness of the reservoir waters, by the splendid architectural display and the multitude of shops offered tourists in Flemington. The valley near Lambertville has absorbed some of the characteristics of tourist-oriented Bucks County across the river.

World news seldom is made in Hunterdon County, although the metropolitan press does look in on such occasions as when county residents bluntly informed state officials and other interested outsiders that they did not feel that a major jetport on the eastern edge of the county would aid Hunterdon's quest for its destiny. It might even be said that nothing really earth-shaking has happened since Bruno Richard Hauptmann was consigned to the electric chair by the jury in Flemington courthouse. Hunterdon people like it that way.

Somerset County's gleaming white marble courthouse in Somerville was completed in 1908. Designed in the Italian Renaissance style, it replaced an old brick courthouse on the same site (at public auction the older building brought $125, with another $700 for the county jail). The sensational "Hall-Mills" trial occurred here in 1926, when a jury found no one guilty in the brutal 1922 murder of a minister and his choir singer.

SOMERSET

THE HANDSOME HILLS

Much of New Jersey's geographical diversity comes together in Somerset County, where northern New Jersey's rolling hills level off into South Jersey's flatlands; where gently flowing streams swell into the Raritan River, long ago christened the "Queen of Rivers," and where widely varied soils have tempted farmers for centuries.

The pleasant land has always attracted those accustomed to the good things of life; for more than two hundred years the Somerset hills have meant, and still mean, landed gentry riding to the hounds, and living on a lavish scale. The fertile valleys along the rivers have meant prosperity for less well-to-do farmers, also. Finally, transportation planners through the years have made Somerset County a mid-state hub where highways and railroads meet.

Thus, in this area apparently destined to be a North Jersey crossroads and a region of expansive living, it seems strange that few paid much attention when a Dutch traveler visited the Raritan Valley of current Somerset County in 1650 and called it "the handsomest and pleasantest country that man can behold." Fine words do not a county make, and the beginning of settlement dated to 1681, when Thomas Codrington and John Royce took up large tracts in the vicinity of what is now Bound Brook. Others followed, particularly

French Huguenots and Dutch farmers from Long Island. Generally, the Dutch stayed in the lowlands near the Raritan, while late-arriving English and Scots favored the hill country.

The Provincial Assembly split Somerset County away from Middlesex on May 14, 1688. The boundaries were loosely defined, although the East New Jersey–West New Jersey line, run by George Keith in 1687, was the westernmost boundary, and still is. Other boundary changes through the years included agreements that settled lines with Essex County (1741) and Morris (1749), a resettlement with Middlesex in 1790, and the loss of a small piece of Somerset to help form Mercer County in 1838.

Such vagueness of boundaries was perhaps related to the unusual reason given for forming Somerset in 1688: "The uppermost part of the Raritan River is settled by persons, who, in their husbandry and manuring their lands, are forced upon quite different ways and methods from other farmers and inhabitants of Middlesex County . . ."

Unique though their husbandry and manuring might have been, the residents of Somerset County were not numerous. All of the county was made one township in 1693, when townships were first established in New Jersey. All the county remained under the jurisdiction of

Middlesex County courts until 1714, when Somerset finally received permission to build its first "gaol and courthouse," at Six Mile Run (now Franklin Park).

Population then centered in the eastern part, near New Brunswick, where a group of Dutch farmers had settled down to farm and to raise large Dutch families. Villages came into being along the Raritan River and its tributaries and in the hills near Basking Ridge. The population was heterogeneous, both in nationality and rank—English and Scottish gentlemen and yeomen, Dutch burghers and peasants, German masters and redemptioners, French Huguenots of high and low fortunes. One historian has pointed out that the abundance of Dutch names in Somerset is no proof that the Lowlanders did all the settling—they merely had the biggest families.

No brood better illustrates that than the family of Christian Van Doren and his wife Altje, who moved from Monmouth County to Middlebush in 1723 and proceeded to boost Somerset's population by seventeen young Van Dorens—twelve boys and five girls. Sixteen of the young Van Dorens carried on the tradition; only one remained single. The sixteen bore 129 children

Old Dutch parsonage built by John Frelinghuysen in 1751, shown in an 1842 woodcut, has been called "The Cradle of Rutgers University."

among them, and when Mrs. Van Doren died at the age of ninety-six she left 352 descendants!

Another Somerset County family, remarkable not for quantity but for quality, started soon after when the Reverend Theodorus Jacobus Frelinghuysen came to establish the Dutch Reformed Church in Somerset County in 1720. His duties extended over three hundred square miles and included four churches. His salary was about $400 a year.

Frelinghuysen brought with him a *Voorleser* (schoolmaster, catechist, chorister, and pastoral assistant, all in one) named Jacobus Schureman. The minister and his aide married the Terhune sisters; the Frelinghuysen-Terhune marriage resulted in five sons. Schureman's descendants became notable in Middlesex County history.

Getting quickly to his duties, Frelinghuysen made sinners squirm and the self-righteous angry with his fiery, evangelical calls for repentance. Religious historians have called this outspoken Dutch minister "the first outstanding revivalist" in the Middle Colonies. His congregation often clashed with him but Frelinghuysen carried on in his blunt, exciting, and exasperating way for twenty-eight years.

Young men desiring to preach in the Dutch Reformed Church had to go to Holland for training and ordination. Three of Frelinghuysen's sons perished while returning after such ordinations: only the second son, John, survived. After the elder Frelinghuysen died in 1748, his followers asked John to become their pastor. He returned in 1750 from Holland, where he had obtained a license to preach. He brought with him a young bride, Dinah Van Bergh, and in 1751 the young Frelinghuysens built at present-day Somerville a home of bricks imported from Holland.

John was the only one of Theodorus Frelinghuysen's five sons who left descendants, with the Frelinghuysen name being continued by John's illustrious only son Frederick—teacher, lawyer, patriot, and statesman. Frederick's three sons, in turn, became lawyers, with son Theodore becoming a United States senator, vice-presidential nominee on the 1844 Whig ticket, and president of Rutgers University in 1850.

Young John Frelinghuysen died in 1754 after only

The Wallace House in Somerville, headquarters of George Washington during the winter of 1778–79. (*N.J.D.C.E.D.*)

four years in the ministry, but before his death he gathered about him in the Dutch parsonage four ministerial students in the first seminary of the Dutch Reformed Church in America. This may properly be regarded as the forerunner of Rutgers University, chartered as Queens College in 1766 to train Dutch Reformed ministers.

After John Frelinghuysen's death his thirty-year-old widow was preparing to return to Holland when Jacob Rutsen Hardenburgh, a seventeen-year-old student of the late Mr. Frelinghuysen, proposed marriage. "Why, child, what are you thinking about!" exclaimed Mrs. Frelinghuysen at first, but they were married and enjoyed a union of thirty years, which ended with

Jacob's death. His widow survived that marriage by another seventeen years. Hardenburgh became the first president of Queens College and his stepson Frederick Frelinghuysen was named the first (and only) tutor when classes opened in 1771.

As Somerset moved toward the Revolution the county grew slowly. Millstone assumed enough prominence to be named county seat when the old courthouse at Six Mile Run burned in 1738. Basking Ridge attracted settlers to the three-thousand-acre tract that John Harrison had bought in 1717 for $50.00, and in 1751 the Reverend Dr. Samuel Kennedy started his famous academy in that village. Johannes Moelich (Mellick) built in 1758 the "Old Stone House" at Bedminster that Andrew

Mellick memorialized a century later in the classic local study, *The Story of an Old Farm*.

Grand estates became an established part of the Somerset scene before the Revolution, with an outstanding early example being Lord Neil Campbell's lavish sixteen-hundred-acre spread at the junction of the North and the South branches of the Raritan. None of the early estates, however, rivaled that of Lord Stirling (William Alexander), who in about 1760 returned to the seven-hundred-acre family holdings at Basking Ridge, intent on "settling a good farm in the wilderness." Lord Stirling lived in the grand manner "and altogether affected a style and splendor probably unequaled in the colonies." During the Revolution he served with distinction in the American forces, although Washington formally addressed him as "My Lord," according to English custom.

The Revolution touched Somerset first at Basking Ridge, where the recalcitrant General Charles Lee was captured in Mrs. White's Tavern on the morning of December 12, 1776. Thirty British dragoons surrounded the house and took the crestfallen Lee off to New Brunswick, "bare-headed, in his slippers and blanket coat, his collar open and his shirt very much soiled from several day's use" (in the words of an eyewitness). Lee was returned to the American lines in a prisoner exchange, and later earned a besmirched page in history for his dilatory tactics at the Battle of Monmouth in 1778.

Brighter episodes remained in the war ledger for Somerset, starting after the Battle of Princeton in early January 1777, when General Washington led his revived army up the west bank of the Millstone River, through Somerville, Pluckemin, and Bernardsville (then called Vealtown) to winter quarters in Morristown. The following May and June his troops occupied positions on the Watchung Mountains, overlooking the plains where General Howe tried in vain to coax the Continentals into battle on an open field.

Nearby, at Camp Middlebrook, tradition says the first Betsy Ross flag flew after adoption of the thirteen-star flag on June 14, 1777. Those who support this theory point out that Washington stayed near Middlebrook before and after June 14—and where but at the commander-in-chief's quarters would the first American flag have flown?

The main body of American troops returned for the quite mild winter of 1778–79. Washington stayed at the newly built Wallace House in what is now Somerville. Here he and Mrs. Washington became warm friends with the Reverend and Mrs. Hardenburgh. Relaxation marked that winter, at least for scores of officers quartered in private homes between Bound Brook and Pluckemin. Washington especially enjoyed a winter party at General Nathanael Greene's headquarters in the Van Vechten house in Finderne early in 1779, when he allegedly "evinced his esteem for Mrs. Greene by dancing three hours with her without sitting down."

Even greater gaiety marked a party given by General Henry Knox at Pluckemin on February 18, 1779, to celebrate the first anniversary of the French alliance. Reviews and fireworks enthralled army officers and their visitors. A pavilion 170 feet long was erected, embellished with thirteen arches for the thirteen states, and that night between three and four hundred gentlemen danced until dawn with seventy of Somerset's handsomest maidens and matrons. Washington led the grand march with Mrs. Knox on his arm.

But there was no such joy in a tiny house in Griggstown where young Mrs. Mary Honeyman lived, left alone much of the time by her mysteriously-wandering husband John. According to a long-held tradition, Mary's neighbors despised John as a Tory and she feared for his life, keeping locked in her Irish heart the knowledge that John Honeyman was in truth an American spy. War's end brought Honeyman the fame he deserved (again according to tradition) after Somerset County learned that John's wanderings and his reports helped to pave the way for the tide-turning Battle of Trenton in 1776. He lived a secretive life until his death at the age of ninety-five, and is now buried in the Lamington Presbyterian cemetery.

The valley of the Millstone River felt the swiftly moving feet of British Colonel John Graves Simcoe and his Queen's Rangers on October 27, 1779. Simcoe led his fast-moving Rangers out of New Brunswick to Somerville and back on the road to New Brunswick in a brilliant fifty-five-mile dash in the course of one night and a

Rockingham, the house in Rocky Hill where Washington stayed from August to October, 1783. (*Earl Horter drawing, The State Library*)

morning. The Rangers coolly drew supplies from an American quartermaster, burned the courthouse in Millstone, and ruined the nearby church. They pillaged the countryside as they went, striking terror in the valley. Pursuers captured Simcoe at Middlebush, but many military authorities have called his raid the most daring single episode of the war.

General Washington came back to Somerset County once more, to draft his Farewell Address while he stayed at the John Berrien mansion at Rocky Hill from August 23 to November 10, 1783. Nearby, in Princeton, the Continental Congress sat to draft peace terms with Great Britain. Congress called Washington to Nassau Hall on August 25 to give him his nation's public thanks. For his part, Washington spoke his farewell to his troops on November 2 at Rocky Hill.

County leaders decided to relocate their county seat after Simcoe burned the Millstone courthouse. Raritan, also called Tunison's Tavern, was selected in 1782. There were then only three houses, a school, the church, and Tunison's bar in town. A general vote of freeholders meeting in Tunison's Tavern accepted a proposition from the Dutch Consistory that the county and their church unite in building a combination courthouse-church in a rare mingling of church and

state. The building was completed in 1783 and a year later the Consistory withdrew, being reimbursed £228 as its share of the cost. In 1798 a new courthouse and jail were built, "similar to that at Flemington." With such dignity in their midst, townspeople renamed the village Somerville.

Life soon centered in Somerville, both because of county business and because the village straddled the Old York Road (Elizabethtown to Philadelphia) and the New Jersey Turnpike (Easton to New Brunswick). Fast-moving stages on the Swift-Sure Line between New York and Philadelphia careened through the town. Drivers of grain-laden wagons stopped overnight at Mrs. Fritt's hostelry in Somerville, then left at dawn for New Brunswick's docks. Many of the wagons trundled back into town on return trips, bulging with supplies for merchants in Somerville and elsewhere on the turnpike.

Attempts to harness the power of the Raritan River moved from the gristmill stage to a broader utilization in 1819, when a dam was built across the river just below the junction of the North and South branches at the town now called Raritan. Twenty-one years later, capitalists invested $150,000 in a raceway to supply power from the Raritan River. Water from the dam and canal moved industry more or less effectively for decades, but the erratic force of Raritan River freshets, and the even stronger force of continued lawsuits over control of the river, eventually ruined the industrial scheme.

Up in the Somerset hills, Lord Stirling's estate fell into ruins, with chickens roosting on his gilded coat of arms and pigs rooting in the courtyard. Nearby Basking Ridge knew both prosperity and intellectual reputation, however—the latter for a widely known academy opened in 1799 by the Reverend Robert Finley, whose students included Samuel Lewis Southard and William L. Dayton, both of whom went on to distinguished careers in the United States Senate. Pupils came from as far away as New York, Maryland, and Virginia. Basking Ridge centered on its noted giant oak tree, already two hundred or more years old in 1799.

Somerville's position as the center of county trade declined after May 1834, when the Delaware & Raritan Canal was completed through the county via the Millstone and Raritan river valleys. The county economy shifted to towns along the canal, particularly Bound Brook. That sleepy little town, with fewer than five hundred inhabitants, quickly became an important point on the cross-state waterway.

The well-conceived, well-built Delaware & Raritan Canal required only fourteen locks between Bordentown and New Brunswick. It was seventy-five feet wide and nine feet deep, wide enough and deep enough to last as a commercial venture into the 1920s. It carried great amounts of coal, and cargo totals often passed two million tons annually between 1860 and 1880. The canal died forever as a commercial venture in 1926, but its calm waterway and some wooden locks can still be seen, south of the Raritan and east of the Millstone.

Every town along the waterway experienced growth,

but the future lay chiefly in railroads. Bound Brook felt its economic pulse quicken when the Elizabethtown & Somerville Railroad (later the Central Railroad of New Jersey) rolled into town in 1841. A year later the "Somerville" part of the road's name was achieved, thus making the county seat an important shipping point for West Jersey grain. But the same year the railroad began to push on to Phillipsburg, taking over most of the upstate grain hauling. Eventually Somerville regained its importance as a local farm center because of the railroad connection and the courthouse.

Somerset County underwent important surgery in 1838 and 1850. On the first occasion the legislature added to newly founded Mercer County a slice of Somerset that included land along all the north side of

Delaware and Raritan Canal at Griggstown in about 1940, when the swing bridge was still in place over the waterway and some commercial boats still used the canal.

Princeton's Nassau Street facing the college buildings. The 1850 excision took away from Somerset and added to Middlesex the triangle in Franklin Township where Rutgers College was located. Thus, within a dozen years, Somerset lost all claim to both its college towns.

Transportation advances marked the 1870s as the Lehigh Valley Railroad built its line across the center of the county and the Delaware & Bound Brook Railroad laid tracks to link Bound Brook with the South and West. Both railroads, plus the Jersey Central, met near Bound Brook, intensifying that town's vitality as a transportation axis.

Upcounty, a new railroad lured a leisure class to the Somerset hills, reviving the days of large estates. The line was completed to Bernardsville in 1871, prompting George I. Seney, president of the Metropolitan Bank of New York, to build a mansion in that town. When the railroad was completed to Gladstone in 1892 many more bankers, industrialists, and stockbrokers discovered that they could enjoy fresh air best when surrounded by hundreds of acres. They created huge new estates in "the far hills." Italians, who arrived simultaneously to lay the tracks or to work on the estates, found they wanted to share the fresh air. They stayed on in Bernardsville and Peapack, reaping whatever small benefits they might from the landed gentry.

Somerset County had no town of more than 3,000 population until 1880. Somerville then had just 3,100 residents, and the county's total population was only slightly more than 25,000. But one of Somerset County's residents might well have been counted as two—Colonel Ruth Goshen of Middlebush, Barnum's Circus giant whose seven-foot nine-inch stature made him the world's tallest man. His death in February 1889 attracted thousands to gape at the largest single grave ever dug in New Jersey.

None of Somerset County's nineteenth-century wealthy set matched either the imagination or the bankroll of James Buchanan Duke, a tobacco tycoon who scorned the natural hills when he came to buy land in 1893. Starting with the four-hundred-acre Vecht farm on the banks of the Raritan near Somerville, he assembled more than twenty-two hundred acres by the turn of the century.

Then, as one writer put it, "he waved his magic wand, the check book" and wondrous things took place on the flat plains. Men and machines built hills, transplanted full-grown forests, made lakes appear where open fields had been before. Hundreds of thousands of rhododendrons and other shrubs brought a woodland atmosphere to the fabulous estate that surrounded Duke's fifty-room "country house." The tobacco king spent an estimated $15 million to remake his flat open farmland into a hilly forest.

Duke's pride in his estate prompted him to open his lands to visitors, but one day in 1915 a party in 180 cars pulled into Duke Park and picnicked on the front lawn of his mansion. Duke threatened to close the park and made good his threat in 1917 when a visiting motorist promised to thrash him if Duke didn't get his phaeton and team of horses off a park road so uninvited automobilists could get through.

Trinity College, an obscure institution in North Carolina, faced a problem in 1924 when Duke signed papers at Duke Park for a $46 million trust fund for charitable and educational institutions. Of the total, $6 million was for Trinity—if it would change its name to Duke University. Trinity didn't hesitate. Duke died the following year, and left the bulk of his $100 million estate in trust for his daughter, Doris, who became the world's richest girl on her twenty-first birthday in 1933.

The early 1900s gave the entertainment world two Somerset County women. First, young Ruth Dennis made her way from a nearby farm in 1900 to dance on the stage of the old Somerset Hall and leaped from there to worldwide fame as Ruth St. Denis. At about the same time Anna Case, daughter of a South Branch blacksmith, impressed churchgoers with her voice in the Flemington village choir. Eventually Anna Case found her way to the Metropolitan Opera House and a great concert career.

Somerset's pride in its noted daughters could not eclipse its shame for its decaying old courthouse, so rundown that it brought only $125 when sold at public auction in 1906. Removal of the 107-year-old building made way for a new $300,000 white marble courthouse, dedicated in 1909 and still in use. It was here that Mrs. Edward W. Hall and two of her brothers were acquitted

One of the gardens in the greenhouse at the Duke estate, where flowers, plants and trees from eleven nations are shown under an acre of glass. (*Irving Tuttle*)

after they faced trial for the 1922 murder of the Reverend Edward W. Hall, rector of a New Brunswick church, and Mrs. Eleanor Mills, a choir singer. The sensational Hall-Mills trial drew every sob sister and crime reporter in the nation to bucolic Somerville.

Fewer than thirty-five thousand people lived in the county when the new courthouse was dedicated in 1909, and most of those either earned their livings from surrounding farms or commuted to New York offices. Just before World War I, the excellent railroad facilities at Bound Brook finally attracted sizable industry to Somerset. In 1912 the Johns-Manville Company built the biggest asbestos plant in the world in the flats southwest of Bound Brook, where the town of Manville has since grown up. Three years later Somerville's Cotta-Lap Company, a manufacturer of floor covering, cautiously began making chemicals on an eighteen-acre

farm at Bound Brook, using the name of Calco Chemical Company.

Somerset County had intimate knowledge of the actual end of World War I. On July 2, 1921, President Warren G. Harding sat down at a desk in the home of U.S. Senator Joseph S. Frelinghuysen in Raritan and signed the Knox-Porter resolution proclaiming peace between the United States and the Central Powers. Harding had come to the Frelinghuysen estate for a Fourth of July weekend of golf and relaxation.

As Somerset moved through twentieth-century transition, it slowly began measures to preserve its illustrious past. Frelinghuysen descendants stepped forward in 1907 after the Central Railroad purchased the old home of Reverend John Frelinghuysen and planned to demolish it for a right of way. The Frelinghuysens bought the house and moved it fifteen hundred feet, and so well built was the old Dutch parsonage that not a crack was caused by the moving.

In Basking Ridge, members of the Presbyterian Church heard the alarming news in 1924 that their four-hundred-year-old oak tree faced rapidly increasing decay. Experts filled seventy-two cavities in the tree with three tons of concrete and stretched 1,150 feet of cable through the tree to hold up the mighty limbs of Somerset County's most noted natural spectacle.

Industry surged forward in the 1920s and 1930s after highway building programs caused three major roads to meet near Somerville. Since World War II Somerset has become one of the fastest-growing industrial counties in the state, with new industry centering in the Somerville–Bound Brook–Manville area. Three foremost names are Johns Manville, whose Manville plant is said to be the world's most varied producer of asbestos products; American Cyanamid, which absorbed Calco Chemical in 1929; and Union Carbide, whose Bound Brook plant for many years won recognition as "the largest single plant in the United States devoted exclusively to plastics production."

North Plainfield, set off from Warren Township in 1872, grew rapidly in the last twenty-five years of the nineteenth century, doubling its population to almost five thousand in 1900. Immediately adjacent to Plainfield (which juts westward out of Union County in the same fashion that North Plainfield juts eastward out of Somerset), North Plainfield early became noted for its residential quality. Twice big Plainfield wooed its smaller neighbor; twice, in 1902 and 1914, North Plainfield residents turned aside proposals to be annexed into a "Greater Plainfield." The building of State Highway 29 (now 22) through the borough accelerated North Plainfield's growth. As a mark of distinction, the famed Washington Rock is within North Plainfield's boundaries.

Despite its key geographical location, the strategic intersection of several railroads, the success of varied major industries, and the unquestionable beckoning of its rolling hills, Somerset County experienced very slow population growth before World War II. County population totaled just under 100,000 in 1950 (99,052). By 1990, the total reached 239,188, but growth had slowed;

in the early 1970s county planners had guessed the county's population would soar well beyond 300,000 by 1990.

Two interstate highways bisecting the county have brought great changes. Route 287 slices in from the east, curves sharply north near Somerville and heads for Morristown. Route 78 cuts through on nearly a straight east-west line. The interstates meet near splendid old Pluckemin, whose placement slightly off the main roads may make it possible for the village to retain some of its charm. Bridgewater and Franklin township farms have taken the brunt of new residential and commercial building.

Industrial and commercial growth has followed the interstates—and in several cases preceded completion. The two most notable are the huge AT&T installations at Basking Ridge and Bedminster. Several other blue-

This old oak in the Basking Ridge cemetery, about 400 years old, has been saved by extensive tree surgery. (*Irving Tuttle*)

The Somerset Hills in the northern part of the county have long been a magnet for horse fanciers, whose pursuits range from fox hunting and polo to quiet canters on wooded trails. (*Walter Choroszewski*)

chip corporations have followed AT&T to the county. Change is subtle. Much of the northern estate country centered on Bedminster and Far Hills appears intact to those who ride quiet country roads past pasturelands where horses and deer often graze together. The modern era edges in slightly; several of the estates have been sold or converted to such uses as schools or institutions. The Veterans Administration Hospital at Lyons, one of the oldest and best-known veterans' hospitals in the United States, is in the midst of one-time estate country.

The aura of wealth and prominence continues to pervade the Somerset Hills, from Bernardsville to Lamington and from Basking Ridge to Gladstone. These hills are a haven for hard-pressed millionaires, ranging from Wall Street warriors to those whose enthusiasm runs to service in state or federal governments. Horses provide much of the relaxation. Red-coated hunters, handsomely mounted, bound over the Peapack countryside most weekends, following sleek hounds that bay at the heels of an elusive fox. The sport reaches its peak each autumn in the annual hunt race meeting staged at Far Hills by the Essex Fox Hounds Race Meeting Association. Thousands of spectators jam into Far Hills, eager to see, to be seen, and to contribute to the Somerset Medical Center. A bit north, the United States Equestrian drivers and mounts are housed at Hamilton Farms near Gladstone.

Somerset maintains much of its heritage, even in the

Interstate Highways 287 and 78 meet in an intricate pattern just north of Somerville. (*Walter Choroszewski*)

face of twentieth-century pressures. Its people have preserved an unusual number of fine historic homes: the Wallace House and the Old Dutch Parsonage (Freylinghuysen House) in Somerville; Rockingham, Washington's "Farewell" house, in Rocky Hill; the Old Farm House of Andrew Mellick, near Bedminster; the Van Vechten House at Finderne, scene of Washington's dancing mood; the Van Horn and Staats houses at Bound Brook; and the Van Doren House in Millstone, all notable during the Revolution.

The valley of the Millstone deserves attention for its many well-kept vestiges of the old Delaware & Raritan Canal, for the beautiful old church at Millstone, for the gristmill at Weston, and for the Millstone Forge. South of Somerville in Hillsborough Township, part of the Duke estate is again open to the public in a unique "Garden of the Nations." Even to those speeding through the county on the new highways designed for itinerants rather than settlers, Somerset County reveals its beauty. Today, three hundred and more years since the first Dutch traveler saw the Raritan valley, Somerset remains "handsome and pleasant to behold."

Shaded in the summertime by towering trees, Morris County's courthouse in Morristown has stood on a sloping hill since 1827. The exterior of the brick and sandstone building has been little changed in nearly 175 years. Ionic columns divide the arched second-floor windows and the simple entrance is more homelike than governmental. The colonnaded and louvered square belfry is topped by a gold dome and weathervane. (*Irving Tuttle*)

MORRIS

IRON BACKBONE

Douglas Southall Freeman, the esteemed Virginia scholar and writer who prepared the classic biography of George Washington, wrote this about Washington's second winter in Morristown:

"A mass of evidence shows that the winter of 1779–80 at Morristown and Jockey Hollow was a period of far worse suffering than the corresponding months of 1777–78 at Valley Forge.

"This evidence is not going to upset tradition. Valley Forge has become emotionally the symbol of patient suffering during the Revolution, and it will remain so, though one finds it somewhat perplexing to know why the hunger and shivering of Morristown have been so nearly forgotten while the miseries of the gloomy camp on the Schuylkill are known to every child in the fifth grade."

Yet, just as Valley Forge has tended to obscure Morristown in a national sense, so has Morristown's vital role in the Revolution tended to eclipse a dramatic Morris County past before and after the Revolution.

History here is many things other than the Revolution: it is more than 250 years of ups and downs in iron mining, the rise and fall of the unique Morris Canal, changes wrought by railroads, and creation of the commuter. It is the roses of Madison, the millionaires of Morristown, the happy Victorian days at Lake Hopatcong. It includes the rise of the dynamite and explosives industry near Dover, the stubborn modern fight to save the Great Swamp and the mushrooming growth of suburbia since World War II.

Iron today is mainly a matter of thinking in the past, but it is the place to begin, for much of Morris County's story rests solidly on "Suckysunny," the "black stone" that Lenape Indians showed colonists soon after 1700. Until then, the course of settlement had been slow: Dutch entrepreneurs from Bergen came in about 1695 to take up fifteen hundred acres near Pompton Plains; a few German and Dutch wanderers headed overland from Philadelphia to New York and stopped at Schooley's Mountain in 1707; former New Englanders came over the mountains from Essex County to settle at Whippanong (now Whippany) in 1710 and to spread westward to start West Hanover (now Morristown).

Hanover Township quickly became the dominant factor because of the old forge built on the Whippany River about 1710. Soon after, a forge began operations in "the hollow" (Morristown), and within twenty years other ironmen followed—at Dover, where John Jackson lit his forge fire in 1722, and at Rockaway in about 1730. Most of the ironworks clustered along the Rockaway River, where proximity to the ore was combined with dashing water power and thick forests—a highly significant factor, since a single forge "fire" alone could consume one thousand acres of woodland annually.

Most of the early ironmakers used ore from the mine opened in about 1713 near Succasunna, where the "blackstone" cropped out on the surface and required little digging. Horses plodded from mine to furnace, carrying ore in leather bags. Then, when the ore was melted, the weary beasts plodded on to tidewater, toting iron bars shaped to their backs.

Jacob Ford, Sr., leader of early Morris ironmen, encouraged agitation in the 1730s to have Morris County cut away from Hunterdon, at a time when Morris had only two settlers per square mile. Hunterdon relinquished a territory encompassing all of what is now Morris, Sussex, and Warren counties in 1739. The new county was named Morris in honor of Governor Lewis Morris, who in 1738 had become the first New Jerseyan to be governor of East New Jersey and West New Jersey. Fifteen years later (1753) Sussex County (including modern Warren) broke away from Morris. The Morris County "freedom" was severely limited; the county had no representatives in the state legislature until 1772.

Morristown assumed both its name and designation as county seat in 1740. Elsewhere the early villages of Pompton, Whippany, German Valley (now Long Valley), Chester, Dover, Rockaway, and Mendham were securely in place north and west of Morristown. Chatham and Bottle Hill (Madison) were modest towns to the east, but Morristown ruled supreme as a commercial center. Ironworkers trekked to Morristown once a week for supplies and most official business, public and private, was done there.

Moribund iron towns such as Rockaway boomed again when the Morris Canal came through in the 1830s. (*Barber and Howe*)

Morris County ironmasters rebelled when a 1750 British decree forbade any rolling or slitting mills to be operated in the colonies. They kept their Morris mills operating in defiance of the decree, and this a full twenty years before violation of British laws became widespread.

The premise might be suggested that the Morris hills gave birth to an early full-scale rebellion, except that the most noted of the surreptitious slitting mills, the one at Boone Town, was run by men who became Tories after the war started. This rebellion of the 1750s was more a rebellion of the pocketbook than of principle.

John Jacob Faesch came to the Morris scene in 1772, when he bought several thousand acres at Mount Hope after leaving the London Company at Ringwood in northern Passaic County. Faesch built a furnace, expanded his holdings near Mount Hope to more than ten thousand acres, and became the county's supreme ironmaster, more powerful even than the Fords, Jacob, Sr., and Jacob, Jr. Faesch's richness did not extend to the spirit, however, since he believed religion was a "very good thing—to keep the lower classes in proper subordination."

Morris County attracted a landed gentry class even before the Revolution. In addition to Faesch and the Fords (who in 1774 completed the mansion that Washington occupied in the winter of 1779–80), great landholders included Peter Kemble, who became a Tory; Lucas von Beaverhoudt, who entertained impartially both British and American soldiers at Beaverwyck in Troy Hills, and Captain Michael Kearny of His Britannic Majesty's Navy, whose Whippany estate was known as the "Irish Lot."

When war flared, Morris County had the iron backbone to stiffen rebellion. General Washington led his bruised troops north to Morristown from Princeton early in January 1777 and remained until late spring. Washington familiarized himself with the ironworks (one of his letters written in 1777 tells of between eighty and one hundred ironworks "great and small" in Morris County).

Munitions poured from the forges and furnaces, particularly those at Hibernia and Mount Hope. Shovels, axes, cannon, cannonballs, grapeshot, and other supplies went to the Continental Army throughout the war. In return, ironworks employees were exempted from service. Colonel Jacob Ford built a powder mill beside the Whippany River near Morristown in 1776, one of the first in the nation and undoubtedly the only Revolutionary War powder mill in New Jersey.

All New Jersey mourned the untimely death of both Fords in January 1777, shortly after Washington led his troops into Morristown. Jacob, Jr., died January 11 of pneumonia; eight days later Jacob, Sr., died of fever. So Morris County lost its most important early leaders at a time when the American cause sorely needed both.

Washington spent his first winter in Morristown at Jacob Arnold's Tavern while his men camped in the adjacent Loantaka Valley to the east. Surrounding hills made the village easy to defend, and even then it must have been a handsome place, since the village green had been set aside as early as 1771. The green is still in the center of Morristown, a tree-shaded reminder of colonial days. The ease of defense, the pleasantness of the village, and the strength of the nearby iron region lured Washington and his army back for the winter of 1779–80.

That winter truly tested the endurance of the American cause. The war had dragged on for more than four and a half years when Washington and his army arrived in town on December 1, 1779. Washington established his headquarters in the Ford Mansion and his men went to endure winter's might at Jockey Hollow.

Everything added up to despair—little food, meager pay, and wretched quarters for the men. Snow fell on twenty-eight separate occasions, and a blizzard between the third and fifth of January 1780 buried men in their tents "like sheep," according to an eyewitness. Washington wrote that the men "ate every kind of horse food but hay."

Mrs. Washington arrived in Morristown on December 28 to spend the winter with the general. The Washingtons shared the mansion with Mrs. Ford, her four young children, and seventeen officers. The twenty-four occupants often gathered near the kitchen fireplace, the only warm place in the house.

To top all else, Benedict Arnold faced a court-martial board in the Dickerson Tavern, Morristown, in December 1779. Accused of favoring Tories in Philadelphia, Arnold received only a mild reprimand from Washington, but it stung him deeply enough to cause him to desert to the British a few weeks later.

Despite the generally low morale, Washington and his staff had some high moments in Morristown. Count Pulaski helped maintain cheer by his exhibitions of brilliant horsemanship. The Marquis de Lafayette, returning from a journey to France in May 1780, reported that a powerful French force was on the way with help. Young Colonel Alexander Hamilton courted Betty Schuyler, who was visiting an uncle just around the corner from the Ford Mansion. Eventually she became his wife.

Hopes for an early peace soared when the army moved out of Jockey Hollow in June 1780. Thus the bitterness of two Pennsylvania brigades, still in service and back in Jockey Hollow the following winter, can be understood. Many of the men had been fighting for more than three years; most had not been paid for over a year. Their grumbling culminated in mutiny on New Year's Day, 1781, when they killed one of their officers, Captain Adam Bettin, and marched off toward Philadelphia. Their commander, General "Mad" Anthony Wayne, followed the mutineers to Princeton and at a series of meetings promised better things for the men. Satisfied, the brigades returned to Morristown.

Out of the mutiny came one of New Jersey's best-known Revolutionary stories, that of Tempe Wick and her horse. The young colonial miss fought off several soldiers from the mutinous Pennsylvania brigade who tried to seize her beloved steed. She galloped home and, according to a persistent legend, led her horse into her bedroom to conceal him from troops who searched in the woods, in the barn, and everywhere but in the house.

War swerved southward to Virginia and the Carolinas. Late in August 1781, Washington sent advance units to Chatham to set up giant bake ovens to delude the British into thinking he would attack New York. The ruse worked perfectly. While the enemy braced for a blow from Morris County, Washington led the main body of his army across New Jersey and on to the plains of Yorktown.

Morris County's isolated position made it stand nearly still after the war. Chartering of turnpikes in the first decade of the nineteenth century slowly increased the county's population and broadened its economy. A toll pike from Elizabethtown to Morristown via Chatham

Built in 1774 by the Ford family, this mansion served Washington and his staff as headquarters during the winter of 1779–80. (*Charles Perry Weimer*)

and Bottle Hill (Madison) encouraged travel (but also prompted the more thrifty to avoid the turnpike via the parallel "shun-pike" a mile to the south). The Washington Turnpike, chartered in 1806 to run from Morristown to Easton, made the Schooley's Mountain "health" business spurt wondrously. Although the Alpha Hotel had been built on the mountain in 1795, it took the turnpike to help make Schooley's Mountain a nationally known health resort.

"The most gay and fashionable company" harkened up Schooley's slopes, to the Alpha Hotel and the Heath House and later to the Dorincourt Hotel. They came for their health (or said they did), and their illnesses vanished after drinking from the miraculous springs, the waters of which contained many minerals and health-giving elements (not the least of which was sodium bicarbonate).

Meanwhile, ironmakers burned timber furiously along the Rockaway River. Forges and furnaces for miles around continued to depend on the old Succasunna mine (renamed Dickerson Mine when the family of Governor Mahlon Dickerson bought the property in the 1780s). From 1826 to 1830, a hundred forges in an area from Hamburg to High Bridge used Dickerson Mine ore. Some other pits—notably Mount Hope—supplied ore, but the easiest digging was at Succasunna.

High costs of transportation and wanton misuse of forest land seemed certain to doom the Morris County iron industry, until George P. Macculloch, a Morristown schoolteacher, went fishing on Lake Hopatcong one summer day in 1822. Gazing eastward over the lake, Macculloch noted the mountains sloping away and his mind played with the thought of a canal, utilizing the waters of Lake Hopatcong and flowing to tidewater down the Rockaway and Passaic river valleys. He looked westward, conceived the possibility of sending the canal down the Musconetcong River valley to Phillipsburg, the approach to Pennsylvania's anthracite coal fields.

Macculloch definitely had Morris County iron in mind when he sought financing for his plan. His scheme seemed fantastic; financial backing came slowly, but by August 1831 the canal—every inch of it dug by hand—linked Phillipsburg and Newark. Never before had such an engineering feat been accomplished; boats literally climbed mountains by an ingenious system that combined inclined planes and locks. Anthracite flowed into Morris County to give new life to the forges and furnaces. Iron again became the king.

Dover, Port Oram (Wharton), Boonton, and Rockaway all revived in the wake of the canal. Henry McFarlan and Joseph Blackwell, New York merchants, expanded the old Dover ironworks. In 1827 they laid out streets and offered lots for sale (with the canal-to-be their chief selling point). Smoke soon bellowed forth in thick columns from the village's two rolling mills, its foundries, its nail and spike factory, its forging shop, and numerous smaller iron-connected enterprises.

Boonton had the most impressive boom of all, however. Grass grew green in that town's rutted streets before the canal cut through. Then the New Jersey Iron Company built a new mill in the village in 1830. The company brought in skilled rolling mill mechanics from England and started to produce in quantity. Paradoxically, as soon as the mill began to benefit from the canal, it began to turn out axles, wheels, and rails for railroads, thus helping doom the canal before it was fairly started.

One of the most famous iron manufactories of all was the Speedwell Iron Works in Morristow[n] achievements included the manufacture in driving shaft for the S.S. *Savannah*, first ve the Atlantic using steam. Samuel F. B. Mc fred Vail brought the old works its greatest ever, by their development of the elec telegraph—with the financial encouragem[ent] Stephen Vail, Alfred's father and owner [of] works. Three miles of wire looped inside carried the first telegraph message on Janu[ary] when Vail ticked out: "A patient waiter is n[o loser]. though he is nearly forgotten now, it was Alfred Vail who perfected the first telegraph transmitter and it was he who devised the dot-and-dash code that erroneously has been called "Morse code."

The Morris Canal was wonderful, but a trip from Phillipsburg to Jersey City took five days. Far more important was the Morris & Essex Railroad. It reached Morristown in 1838 and snaked its way to Dover within ten years. Morristown, Madison, and Dover all picked up pace, and by 1850 the earliest and most hardy commuters were living in Morris County and working in

Legend says that Tempe Wick hid her horse in a bedroom here when rebelling American troops tried to seize the steed. (*Earl Horter drawing, The State Library*)

The Dickerson Mine near Dover, one of the earliest sources of Morris County iron ore. (*State Geologist's Report*, 1855)

Newark or New York. That called for patient waiters: a one-way junket from Morristown to New York took three hours.

Quick transportation encouraged extensive mining and exportation of iron ore. In 1855 Morris County mines produced 100,000 tons of ore; twelve years later that total jumped to 275,000 tons, and by 1880 Morris was the third county in the nation in amount of iron ore mined, with 568,420 tons.

The old Dickerson Mine continued at full pitch, but it could not begin to meet demands. Iron mines pockmarked the entire backbone of western and northern Morris County; operators dug deeper and deeper for the precious black stone. As many as fifty mines operated simultaneously in the region from Long Valley to Hibernia. Then the national iron industry discovered in 1882 that iron ore could almost literally be picked off the surface in the Mesabi region near Lake Superior. The iron crown moved from Morris to Mesabi.

The New Jersey iron dynasty faced ruin, although full effects of the Mesabi interloper took years to develop. Nevertheless, the ancient Dickerson Mine closed in the 1890s after giving up more than a million tons of ore. Hurdtown's famous mine closed in 1898, after going down twenty-six hundred feet for elusive iron. Hibernia,

once the heart of the industry, heard the sound of the pick for the last time in 1913, seven years after thirteen miners had drowned in flooded shafts.

The iron mines attracted allied industries. Dover had an extensive plant in the 1870s for making mine equipment, in addition to its rolling mills. Boonton's iron processers gained additional fame for nail production, while Wharton (formerly Port Oram) attracted the tremendous foundry of the Replogle Steel Company (whose closing in 1919 brought devastating economic collapse to Wharton).

Mines enticed the Giant Powder Company of California to Kenvil in 1871 to make dynamite. First devoted exclusively to dynamite, Giant turned to smokeless powder and during World War I (as Hercules Powder Company) added TNT.

Hercules strengthened Morris County's long-established role as an "arsenal of freedom," and the title became fixed in September 1880, when the War Department purchased 1,866 acres east of Green Pond Mountain to build mighty Picatinny Arsenal (which now spreads over 5,125 acres of ground with installations valued at considerably more than $100 million).

More than anything, the Morris & Essex Railroad changed the county's character by offering increasingly rapid and dependable train service. Men of wealth recognized that they could work in New York and live in the healthful Morris hills: in Morristown, Madison, Convent, Chatham, and surrounding areas. Morristown's handsome streets were adorned with great Victorian mansions, and splendid estates on the surrounding slopes harbored the wealthy and the famous.

Opulence was a Morris County tradition. William Gibbons of Elizabeth, one of the nation's early millionaires, completed the finest mansion in the county at Madison in 1836, far grander than even the Ford Mansion, the standard of previous generations. The palatial brick home, 150 feet wide and 100 feet deep, rose in the high-pillared Southern tradition that Gibbons cherished. Daniel Drew, noted New York financial scoundrel, bought the mansion and grounds in 1867 and donated it to a newly-founded Methodist seminary. In gratitude, the Methodists named their school Drew University. The Gibbons Mansion, completely refurbished after a major fire in August 1989, remains the heart of Drew.

As the twentieth century dawned, Morristown boasted that within a radius of one mile of the green more millionaires lived than in any other equal area in the world. A *World Magazine* article in 1905 reported that ninety-two persons each worth a million dollars or more called Morristown home. Their fabulous estates were numerous enough to fill the pages of a World War I vintage picture book, *Beautiful Homes of Morris County.*

Heading the millionaires in total assets were Mr. and Mrs. Hamilton McK. Twombly, worth $70 million between them. The Twomblys called their hundred-room house and nine-hundred-acre estate Florham (for Florence and Hamilton) and in 1899 urged the little village of Afton—where they paid most of the village taxes—to change its name to Florham Park. Afton's town fathers found no difficulty in complying.

Although the Twomblys had the most money, the most opulent spender seemed to be the international banker, Otto H. Kahn. His Cedar Court in Normandie Heights was so lavish that a 1905 fire, which destroyed only the east wing, caused damage estimated at $750,000.

The moneyed families imported large numbers of people to serve, particularly Southern blacks who came to work in the mansions and Italian immigrants who labored in the greenhouses and on the rolling lawns. Large numbers of area people depended on the estates for their living, and continued to do so until the Depression days of the 1930s.

Once the "summer residence" of the ultra-rich Hamilton K. Twombleys, this mansion is now the centerpiece of Fairleigh Dickenson University's campus in Florham Park and Madison. (*Walter Choroszewski*)

Lake Hopatcong, shared by Morris and Sussex counties, is New Jersey's largest lake, seven miles long with a shoreline of more than forty miles around.

Monied families also contributed an air of serenity that artists and writers found pleasant. Bret Harte and Rudyard Kipling both wrote for short periods near Morristown. The most famous names among permanent residents were A. B. Frost, a painter of outdoor and sporting scenes; Frank Stockton, prolific writer of books and short stories; and Thomas Nast, the greatest of nineteenth-century cartoonists and the originator of both the Republican elephant and the Democratic donkey as political symbols.

Another by-product of the wealthy families was the beginning of the rose industry that for decades became a way of life in Madison, Chatham, and Chatham Township.

Roses had been grown for sale in Madison as early as 1856, but the rise of the "Rose City" specialty really began in 1877 when T. J. Slaughter, a rich cotton broker, bought the luxurious Dellwood estate. He built greenhouses, hired John N. May as superintendent, and by 1886 the Slaughter greenhouses shipped as many as four hundred thousand rosebuds annually.

Within fifteen years, between forty-five and fifty small greenhouses were built in Madison and Chatham, most of them within hailing distance of the Railway Express offices. These leading growers were respected everywhere: Louis M. Noe of Chatham Township, the nation's foremost grower of the great *American Beauty*; Frank L. Moore of Chatham, originator of the *Bridesmaid*; and Charles Totty, a Madison rose man whose name was famed throughout the world.

The pleasant, simple days of the late nineteenth century also brought increasing numbers of vacationists to the Morris County lakeland. A few built huge cottages on the shores of Lake Hopatcong, but for most people, a lake vacation was a camping trip. Sunday "excursion" crowds flocked to the lake in the 1890s and on through World War I days, mainly on Jersey Central Railroad cars from Jersey City by way of High Bridge and Long Valley.

In the midst of all this, farming was the major theme. The population of 65,156 in 1900 was widely scattered; only Morristown, with 11,267 people, had more than 6,000 people. Villages west of the county seat clung to rural ways through the 1920s, scarcely touched by the

changing world, even to electricity or running water. Fourth and fifth generations of the same families occupied the farms of their forebears.

It couldn't last. Automobiles chugged outward from Morristown and by 1930 Morris County felt its first growing pains: population had nearly doubled since 1900. Raw statistics tell the story: population in 1940, 125,732; in 1990, 421,353. Parsippany–Troy Hills, a sprawling township whose population was only 10,976 in 1940, has leveled off at about 48,000 residents and is about three times as big in population as Morristown, the long-time leader.

Morris County's population has leaped by 160,000 persons since 1960, an average of about 53,000 new people every decade. However, 120,000 of those newcomers arrived in the single decade between 1960 and 1970—fleeing the evils of the cities, real or imagined; following the newly completed Interstates 80 and 280, and heeding the lure of builders who found ample money to turn pastures into developments. Since 1970, in contrast, the influx of population has averaged fewer than 2,000 new people annually.

Population growth has spread through nearly every municipality, remarkably well distributed. Fifteen towns have populations of more than 10,000: among them, only Parsippany, Mount Olive, Randolph, Roxbury, and Morris Township exceed 20,000. Of the fifteen, eight are within easy hailing distance of Routes 280 or 80, both completed in time to accelerate the flight from the cities.

Transition is easily seen. The iron mines, after a spurt during World War II and for a decade later, are completely dormant. Even the Mount Hope mine, acclaimed when dug in the 1940s as the "deepest mine shaft east of the Mississippi," is shut. The lakelands are more crowded than ever, and nearly all of the lakefronts are occupied by year-round homes. The great estates of the millionaires are nearly all gone, although several live on in other forms.

Allied Signal occupies the former Otto Kahn estate. Fairleigh Dickinson University occupies the Twombly mansion and part of the estate grounds, sharing the latter with Exxon Research Laboratories. Mead Hall in Madison, the William Gibbons mansion, is the

Each May the campus of Drew University comes alive with the white of dogwood blooms, especially in front of Mead Hall, completed in 1836, now a beautifully restored national landmark.

administration building for Drew University. A few blocks away, Bayley-Ellard High School is housed in another old mansion. Nearby, in Convent, St. Elizabeth's College is set in an area that is still predominantly estate country.

The clash between those who pursue growth and those who seek to retain historic and natural charm have been inevitable. Planners occasionally mutter wistfully that Morristown traffic would be speeded if the town's colonial green were to be paved over, forgetful that the town's uniqueness depends entirely on that center. The new highways relieve some old problems and create even greater ones by bringing in more industry, more population, and more traffic. Area residents fought bitterly (and futilely) in the early 1960s to keep new Interstate Highway 287 from slicing through Morris-

64

The Great Swamp, in southeastern Morris County, the remains of ancient Lake Passaic, became a landmark in the campaign for land preservation after a threat in 1960 to convert the site into a jetport was turned back. (*Walter Choroszewski*)

town, within less than a stone's throw of the Ford Mansion, one of America's historical shrines. The cries of historians were ignored.

Road builders won the highway fight in Morristown, but local conservationists gained national attention and praise by repulsing the Port of New York Authority's determined bid to build a giant jetport in the Great Swamp. Announcement in 1959 that the Authority wanted the swamp caused such an outpouring of emotion and enthusiasm that some three thousand acres of swampland were purchased and donated to the federal government to create a national wildlife refuge. The Great Swamp, a portion of the lake bottom of prehistoric and long-forgotten Lake Passaic, lives on. Its survival has been hailed as one of the most successful conservation fights in American history.

Thus Morris County has moved far away from the days when the "Anvil Chorus" and "Yankee Doodle" could suffice as Morris themes. Still, the Revolutionary and Great Swamp heritages grow ever more cherished—and never forget that the iron is still there: more than six hundred million tons lie in the closed mines. King Ferro could return some day, to greater glory, but Morris County has no intention of standing idly still to await that day.

Paterson was at the height of its industrial prosperity in 1903, when this massive Passaic County courthouse, as grandiose as many state capitols, was finished. The white marble structure is topped by an impressive dome and cupola and the front entrance is in the then-popular neoclassicist tradition. This old courthouse was completely renovated in 1965 when a new six-story courthouse was built closer to the city center.

PASSAIC

WASP-WAISTED

Elbridge Gerry's early nineteenth-century philosophy that land areas should be manipulated in a manner most beneficial to politicians (forever remembered as "gerrymandering") found full favor in February 1837 when New Jersey legislators labored in Trenton to establish Passaic County. No area ever was more gerrymandered territory than wasp-waisted Passaic.

First, South Jersey votes held back Passaic County until Atlantic County could be created to maintain a balance of power. Then, by linking the little-settled country north of Pompton Lakes with the heavily industrial regions along the Passaic River, South Jersey politicians killed a long-heard clamoring for two small, logical new North Jersey counties proposed under the names of "Pompton" and "Paterson." The Pompton and Paterson counties clearly recognized the striking geographical and economic differences between the rugged hill country of the north and the emerging factory area in the crook of the Passaic River. But only the one hourglass-shaped county could be slipped by the legislature. Few worried that North Passaic's forestlands had little in common with Paterson's factories. Intervening years have failed to make the two areas on either side of the narrow two-mile connecting corridor completely one. The waist divides as much as it connects.

Water is a common denominator between north and

south, for the ponds and reservoirs that fill the forested valleys of the north drain through the Pompton River to swell the mighty Passaic River. Those combined waters spill precipitously over the Passaic Falls at Paterson, in tribute to a common heritage. The "Great Falls" also are a reminder of glacial days. Some twenty thousand years ago, when Lake Passaic spread for thirty miles to the south because ice had clogged natural outlets of the Passaic River, the pent-up waters smashed through a new outlet over the rocky cliff. Passaic County's history would be linked to that cataract.

Indians spoke with awe of the falls, calling it Totowa, meaning "heavy, falling weight of waters." Passaic was a Lenape word, too. Some say it meant "place where the land splits" or "place where the river splits." Others claim the word meant "valley" to the Lenape. Under any circumstance, "Passaic" troubled the early settlers who tried to spell it. Variations included Passaick, Passawicke, Passaya, Fishawack, and dozens more.

Dutch settlers came early, meandering up the river to a spot below the falls. The earliest of record was Hartman Michielsen, who bought an island in the river in 1679 from Captehan Peeters, an Indian with an anglicized name. That same year two Dutch missionaries wrote an awe-filled account of the grandeur of the falls, "a sight to be seen in order to observe the power and

A reminder of old iron glories is the state-owned Ringwood Manor. (*N.J.D.C.E.D.*)

wonder of God." Then, in 1682, fourteen Dutch families acquired the Acquackanonck Tract, comprising most of modern Clifton, Passaic, and Paterson. Acquackanonck was another Indian name, meaning "place in the rapid stream where the nets are set."

Arent Schuyler and Anthony Brockholts, a former acting governor of New York, bought fifty-five hundred acres near Pompton in 1696. Schuyler promptly began to build a house, which still stands in Pompton Lakes. All of the land in modern Passaic County had been purchased from the Indians before 1711, including the acres on the forbidding Bearfort, Kanouse, and Ramapo mountains to the north. Settlers stopped at the "little falls" (west of modern Paterson) in 1711, and Simeon Van Winkle built his "white house" on a river ford two miles below the "great falls" before 1719. German and Dutch families lived in the rough northern country by 1730, among them John Jacob Kanouse of Holland, whose name is perpetuated in Kanouse Mountain.

Cornelius Board, tramping up and down the Ramapo

Valley seeking copper, found iron instead, and built a forge near Ringwood before 1740. Board sold out to the Ogdens of Newark in 1742. Styling themselves the Ringwood Company, the Ogdens commenced the smelting of iron. The name Ringwood probably came from an estate in Hampshire, England.

Word of the rich iron deposits spread to England, where the American Company (sometimes called the "London Company") commissioned an energetic German, Peter Hasenclever, to represent them in American iron ventures. Hasenclever sailed for America in 1764 and quickly acquired fifty thousand acres, including the Ogden's "decayed iron works" at Ringwood. He imported 535 Germans to run his mines and smelting furnaces and created a thriving iron community within two years. Roads spread through the forestland to connect the Ringwood mines with company-owned furnaces at Pompton, Charlotteburg, and Newfoundland. Hasenclever lived so much like a feudal lord in the mountains that visitors called him "Baron."

In the surrounding forests deeply religious German colonists eagerly welcomed the Reverend Ferdinand Farmer, the indefatigable Catholic priest who conducted services at Macopin (Echo Lake) in the 1750s. Father Farmer's impromptu services in those wild northern hills were among the earliest Catholic masses in New Jersey.

The Baron spent £58,000 in two years, returned to London for more money, only to be bankrupt by 1769. John Jacob Faesch succeeded Hasenclever, and Faesch in turn yielded control to Robert Erskine in 1771. Erskine's diligent efforts at Ringwood mines provided munitions for the Revolutionary cause, and the young Scotsman rendered yeoman service as surveyor general and map maker for the Continental Army. Before his death in 1780 at the age of forty-five, Erskine had drawn more than two hundred detailed maps.

General Washington often stayed in what is now Passaic County. The main American army encamped at Pompton, Wayne, and Totowa in the summer and fall of 1780. Washington and his officers lived in the big redbrick Theunis Dey Mansion at Preakness from July 1 to 29 and from October 8 to November 27, 1780. The gambrel-roofed house, already forty years old when

Washington slept there, still stands and is open to visitors.

Nevertheless, Washington's most important visit of all possibly was on July 10, 1778, when the general stopped for lunch at the foot of the majestic "Totowa Falls." One of his officers, young Alexander Hamilton, particularly exulted in the pounding volume of the falls as they plunged seventy feet into their rocky gorge.

Thirteen years later Hamilton, then secretary of the treasury in Washington's Cabinet, sent to Congress his vital "Report on Manufactures." He insisted that the new nation could never be truly free until it manufactured its own products. Unquestionably he envisioned an industrial city beside the falls that he had first seen as an army colonel; he knew the power potential. Certainly he rejoiced on November 22, 1791, when New Jersey's Governor William Paterson signed the charter for the Society for Establishing Useful Manufactures.

The society (even then abbreviated as S.U.M.) invited proposals from New York, New Jersey, and Pennsylvania—but Hamilton offered no objection to an engineer's declaration that the Passaic falls offered "the best situation in the world." An S.U.M. committee accepted that appraisal on May 17, 1792, bought seven hundred acres at the falls, and named their projected city in honor of Governor Paterson. Hamilton modestly, and with political sagacity, rejected suggestions that the place be named for him.

The society hired Major Pierre Charles L'Enfant to design the city in a manner to "surpass anything yet seen in the country." L'Enfant sketched elaborate plans, with streets two hundred feet wide branching out like spokes from a hub, but the S.U.M. budget failed to match L'Enfant's imagination. The major took off with his plans, which proved very valuable when he laid out Washington, D.C., in 1801 on the flat land near the Potomac.

Peter Colt, treasurer of the State of Connecticut, succeeded L'Enfant in February 1793, taking over a moribund organization that had raised only $275,000 of its anticipated $500,000. He started digging a raceway to lead the powerful river to the Society's cotton mill, which became known as the "Bull Mill" because Colt operated it with oxen while awaiting water power.

America had few skilled craftsmen; Colt imported them from England, Scotland, and Ireland.

Gloom descended on the budding city when the S.U.M. ran out of money in 1796, thanks largely to an employee who absconded with $50,000 when sent to England to buy machine parts. The society's mill ground to a stop, but individual operators came to the city to lease S.U.M. property. John Clark, for example, started Paterson's first machine shop in about 1800. His plant became a noted training school for mechanics. John Parke built a small cotton mill of his own, then in 1810 erected a large stone mill.

Parke disdained sending his products to New York via the sloops tied up at nearby Acquackanonck Landing. Instead, he packed his cotton in "gorgeously painted" covered wagons and went overland to Philadelphia. It cost more, but Parke found it paid to advertise. Business boomed for Parke (and the city's six or seven other cotton millers) in the War of 1812, but industry collapsed again when peace came. A new national tariff in 1816 pumped life back into the cotton mills; Paterson's ever-recurring boom-and-bust cycles had begun.

A dozen cotton mills prospered in S.U.M. facilities in 1825 and twice that many used the power of the falls by 1829. Moneyed men invested in the mills and built fine homes on the hillsides surrounding Paterson. The big industrial leaders scorned free schools, although they

Dey Mansion at Preakness, where Washington spent eighty days in the summer and fall of 1780. (*Earl Horter drawing, The State Library*)

69

Winter fashions a tight grip on Paterson's "Great Falls," which in warmer weather plunges seventy feet to create the awesome power that in 1791 led to the founding of Paterson as the nation's first planned industrial city. (*Walter Choroszewski*)

allowed Sunday schools where youngsters working in the mills could study on their day off without hindering production. In 1832 Paterson had twenty "pay" schools, one free school.

Paterson broke away from Acquackanonck Township in a mutually satisfying separation in 1831. Paterson leaders decided they wanted to keep their own tax revenues. Acquackanonck people found satisfaction in the thriving trade carried on by Passaic River steamers which touched at their docks—and saw no reason why Paterson votes should run their little community.

A fearsome cholera epidemic struck the Passaic River lands in 1832, killing 140 in Paterson alone, but it failed to stop full operation of the Morris Canal through the county via Paterson and Little Falls. Nor did it stop work on the Paterson and Hudson River Railroad, chartered on January 21, 1831, and completed to Jersey City in 1834. Steam locomotives ran over the route for the first time in June 1835. Paterson's mills absorbed coal brought in by the Morris Canal and sent increasing quantities of goods to tidewater on the railroad.

The new transportation eventually helped upcounty farmers, too, by opening great new markets. The Morris Canal boosted Little Falls industry and gave it enough prominence to entice Robert Beattie's carpet company out from New York to build a "capacious" mill in 1842. Only Acquackanonck (Passaic) suffered, because the canal and railroad doomed its dockside trade.

Meanwhile, in Paterson, the Colt family took over complete control of the S.U.M. by purchasing 1,991 of the society's 2,620 shares. Roswell L. Colt, largest shareholder and "the greatest of the Colts," became governor of the society in 1814 and served until his death in 1856.

Other Colts had genius, too. John Colt started to make cotton in Paterson in 1814, and in 1827 he became the first man ever to substitute cotton for flax in sail duck. The yacht *America*, sporting the legend "Colt's Duck Mill" on her sails, won for this country the coveted America's Cup. Samuel Colt made his first Colt revolver in the Paterson "Gun Mill" in 1836. Sam's gun seemed a failure, so he sold his last Paterson model to an Indian trader in 1842. When the government finally recognized the gun's merits in 1847 and gave him a large order in time for the Mexican War, Colt had no model from which to work. He redesigned the revolver and resumed manufacture in Hartford, Connecticut, where he made his fortune.

Another Colt, Christopher, established Paterson's first silk mill in 1839, but the true "father" of the Paterson silk industry was John Ryle. Colt sold his silk plant in 1840 to George W. Murray, who brought Ryle from England to superintend operations. Ryle set up a battery of silk looms in 1842 and bought out Murray in 1846. Soon Ryle was hiring three hundred people to make one thousand pounds of silk weekly. The "Silk City" was born.

Cotton supremacy gravitated from Paterson to New England after the Panic of 1837, but the mechanical know-how and the pool of experienced male and female hands remained behind. Thus, when several companies began to make railroad locomotives in the 1830s, Paterson had an edge on all the nation: its machinists could make anything. It was no anomaly that Paterson became the "Iron City" and the "Locomotive City" at the same time it became the "Silk City."

Thomas Rogers, Paterson mechanic, made the city's first locomotive in 1837, finishing the "Sandusky" for an Ohio railroad. In 1838, Rogers boasted that he had built five railroad engines in a single year and by 1850 the plant turned out more than one hundred locomotives a year. Others followed; by Civil War times Paterson and Philadelphia between them made 75 percent of all American locomotives, with Paterson holding a slight lead over its big-city rival. Horses pulled completed locomotives along Market Street to the Erie Railroad freight yards.

Paterson and Passaic County were synonymous before the Civil War. No one challenged the city's right to become the county seat in 1837. Seventy percent of Passaic's 16,734 people lived in or adjacent to Paterson in 1840—a ratio between upcounty and downcounty that continued unchecked for almost another fifty years.

Amidst the clanging of factories and the whirring of looms, Paterson Township officially became a city in 1851. Its 11,341 people had great pride. In fact, too much pride and too much sense to permit aldermen to continue wearing on their hats the leather badges that proclaimed: ALDERMAN, FIRST WARD (or any other ward). That was too much for democratic Paterson, whose citizens ridiculed the show of snobbishness. The badges disappeared.

Down the river, people living in sight of Dundee Island clung to their quaint name of Acquackanonck and stubbornly demanded ridiculously high prices for their land. There were few buyers. Finally, after thirty years of fruitless attempts to harness the river as Paterson had done seventy years before, the Dundee Manufacturing Company gave in to exorbitant demands and bought two key farms in 1858. The company built a 450-foot dam across the river and let it be known that open arms awaited manufacturers.

A small brick and anvil factory responded initially, and the New York Steam-Engine Company works, a

Looking eastward from Garret Mountain Reservation toward Paterson, the viewer is rewarded with a panorama that includes both the historic city and the countryside for miles around. (*Walter Choroszewski*)

Oak Ridge Reservoir, shown here, is one of several Passaic County water storage areas built to supply the needs of half a dozen nearby counties.

wire mill, and a printworks followed. By 1871, when the state legislature permitted the village of Passaic to split away from Acquackanonck Township, about fifteen mills fringed the Dundee water power canal. Fewer than three thousand people lived in the area.

All Passaic County expanded in the last three decades of the nineteenth century. Wayne Township boasted in 1880 of the Laflin & Rand Powder Company (capacity, six hundred kegs daily). H. Julius Smith broke away from Laflin & Rand in 1886 to found his noted blasting cap factory in Pompton Lakes. Mountain View had four brick factories producing more than one hundred twenty thousand bricks daily. The Beattie Company greatly en-

larged its carpet plant at Little Falls, and four other mills and an iron molding plant built near the Beattie factory.

North of the "wasp waist," iron and water paced the advance. Martin Ryerson and family took over the old Ringwood works in 1807 and operated them sporadically until 1853, when Peter Cooper bought the twenty-two-thousand-acre property at public auction. Cooper, New York glue magnate, inventor, and promoter, pushed the old mines to their greatest prominence—aided by Abram Hewitt, who merged his personal and business fortunes with Cooper in 1855 by marrying Peter's daughter Amelia.

The Cooper-Hewitt combine made the mines pay.

The 1880 census showed that up to then a total of 896,000 long tons had been taken from twenty Ringwood mines. Some estimates today say 2,500,000 long tons have been taken from the mines since colonial days—a great percentage of it during management by Cooper and Hewitt interests. The mines, worked on and off since 1931, have been idle now for nearly fifty years.

New life came upcounty in the 1870s, when the New York Susquehanna & Western Railroad and the Montclair and Greenwood Lake Railway both laid their tracks through Passaic County's narrow waist at Pompton Lakes. Excursion trains sped northward, carrying crowds to Greenwood Lake from Jersey City— with twenty-seven stops along the way. Greenwood Lake was Baron Hasenclever's old "Long Pond" of the 1760s, much enlarged by a dam built in 1834 to raise the level to supply water for the Morris Canal.

Northern Passaic County streams and ponds were much envied. Late in the 1870s, Newark leaders eyed the crystal-clear waters in the Pequannock and Wanaque watersheds, convinced of the practicability of tapping upper Passaic to provide drinking water for their city. While Newark politicians debated the proposal, a syndicate known as the East Jersey Water Company quietly bought up most of the land in the Pequannock watershed.

Accordingly, when Newark finally decided in 1889 to build reservoirs in Passiac County, it found the East Jersey interests held a monopoly on the land. The city negotiated with the water company to build dams at Oak Ridge, Echo Lake, Clinton, and Macopin at a total cost of $6 million. East Jersey lived up to its agreement; by May 1892 the three reservoirs were built, and a forty-eight-inch steel pipe carried a daily flow of twenty-five million gallons of Passaic County water twenty-one miles to Newark faucets.

Construction of another reservoir at Canistear before 1900 and improvements to the other reservoirs through the years have raised the current Pequannock River storage area to more than eleven million gallons. All of it came under complete Newark control in 1900, when court decisions forced the East Jersey Water Company to convey its water rights to the city.

Even greater plans engrossed Newark water men in 1907 when the city revived study of the Wanaque River watershed as the location for a fifty-million-gallon-per-day reservoir. This time Passaic County interests reacted strongly, alarmed that the Pequannock watershed had slipped completely away from county control. They were determined to share in their valuable liquid assets.

Eventually, eight municipalities combined to build Wanaque Reservoir: Paterson, Passaic, and Clifton in Passaic County; Newark, Montclair, Bloomfield, and Glen Ridge in Essex; and Kearny in Hudson. Much legal maneuvering delayed the project, most of it occasioned by the stubborn refusal of large property owners to give up land which they wanted to preserve as grazing pasture for their prize cattle.

Despite the legal battles, work began on November 23, 1920, on the tremendous reservoir capable of supplying a hundred million gallons of water daily. A dam fifteen hundred feet long and a hundred feet high was completed in 1928. Water started to back up through the valley for seven miles. Work on the $26 million project was completed in 1930.

Paterson, self-styled "fastest-growing city in the East" in 1880, had a tremendous influx of European immigrants in the 1880s. Emigrant trains stopped nightly in town. Many of the newcomers also made their way to mushrooming Passaic, whose population jumped from about 1,000 in 1873 to 6,632 in 1880 and 27,777 in 1900. Passaic led all American cities in the proportion of foreign-born residents in the 1910 census. Its famed woolen mills, started in the 1890s, kept the immigrants busy.

Locomotive production began to decline in Paterson during the 1890s and was gone by World War I. Silk production and silk processing took up the slack. Paterson also became one of New Jersey's prime shopping and entertainment centers during the 1920s and 1930s, with scores of small shops and supply houses lining the city's old streets.

Celebration of the S.U.M.'s hundredth anniversary in 1891 served as the occasion to "remember in passing"—to remember that the American process for making paper in a continuous roll was developed in

The 300-acre Skylands Botanical Garden at Ringwood Manor, New Jersey's first official botanical garden, provides additional incentive to visit Ringwood Manor State Park. (*Walter Choroszewski*)

Paterson, that a Paterson man invented the steam radiator, and that Paterson made nearly all the railroads' rotary snowplows as well as a big percentage of the nation's fire engines.

Most residents in 1891 clearly recalled John Philip Holland, the supposedly eccentric teacher at St. John's Parochial School. On July 23, 1878, he tried out in the Passaic River his first fourteen-foot cigar-shaped submarine, proclaimed a modest success chiefly because he survived. His 1881 launching of the "Fenian Ram" (paid for by Irish Fenian sympathizers) raised him somewhat in the city's estimation—but not until submarines wreaked havoc on shipping in World War I did Paterson and the world understand the true significance of John Philip Holland's invention. Ironically, he thought sub-

marines would make warfare too horrible for civilized nations to contemplate.

Active in the S.U.M. celebration in 1891 was Garret A. Hobart, prominent businessman and politician who had been a lawyer in Paterson since 1866. Hobart had been, among other things, the prime spirit in the successful East Jersey Water Company coup. Less inspired was his horsecar syndicate, put together in 1890, the year that New Jersey's first electric trolley cars operated between Passaic, Garfield, and Clifton. Hobart's political star ascended rapidly in the early 1890s and reached its zenith in 1896 when he was elected vice president to serve with President William McKinley. His death in 1899 cut short a promising career in national politics.

Everything was shoved out of mind in 1902 and 1903

when the elements tried vainly to eradicate Paterson. First a fire on February 9, 1902, swept through fifty-four acres and destroyed 456 buildings, fanned by sixty-mile-an-hour winds. Some five hundred families were homeless amidst damage estimated at more than $10 million. Three weeks later violent floodwaters surged through the streets, standing fifteen feet above normal level, and soon afterwards a tornado twisted through the city. Finally, in October 1903, floodwaters again inundated the city after an incredible 15.04 inches of rain fell in less than three days. Miraculously, however, in every instance—fire, wind, and water—the silk mills escaped damage.

Although they had survived the elements, the mills suffered drastically from a violent strike in 1913. When Paterson's 25,000 silkworkers struck, led by the International Workers of the World (I.W.W.), all of the city's 350 silk mills came to a standstill. Millowners railed against the "red" strike leadership, but the trouble had roots reaching back to 1794, when Paterson had its first mill strike. Intermittent small strikes through the nineteenth century pointed up the tremendous economic and social gulf between worker and millowner. Industrial strife was inevitable, but labor and management both suffered bitterly from the five-month-long strike in 1913.

Paterson's silk-mill owners were caught napping in the 1920s when synthetic rayon swept the country. In 1934, out of forty-seven thousand rayon looms in the United States, Paterson had none. Silk management began an exodus in 1925; Silk City was little more than a nickname by 1935. But another Paterson industrial era was spawned when the then little-known Wright Aeronautical Corporation moved into a deserted silk mill to start making airplane engines. Wright's engines gave Paterson worldwide fame when Charles M. Lindbergh used a Wright Whirlwind engine on his epic solo flight to Paris in May 1927. Paterson went into its fourth distinct cycle: from cotton to locomotives to silk, and now to airplane engines. The city's industrial eggs still remained largely in one basket.

As Paterson and Passaic grew, their populations and industry spilled over into the farmlands of Clifton,

whose greatest early prominence had been from 1886 to 1891 when a racetrack flourished in the village. After Clifton proclaimed itself a city in 1917, it had an amazing growth. Even in the doleful 1929–1934 days, fifteen hundred new homes were built in Clifton; five thousand more were added from 1934 to 1940. The years since World War II accelerated the increase, reaching a population peak of 82,437 in 1970. Although that dropped to 71,742 in 1990, Clifton is second to Paterson in the county. Textile, steel, and chemical plants prosper within its borders.

Paterson remains the county's most important city. Hundreds of smaller industries hum in the many factories where in the recurring cycles of the past only a single product was made. City leaders believe that diversification is good; too long has Paterson risen and fallen on a single industry—the latest blow being when Wright moved out after World War II.

Local citizens are determined to preserve Paterson's unique industrial history. They have had eighty-nine acres surrounding the Great Falls designated as a Historical District, included in the National Register of Historic Sites. More than forty historic structures are included in the area, ranging from a raceway designed by Pierre L'Enfant in 1792 to several of the old locomotive works. Each summer a festival is held at the falls to call attention to its thundering beauty.

More than anything, Paterson has managed to keep a stable population over the past forty years, one of the rare American cities to do so. Its population has changed and become considerably more diversified, but in 1950 city residents totaled 139,386. In 1990, the total was 140,891. Passaic County's pickup of nearly 150,000 new residents since 1950 has not been at the expense of ruining its core city, as has been the case with so many cities in the nation.

Wayne Township, south of the "waist," has had startling growth since 1940, when the township had only 6,800 residents. In 1990, the total was 47,025. "Fortune 500" industries have found the woods and scenery compatible with business, including American Cyanamid and U.S. Rubber.

Passaic County's growth has been upcounty. Just after

John P. Holland's first successful submarine, the *Fenian Ram*, launched in 1881, is exhibited in Paterson's West Side Park. (*Irving Tuttle*)

World War II, much of that region remained as wild and unsettled as it had been when Baron Hasenclever lived high in the hills. Only one major road pierced the mountain land, linking Pompton Lakes and Greenwood Lake. Primitive roads, often impassable, pierced the Kanouse and Bearfort valleys. The road westward from Oakland over Ramapo Mountain was not even on any drawing board.

In 1900, only 5,353 people of the county population of 155,202 lived north on Pompton Lakes. Today about 25,000 people live in the mountain regions. The up-county region abounds in lakes, reservoirs, woodlands, and quiet isolation. The gap between the regions remains. That may come to crashing change. Completion of long-delayed Interstate 287 opens the possibility that real estate interests may lure scores of thousands of people into the woodland. The possibility is not high; Route 287 veers sharply east just north of Pompton Lakes and heads over Ramapo Mountain on the way to Suffern, New York. To the north, major governmental holdings in Ringwood State Park and in the Wanaque Reservoir watershed discourage exploitation.

Still, the threat is ever-present, so pressing that more than forty local, state, and national environmental groups and New Jersey admirers banded together in the early 1990s as the Highlands Coalition aiming to protect as much of the region as possible in the Highlands National Reserve. (The National Reserve would cover about one million acres in New Jersey and New York, basing its strength on the fine watersheds that bubble through the Highlands, on the largely undisturbed hardwood forests, and the area's varied historic regions and parklands.)

Seeing is believing. Paradoxically, completion of Route 287, which pointed an ominous finger at the Highlands, also offered the best time in all history for the average person to get a view of the Highlands, visible before only to soaring hawks or plane passengers. Unless the highway builders fence in the highway with the high roadside walls that threaten to shut off all New Jersey scenery, the motorist will have vistas that many would consider unlikely in New Jersey.

Water remains the dominant county theme. Reservoirs slake big city thirsts. Ponds and lakes of varying sizes up to Greenwood Lake (which is shared with New York) attract those seeking surcease from traffic's roar. Water shapes Passaic County's destiny, keeps both sides of the wasp waist different. The political expediency of 1837 now seems a blessing. Diversity never hurt any county.

THE CITY BELT

At one end there is New York, at the other there is Philadelphia. Between, on either side of a fifteen-mile-wide corridor linking them, live nearly two-thirds of all the people in New Jersey.

This is the City Belt . . .

Where trains thunder over what was once the busiest stretches of railroad tracks in the world, where heavy trucks and millions of cars grind away at cement and macadam, where factories and research laboratories and chemical plants combine to make New Jersey one of the most important industrial states in the land, where docks take from all the world and give back "Made in New Jersey" wares.

This is the City Belt . . .

Where the upper half revolves around New York, where the lower half sees Philadelphia as its axis; where transportation has been the key ever since the first footpaths linked the Dutch village of New York and the Quaker village of Philadelphia.

This is the City Belt, where "dormitories" for New York and Philadelphia have become a way of life, where teeming waterfronts reflect the vigor of the state, where most of New Jersey's colleges and universities have been born and brought to maturity. This is the City Belt, all that most of Jersey's millions of visitors ever see. This is a land of industry, of slums, of housing developments, of progress, of noise, of culture, of vitality, of promise, and of problems. This is the land that Benjamin Franklin likened to a barrel "tapped at both ends."

This is New Jersey's City Belt . . .

Bergen County's courthouse in Hackensack has been called "architecturally one of the most success-ful buildings in the state." Erected in 1912, when Hackensack was merely an overgrown town, the huge stone structure was ready for the county's meteoric rise in population. Around the exterior of the pillared and gilded dome, sculptured figures record the history of families prominent in colonial Ber-gen County history.

BERGEN

NEW JERSEY'S GATEWAY

Genuine Dutch colonial homes and the George Washington Bridge are nearly three centuries apart in Bergen County time, but both are very much a part of the same heritage. The Dutch who came in the seventeenth century to build houses with thick stone walls and strong gambrel roofs sought a place to live close to New Amsterdam. The bridge merely quickened the search by making it easy for many thousands more to live in Bergen and work across the Hudson River in New York.

Live in New Jersey, look across the Hudson for income, inspiration, and even political thought: that has been the Bergen story in capsule from the start to the present. Dutch traders and fur trappers who slipped across the river during the 1620s depended on New Amsterdam for their fur markets and for military help if they blundered in their dealings with the Indians on the west shore of the Hudson River.

Fortunately for those fortune-hunting Dutch, one of Bergen County's all-time great citizens welcomed them. He arrived ahead of the fur trappers by the simple expedient of being born on the banks of Overpeck (Awapaugh) Creek in about the year 1577. He was Oratam, the great sagamore and sachem of the Hackensack (Achkinkeshacky) Indians, and his decision to live in peace with the usurpers of his land eased the way for settlement of Bergen.

Oratam had help from some of the Dutch in his peaceful intentions, although most of them, like most European interlopers, held the arrogant view that the land was theirs for the taking. Mrs. Sarah Kierstede, wife of a Dutch doctor on the Island of Manhattan, took the trouble to learn the Indian language, and as an interpreter she helped conclude treaties. Oratam, in gratitude, granted her title in 1638 to 2,120 choice acres on the banks of the Hackensack River.

Captain David Pieterszoon de Vries, an adventurer and mariner of considerable note, promoted settlement on the Hackensack in 1640 and quickly earned Indian trust. His interest in the fertile lands west of the Palisades was combined with the awareness that the panthers and wolves in the Bergen woods were more dangerous than the Indians.

Unfortunately, not all the Dutch sought peace and understanding. A brutal massacre of Indians in Bergen County in 1643 touched off bloodletting that not even the wisdom of Oratam and the sympathy of de Vries could stem. In that year, Dutch soldiers from New Amsterdam slaughtered eighty sleeping Indians near what is now Jersey City and started a war. Indians retaliated by rampaging through the countryside against all settlers. Fighting continued almost until 1664, the year the English took New Amsterdam from the Dutch and renamed it New York.

Colonization proceeded quickly in Bergen under the

English, mainly because they dealt in friendly and reasonably just fashion with the tribes of the aging Oratam. The great Indian was nearing the end of his days—he was too old to go to Newark to sign a treaty in 1666—but when he died in 1669 at the age of ninety-two he had seen peace come to the land he loved. The price had been high: the Indians had lost their land.

Oratam's deeds are commemorated on Hackensack's official seal, which bears his likeness. Enough Indian names have survived to remind present-day residents that followers of Oratam also slept here—Hackensack, Ho-Ho-Kus, Pascack, and Mahwah, for example.

One of the first English landholders was Captain William Sanford of Barbados in the West Indies, who in 1668 acquired for himself and Nathaniel Kingsland a huge 15,308-acre tract between the Hackensack and Passaic rivers south of Sanford's Spring (today's Rutherford). A year later, Captain John Berry, also of Barbados, bought ten thousand acres "six miles up into the country" from Sanford's property. Eighteen of today's Bergen County towns lie within that Berry tract between the Hackensack and Passaic, from Wallington, East Rutherford, and Little Ferry on the south to parts of Paramus and River Edge on the north.

Neither the Dutch nor the English established Bergen's first permanent settlement. That honor fell to David des Marest, a French Huguenot who objected to contributing in support of the Dutch Church in New York. He sailed with his family up the Hackensack River in 1677 to what is now New Milford and settled down to

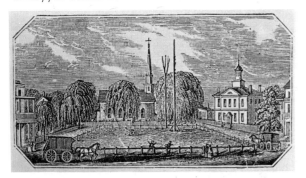

This 1868 woodcut shows the courthouse and the Dutch Reformed Church on the green in Hackensack. (*Barber and Howe*)

farming and religious peace. He owned about five thousand acres.

Bergen had been established as a county in 1675, its borders were vaguely fixed between the Hudson and Hackensack rivers and from the New York province line to the Kill Van Kull and Newark Bay. This included all of present-day Hudson County.

Population pushed slowly westward. By 1700 enough people lived in Yaughpaugh, now Oakland, to require the services of a circuit-riding dominie. A syndicate bought the Ramapo Tract in 1709, a sprawling piece of real estate that covered 42,500 acres and included everything in the county west of a line drawn from today's Glen Rock through Ridgewood to Upper Saddle River. That was a year of growth, for in 1709 Essex County ceded to Bergen the old Sanford and Berry purchases known as New Barbadoes Township.

The thriving village of Hackensack dominated New Barbadoes and it became the county seat. Port of call for ocean-going ships and center of a rich agricultural section, Hackensack boomed. New settlers built splendid brick and red sandstone homes, shops lined the shaded streets, and stagecoaches regularly brought new faces and the mail. Life in the religious-minded colonial village centered in the stately Dutch Reformed Church on the green, built in 1696 on two-and-three-quarters acres of land donated by John Berry. The old Demarest hearthstone bearing that date is still in the east wall of the church.

So well established and pleasing was Hackensack that in 1767 the state legislature debated the merits of the village, along with New Brunswick's advantages, for the location of Queens College (Rutgers). The vote ended in a deadlock when the Bergen County delegate to the legislature, Dr. David Wilson, scrupulously refused to vote. New Brunswick won on the tie-breaking vote of Governor William Franklin. Dr. Wilson returned to Hackensack to establish in 1768 the widely renowned Washington Institute to work "for the preservation of the morals of youth" (and to educate them, too).

Bergen's Dutch and English lived harmoniously, respecting one another as well as other nationalities who came to the shores of the Hackensack and Passaic rivers in the eighteenth century. Dutch culture was predominant, as witness the building of the Dutch Church on English land in Hackensack. Whatever their nationalities or sympathies, Bergen residents prepared themselves for the Revolution. They were fully aware from the first crackling of guns at Lexington that the British in Boston would find Bergen was the gateway to New Jersey and the mid-Atlantic strongholds.

They had not long to wait. Lord Cornwallis led five thousand British regulars and Hessians across the Hudson in mid-November 1776 in pursuit of George Washington's army. Cornwallis overwhelmed the garrison at Fort Constitution (Fort Lee) on November 19 and sent the Continentals reeling across Bergen toward the little span over the Hackensack at New Bridge. In what historians regard as a colossal blunder, Cornwallis failed to follow up his advantage. One writer declared that "the crossing of the Delaware was made safe by the crossing of the Hackensack a month earlier." Washington regrouped his ragged and despairing troops in Hackensack and led them fully across New Jersey to Pennsylvania, the base for the inspiring American attack on Trenton on Christmas night, 1776.

No great battles brought fame to Bergen, but the county constantly felt the cruelty of war. Caught between British and American forces, the innocent suffered as well as the guilty. Bergen has aptly been called "The Neutral Ground." Foraging parties stripped its fields and orchards. A raid on September 28, 1778, was particularly chilling.

About 120 American soldiers in the Virginia Light Horse regiment, led by Colonel George Baylor, took refuge that September night at a farm between River Vale and Old Tappan. Just before 2 A.M., British General Charles Grey sent his troops smashing into the American position with orders to "take no prisoners." The British managed to kill about fifty soldiers, bayoneting them to death in response to Grey's order that they take the flint from their muskets to ensure that none would be fired. The massacre earned Grey both hatred and the enduring nickname of "No Flint" Grey.

Washington was often in the county, staying in Hackensack, Ridgewood, and Englewood, among other places. He was in Morristown, however, on March 23, 1780, when British troops slashed into Hackensack to burn the county courthouse. They failed in efforts to put the torch to the Dutch Church on the green. Frightened county officials soon transferred government into the hills at Yaughpaugh.

Bergen residents wavered in their loyalties. One important defection from the American cause was that of John Zabriskie, who occupied a large house that the Ackerman family had built at New Bridge before 1700. Zabriskie grew prosperous from his big gristmill and his extensive dock on the river after he bought and enlarged the Ackerman farm. He remained loyal to King George. In retaliation after the war, his home was taken from him by patriots and presented in gratitude to Baron Freidrich von Steuben for his services in the American cause. Von Steuben never occupied it.

War wounds healed in time. Peace brought freedom to till the Bergen fields again and the county's Dutch farmers moved to the fore. There was some industry, but it consisted mainly of such strictly local enterprises as gristmills, smithies, and sawmills powered by the county's many streams. An exception was the sporadic copper mining in North Arlington, started in 1719 by the accidental discovery of a vein of ore on Arent Schuyler's farm.

Up Park Ridge way, John Campbell and his sons made plenty of wampum—literally. John took over an abandoned mill in 1775 to fashion Indian money from seashells. He found wampum could be sold for good hard American dollars to such adventurers as John Jacob Astor, who came to the Campbells for the Indian wherewithal to conduct his vast fur-trading ventures in the West. Indian traders from all over the country looked to Park Ridge for wampum until 1889, when the Indians decided that American dollars had come to stay.

Agriculture was Bergen's nineteenth century way of life. County farmers depended on slaves; in 1790 Bergen counted 2,301 slaves, more than any other New Jersey county. Even the slicing away of sizable chunks of land to help form Passaic County in 1837, and the creation of Hudson County from Bergen in 1840, failed to cut appreciably into farm emphasis.

And small wonder, if you would believe the chroniclers of the day, who boasted that the lush soil yielded pears a pound in weight, celery more than three feet

Now state-owned, this house was built before 1700 and offered after the Revolution to Baron von Steuben. The baron never lived in the house.

long, and pumpkins weighing a hundred pounds, give or take a few inches or pounds in all cases. Hackensack melons and "Chestnut Ridge" peaches brought further fame to Bergen growers. New Yorkers eagerly bought this "Jersey Dutch" fare, ferried across the Hudson in small boats.

Most important of all was the strawberry trade, which started about 1800 and reached a peak just before the Civil War. This was a fabulous era, when buyers, sellers, and pickers congregated in the inns at the strawberry centers in Ramsey and Allendale. Most of the strawberries went by the wagonload over rutted roads to New York, Paterson, and Newark. The last week of June 1858, for example, saw eleven hundred wagonloads car-

rying a million and a half baskets of the ripe red fruit trundle through the tollgates of the Bergen turnpike on the way to market. The strawberry rash faded quickly after the Civil War and disappeared completely by 1880.

Farm prosperity brought demands for improved turnpikes, but railroads supplied the needed fast movement. Strawberries helped lure the Paterson & Ramapo Railroad north from Paterson to a link with the Erie Railroad just over the New York border at Suffern. The P. & R. ran through present-day Glen Rock, Ridgewood, Ho-Ho-Kus, Waldwick, Allendale, Ramsey, and Mahwah. During strawberry season, the railroad took as many as eight specially painted white boxcars out of Allendale and Ramsey every morning, each loaded with rich, red fruit. There was little other traffic along the sparsely settled right of way.

Railroad builders laid track on hope. During the middle 1850s, John Van Brunt and others tramped through the valley west of the Palisades trying to drum up interest in their Northern Railroad. Prosperous farmers showed scant interest but the first Northern Railroad train ran from Jersey City to Nyack, New York, in 1858. As it whistled up the valley, it ensured the future of such towns as Englewood, Tenafly, and others—some of them little more than dreams in 1858.

The railroads gave sudden birth to a new type of businessman, one who ever since has risen and fallen in good times and bad in Bergen—the real estate man, quick to envision a paradise in fields "within five minutes' walk of the station" (which he hoped would be built).

Bergen's first official real estate development came in 1854 when Dr. Carl Klein led a group of New York Germans to a hillside north of Boiling Springs, as Rutherford was then called. They bought 140 acres, split it up into 270 plots, and appropriately enough called the place Carlstadt (Carl's Town). Nearby, at Boiling Springs, Floyd W. Thompkins began buying and selling home plots in 1858. He had only moderate success, for the country stood on the edge of the Civil War.

The war temporarily shelved the building boom and all else. Bergen residents split in heated wrangling over the conflict. Much of the bitterness was occasioned by the tight political hold that Garry Ackerson's Democratic political machine had on the county. Strong antiwar sentiment in 1860, combined with the cynical Ackerson machine, resulted in Abraham Lincoln's losing Bergen's presidential vote to John G. Breckinridge, 2,112 to 1,455. This prompted a New York editor to declare that "Bergen people feel and think much as they do in South Carolina."

The minister of the Paramus church, the Reverend E. T. Corwin, had to enlist twenty-five men armed with shotguns to keep flying the American flag that he had hung in the church after Fort Sumter was fired on. In 1861, the editor of the Democratic *Bergen Journal* was threatened by Copperheads after he wrote articles supporting the Union. A militia unit at Schraalen-

burgh (now Bergenfield) expressed sympathy for the South. Later in the war, Bergen Democrats in the state legislature, particularly the poet Thomas Dunn English, vigorously criticized the war effort.

But Northern sympathies prevailed. Bergen's young men enlisted and their parents supported the Union cause. Freeholders voted nearly a million dollars in 1863 and 1864, particularly to help fill draft quotas through bonuses for substitutes or volunteers. A freeholder resolution in 1865 said this "saved our friends and brothers who had no desire to leave their homes and go live a soldier's life or die a soldier's death."

Bergen County was nearly 200 years old by the end of the Civil War, and people had lived there for some 230 years. The area was rural and Dutch. Some churches still conducted services in Dutch, with only occasional sermons in English. Old residents in a few places spoke "Jersey Dutch," a strange mixture of Dutch, English, and Indian words. Dutch was not spoken in the larger towns, but there was little sophistication anywhere.

Political excitement was about all that the agricultural county enjoyed, if the words of an editor of the *Bergen Journal* were true. He rued the "monotony of bucolic existence" in Bergen and cried that "lawyers cannot incite the people to contention during the six days nor the preacher keep them awake on the seventh."

Then, thanks to the railroads, "outside folks" flocked in to stay. J. Wyman Jones, a lawyer, saw possibilities in golden orchard country, that rolling land where Englewood now stands. His city friends came, settled on the land near the Northern Railroad, and commuted to New York. Local stores failed to meet early demands of the newcomers, it is said; commuters from Englewood in the 1860s carried market baskets to and from the train each day.

Another outsider, William Walter Phelps, made Teaneck his home in 1865, settling in the old Garrit Brinkerhoff house on Teaneck Ridge. Within thirteen years he and his Palisades Land Company owned four thousand acres as far east as the Palisades and north to Alpine, pinning hopes for land sales on Northern Railroad service. Phelps became one of Bergen's noted citizens before his death in 1894. He personally defrayed the cost of thirty miles of road, paid half the cost of his town's railroad station, and ordered the planting of more than a half-million trees—plus being elected to Congress and serving as minister to Austria and Germany.

Other promoters laid their rails and their plans. An excursion train service was inaugurated on March 8, 1870, on the Hackensack & Northern between Jersey City and Hillsdale. It foretold rapid expansion, and it tied the county seat to the big city, thus freeing it from reliance on windjammers plying the Hackensack. Four years later the Jersey City & Albany, a branch of the New Jersey Midland, opened service up through Teaneck, Schraalenburgh, and Dumont to Tappan, New York. Tiny stations rose in pastures; one near Schraalenburgh was simply called "Bergen Fields," and so a town was named.

Out along the Passaic River, Gilbert D. Bogart and Henry Marsellus bought property and laid out a town that was called East Passaic until James A. Garfield was elected president in November 1880. The next day Bogart strode into the office of the editor of the Passaic newspaper and announced: "From today on we're Garfield. No more East Passaic." Other towns and villages lost old Dutch and Indian names under the influence of the new arrivals. So much so, in fact, that in 1872 the Bergen County Historical Society, according to contemporary newspaper stories, sought to prevent "the old historic names of the county from being blotted out by namby-pamby sentimental 'Ridges,' 'Woods' and 'Parks.'" They failed, and such names as Boiling Springs, English Neighborhood, Weerimus, Red Mills, Schraalenburgh, and Pamrepaw disappeared.

Bergen was attractive by any name. Summer people flocked to such popular spots as the Norwood Hotel and Edgewater's Buena Vista Hotel to enjoy the county's well-advertised healthful air. These visitors were of course desirable. Somewhat less welcome, but apparently tolerated because they helped the economy, were "hordes of New York ruffians of the lowest degree" who came to the illegal cockfights and the illegal horse race betting rooms in the area surrounding Fort Lee. More than three hundred thousand visitors came to Fort Lee by ferry in 1879 alone, and a goodly number of them came for more than the Jersey air, enforcement officials admitted. Such visitations by New York's gambling fraternity became accepted, even into the middle of the twentieth century.

But sweet, dreamy hours could be enjoyed at Fort Lee's Park Hotel and pleasant times at Clahan's Hotel in Edgewater. Francis R. Tillou's estate, Tilliedudlum, attracted New York's Very Important Persons, including the unsavory Boss Tweed, King of Tammany Hall. Above all, the Octagon Building at Edgewater was a mecca for the fun seekers. Upcounty, the Park Ridge Town Improvement Association ran a big amusement center—and used the proceeds to defray the costs of streets and sidewalks and to pay the boy who lighted the oil lamps in the streets.

An acute attack of what has been called "boroughitis" seized Bergen County in the 1890s, spurred when the legislature voted a new borough act that made each township a separate school district, wherein taxpayers were obliged to pay, pro rata, existing debts of old school districts, as well as future school debts. Importantly, the act applied only to townships. Boroughs, towns, villages, and cities all were exempted.

Small wonder then, that between January 23 and December 18, 1894, Bergen gave birth to twenty-six new boroughs, or that the county today has seventy separate municipalities in its 233 square miles.

The changes often took place in charged atmospheres. Bitter words were exchanged. A few noses were bloodied at polling places. Balloting was close, school taxes or no school taxes, for many people hated to see their old towns broken up. Of all the misunderstandings, however, none was more cruel than that visited upon one Russell Jones, whose border-line house burned down while firemen of Bogota and Teaneck argued over who had a right or duty to extinguish the fire.

Real estate men rode high. They ran special trains and offered hot chowder and lukewarm music to induce prospective buyers to take trains out to see the Bergen County of 1890. Landsellers expressed joy in 1900 when the federal government approved plans for a double-decked $60 million bridge over the Hudson River from New York City to West New York. The bridge was not built, but population in Bergen zoomed from 78,441 in 1900 to 139,002 in 1910. In 1905 the editor of the New York *Tribune* summed it up: "Alas, the days of the Ber-

The rugged Palisades have impressed travelers for nearly four hundred years, but only determined action by state women's clubs saved its natural beauty from ruin in 1896.

gen farmer are numbered. Land that is worth $1,000 to $5,000 per acre is too valuable to be devoted to the raising of corn and cabbage." Newcomers eagerly bought the cabbage fields and corn patches for homesites.

One piece of Bergen County land challenged both those eager for beauty and those dedicated to "progress." That was the magnificent Palisades, first noted and praised by Henry Hudson in 1609, but by 1890 just a mound of rock to quarrymen who steadily blasted away

at the grandeur. The State Federation of Women's Clubs took a bold, unyielding stand against the destruction in 1896, forcing the all-male New Jersey legislature to suspend dynamiting in the Palisades. This led in 1906 to formation of the Palisades Interstate Park.

The Palisades also were appealing to the new breed of movie makers. Magnetic names were attracted to Fort Lee, motion picture capital of the world from 1907 to World War I. Pearl White emoted much of her

Gateway to Bergen County and New Jersey, the George Washington Bridge opened in 1931 to link New York City with northern Jersey commuter towns, radically changing living and travel patterns. (*Walter Choroszewski*)

anguished and nearly interminable series *The Perils of Pauline* in the rugged Palisades. Edwin S. Porter made *Rescued from an Eagle's Nest* in 1908 with young David Wark Griffith in the role of a mountaineer. Mack Sennett and his pie throwers arrived at Fort Lee in 1908, and in 1909 the winsome Mary Pickford made her debut there in *The Violin Maker of Cremona*.

Fort Lee enjoyed its position as the film capital. Samuel Goldwyn, William Fox, and Carl Laemmle all started movie careers nearby, and such stars as Rudolph

Valentino, Lon Chaney, Charlie Chaplin, Fatty Arbuckle, Theda Bara, Lillian Gish, Marie Dressler, and Clara Kimball Young faced Fort Lee cameras. It was a sad day for the livery stables, the hotel, the restaurants, and the town extras when movieland moved to Hollywood. Richard Barthelmess and Ina Claire starred in Fort Lee's last important film, made in 1923.

World War I gave Bergen County both fear and importance. Fear, coupled with anguish, swept the area on January 11, 1917, when a fire roared through the sprawling munitions plant of the Canadian Car & Foundry Company at Lyndhurst. A half-million exploding shells terrorized the section during the next twelve hours, causing $16.7 million in damages. Amazingly, there were no casualties.

Much more pleasant was Camp Merritt at Cresskill and adjacent towns. Some 700 acres comprised the hastily built camp, designed to speed soldiers to France. Between November 1917 and November 1918, a total of 578,566 men shipped out of Camp Merritt. After the Armistice, 466,805 men were returned home through the camp. Thus, slightly more than a million young men came to know the county, its young women, and its opportunities.

Explosion, war, camp, movies, Palisades, real estate booms, strawberries, Revolution, colonization, Indians —those are varied elements in Bergen's past. Yet, no Bergen happening was more important than that on October 24, 1931, when Governor Franklin Delano Roosevelt of New York and Governor Morgan F. Larson of New Jersey jointly snipped a ribbon to open the $80-million George Washington Bridge. Bergen and New York City were joined in fact as well as in spirit.

Bergen had been dreaming of a bridge since 1834, when the New York and New Jersey legislatures first set up a commission to study the spanning of the Hudson. Now, just three years short of a century later, the bridge was ready, thanks to the available millions poured into the project by the Port of New York Authority.

Ready, too, were the energetic real estate men; Bergen's phenomenal population growth since 1931 can be attributed both to the bridge and to the successful selling of Bergen as a place in which to live. Today home developments spread far and wide, with split levels and "Modern Dutch Colonials" edged up tight to two-hundred-year-old Dutch stone houses.

Industry is important in Bergen, of course (and most of the development-swelled towns would give anything for a couple of nice clean little factories to help ease taxes). Industry is principally concentrated along the Passaic (Fair Lawn, Garfield, Lodi), near the important Teterboro Airport (Wood Ridge, South Hackensack, and Moonachie) and along the Hudson, particularly at Edgewater (called the spot "where homes and industry blend"). Research laboratories and offices of erstwhile New York firms have been relocated in Bergen. All are rich sources of employment and county prosperity.

Still, Bergen must be looked upon mainly as "home," or at least as a bedroom where continuing tides of "work in New York, live in New Jersey" enthusiasts try to escape the city for a while—only to find themselves caught in the mounting volume of traffic on highways leading to the George Washington Bridge. Double-decking of the bridge merely encouraged more automobiles. More than fifty million vehicles use the bridge annually.

Boosters of boom for Bergen enthusiastically greeted news in 1976 that county population had soared to 911,000, freely predicting that Bergen, already first among New Jersey counties in total population, soon could boast of being the first to top one million. It was

Meadowlands Stadium in East Rutherford hosts the Giants and the Jets, neither of whom acknowledge their New Jersey home. Nearby are a racetrack and Byrne Arena where the New Jersey Nets and Devils play.

Considered by most people to be merely a sports complex, the Meadowlands has also become the center for impressive corporate offices and residential development. (*Walter Choroszewski*)

not to be. By 1990, population had dropped to 825,380. Fifty-one of the seventy municipalities showed declines, most of them minuscule but declines nevertheless.

It was not so much disenchantment with Bergen as it was a settling down to awareness that too much traffic could become a heavy burden. Boom areas that had swept aside the vegetable farms and woodlands became stabilized. Older, prosperous towns showed scant declines or increases of perhaps twenty-five to fifty, indications of long-time, intelligent planning.

Despite the huge population influx since World War II, Bergen has managed to retain some open space. Most notable is Palisades Interstate Park that runs from the George Washington Bridge northward to the New York State border. It is the state's most impressive landmark, a splendid evidence that even a century ago people cared enough about New Jersey to preserve a geological wonder.

Another geological gift was the Hackensack Meadows, a stretch of 19,730 acres that until 1969 had been victimized by fragmentation among fourteen communities, little or no planning, and a long-standing reputation as a sordid, odoriferous eyesore. In 1969, state legislation created the Hackensack Meadowlands

Development Commission, charged with bringing order to a huge area that often had been described as potentially "the most valuable real estate in the world."

The commission has the delicate job of balancing proper environmental concerns with pressures for real estate development. The meadows are, more than anything, precious wetlands, one of nature's fundamental links to human existence. The region calls for imagination and caution. For those who have taken the time to look carefully, these "meadows" are far more than swamp to be eliminated.

"Enchantment" in the meadows took on new meaning in 1972 when work began on converting 588 acres of marshland in East Rutherford into a major sports complex. A mile-long oval racetrack opened in the summer of 1976. On October 10 of the same year, the football Giants kicked off against the Dallas Cowboys in the new 78,000-seat stadium (named Giants Stadium). The Giants had crossed the Hudson from New York, a continuance of a westward transmigration more than three centuries old in Bergen. Then, in 1981, the 19,000-seat Byrne Arena opened for the basketball Nets, hockey Devils, and most prominently among college teams, the Seton Hall Pirates. Later, in 1984, the football Jets moved their home games into the stadium. Still, no matter what the television networks and newspapers make of the sports complex, the county for most Bergenites remains a homeland, as always.

It is homeland, combined with the closeness of the cultural, economic, and financial might of New Amsterdam, better known as New York these days. If crossing the bridge, either way, can often take far longer in an automobile than an old-fashioned ride on a train and a ferry, well, that's progress, twentieth-century style.

Few courthouses have won the attention accorded the Hudson County landmark in Jersey City. When the county finished a new courthouse nearby in 1960 and planned to raze this structure, stormy protest greeted the proposal. That saved the classic Greek-style courthouse, whose grand 1910 features include granite walls, bronze window frames, high Corinthian columns, and a flat dome.

HUDSON

MANTLE OF WHEELS

Perhaps Dutch Burgomaster Michael Pauw, comfortably at home in Holland, really believed that peacocks strutted over the land he bought on the shores of Henry Hudson's River in 1630. Certainly the glowing accounts brought back by Henry Hudson after his 1609 voyage would have convinced a burgomaster that peacocks (at the very least) dwelled on the west bank of the river.

More likely, since Pauw means "peacock" in Dutch, the Hollander was honoring himself when he purchased sight unseen an area comprising much of what is now Hudson County and named it Pavonia—"The Land of the Peacock." He never saw his land, never knew if peacocks really preened their feathers by the Hudson River, but early Dutch settlers agreed that Pavonia was handsome, pleasant enough even for peacocks (or Pauws).

Pavonia was destined to become one of America's key transportation centers, and once the railroads rolled through Bergen Hill to the Hudson River in the 1830s, the riverbank brilliancy faded. The county became a willing victim of machines—both coal-fired and ballot-stuffed. Although neither of these machines was invented in Hudson County, both unquestionably attained their greatest perfection on the banks of Henry Hudson's river.

Hudson, an English captain working for the Dutch

East India Company, discovered "his" river and the surrounding land accidentally as he poked about looking for a shortcut to the Indies. No shortcut existed, but glowing word pictures of the wealth of land convinced Dutch sponsors that Hudson's voyage had not been in vain. The Dutch West Indies Company set out to exploit the New World.

The Dutch disregarded any rights of the Lenape, who came each summer to fish in the river and the back bay. Piles of oyster- and clamshells told of centuries of summer visits. Maize fields on the hillside spoke of a way with the land. Indian names—Hoboken, Communipaw, Secaucus—gave evidence of settlement.

A few Dutch trappers may have slipped westward across the river from New Amsterdam in the 1620s. Real settlement began after Pauw's purchase, although he failed in his agreement to "plant a colony of fifty souls, upwards of fifteen years old." It is likely Pauw had representatives on the land as early as 1633. Jan Evertsen Bout came early to what is now Jersey City. Aert T. Van Putten established America's first brewery at Hobocan Hackingh (Hoboken) in 1642.

The stupidity of William Kieft, director-general of New Amsterdam after 1638, threatened to ruin all Pavonia. He sent eighty soldiers across the river on February 25, 1643, with orders to massacre Indians peacefully gathered there. Kieft concluded his order by asking that "our God may bless the expedition." His soldiers massacred eighty sleeping innocents and unleashed Indian retribution on the land for years.

Governor Peter Stuyvesant arrived in 1646 and forbade all settlement in the outlying plantations. He approved the establishment of the town of Bergen in 1660 as New Jersey's first regular village. Dutch colonists built their town behind a square wooden barricade to fend off attackers. This eight-hundred-foot square is now Bergen Square, in the heart of modern Jersey City. New Jersey's first municipal government was started here in 1661, the same year that the first organized church and school were begun.

The solid Dutch settlers watched with only token interest as their overlords and the English bounced the province around after 1664. The English took all of New Amsterdam (including New Jersey) from the Dutch in 1664. The Dutch took it back in 1673, but finally a treaty between England and Holland ensured New Jersey for the English in 1674.

All of modern Hudson County was included in Bergen County when it was created in 1675 and redefined in 1682. Dutch traditions and the Dutch way with the land persisted. The ready market across the river made the Dutch cabbage growers successful; they cared little whether the market was called New Amsterdam or New York. Down on Bergen Neck (Bayonne), Dutch farmers raised cabbages so big they were called "Governor's Head" (referring to size, not quality), and fishermen hauled in oysters so large they were called "Governor's Foot."

A few settlers ventured westward from the river, although such natural barriers as rocky Bergen Hill and the soggy meadows to the west made it much easier to stay near the Hudson. Captain William Sanford and Major Nathaniel Kingsland, retired British colonial officers, bought all the Harrison-Kearny area in 1668. Fifteen years later a few adventurers moved over the boglands to the high ground at Secaucus. That name came from the Indian Siskakes—"where the snake hides." Indians avoided the area, particularly the rocky "Snake Hill."

Almost a century slipped by before the county began to assume the transportation role that would have such tremendous significance for this west bank of the Hudson. Philadelphia-bound stage wagons began to roll in 1764 from Paulus, or Powles, Hook (now Jersey City), down over Staten Island and then over to Woodbridge via the Blazing Star Ferry. The new route broke the monopoly formerly enjoyed by Elizabethtown and Perth Amboy and gave travelers the advantage of a speedy two-day trip (weather permitting) to Philadelphia.

As many as twenty stages moved in and out of the Hook daily, but westbound passengers found themselves on the short end of a neat tavern-ferry parlay. Morning ferries, despite improvements inaugurated in 1764, usually arrived just too late to catch the westbound stage. The solution, naturally, was to stay in the tavern overnight and start off refreshed the next morning. A sus-

Statue of Peter Stuyvesant in Jersey City's Bergen Square marks the site of old Bergen, laid out in 1660 as New Jersey's first town.

picious traveler could hardly help thinking the ferry would have caught the stage had the same entrepreneur not owned both ferry and tavern.

Ferries and stage wagons made Paulus Hook, Hoboken, and Bergen Neck vital during the American Revolution. George Washington ordered two forts built at Paulus Hook, and on July 2, 1776, two days before the official Declaration of Independence, General Hugh Mercer sent hundreds of New Jersey militiamen to fortify Bergen Neck. New York's capitulation to the British in that summer made the forts untenable. The Paulus Hook fort fell into enemy hands on September 23, 1776, as Washington's battered army reeled back across the Hudson River from New York.

Except for a few dramatic hours in 1779, most of the riverfront remained in royal control throughout the Revolution. The exception came in the predawn hours of August 19, 1779, when Major Harry (Light Horse) Lee led four hundred American troops over the marshes from Hackensack for a bold smash at Paulus Hook. Lee's men routed the surprised British, but the position could not be held with the rest of the area in enemy hands, so Lee retreated quickly. His troops took along 159 prisoners, at a cost of only two killed and three wounded.

The nearness of the British and the apparent hopelessness of the American cause prompted many riverfront "summer patriots" to embrace the Loyalist side after the fall of Paulus Hook. William Bayard, son of one of the earliest settlers of the Hoboken area and one of the most active prewar promoters of the Revolutionary movement, made a fantastically wrong guess when he switched allegiance late in 1770 and accepted a colonel's commission in the British army.

That cost Bayard his estate at war's end and brought the county its most famous son, Colonel John Stevens, who bought the Bayard holdings for $90,000 at public auction in 1784. Just before the sale Baron Friedrich von Steuben, Prussian military expert revered for his wartime services to the Americans, tried to buy the estate. Governor William Livingston replied that such a private sale could not be arranged because of the state legislature's having approved an auction. Anyway, Livingston added in his consoling letter to the baron, " . . . never was there a place where mosquitoes are more numerous."

Mosquitoes didn't bother the versatile John Stevens. On the slopes of Castle Point he raised New Jersey's most illustrious engineering family, and in the study of Stevens's villa his fertile mind ranged through projects far in advance of his day. The Stevens family's engineering saga has highlighted all the history of Hoboken and much of the story of New Jersey railroads. Many of Stevens's dreams came true through his energetic sons; others materialized in the work of Stevens Institute of Technology, founded by his family in 1870.

The beauty of his holdings prompted Stevens to gauge correctly that New Yorkers would like to visit and live in Hoboken. Accordingly, in March of 1804 he mapped "The New City of Hoboken" and offered eight hundred lots at an auction in New York. Soon after the Hoboken auction, speculative New Yorkers cast envious eyes on Paulus Hook in the belief that if John Stevens could be successful at Hoboken, they could be even more successful at the old ferry site. Encouraged by the advice of their distinguished attorney Alexander Hamilton, a syndicate of city lawyers led by Anthony Dey bought the present site of Jersey City in 1804. The area had little to recommend it except the ferry slips and the racetrack, where ponies had been competing on and off since 1769. Dey and friends paid six thousand Spanish milled gold dollars to the Van Vorst family.

Only thirteen people lived permanently in the sand hills of the Hook when the so-called Associates of the Jersey Company acquired the land, but Hamilton envisioned a great metropolis, pointing out that in all history great cities usually arose on the west rather than the east bank of a navigable river. Five months later, on July 11, 1804, Hamilton fell mortally wounded in a duel with Aaron Burr up the river on the famous Weehawken dueling ground (where, incidentally, more than fifteen duels were fought before the pistol play was outlawed in 1835).

The loss of Hamilton stunned the Paulus Hook real estate developers, and in the years ahead, as their venture seemed perilously close to failure, they wished often for Hamilton's counsel. The Jersey Company offered many inducements—a red-brick tavern, 600 poplar trees along the streets, and 1,340 lots for sale at only $100 apiece. Few buyers came. After the first thirty years

Named for the noted Stevens family, pioneers in railroads and other engineering advances, Stevens Institute of Technology began rising on the banks of the Hudson in 1871. (*Walter Choroszewski*)

of its existence, the town had grown to only 1,500 persons. Changing the settlement's name to Jersey City in 1820 caused no spurt in sales.

Dey and his friends could look across the river to find the principal reason for their slow progress. New York's tight monopoly on water rights gave that state control up to the low-water line on the New Jersey side. However, the fact remained that the Associates also maintained too tight a grip on their land, refusing even the possibility of ferry rights to purchasers and subjecting property holders to governmental as well as economic control by the company.

Everything changed for the better in 1834. First, a treaty that year set the boundary line between New Jersey and New York in the middle of the Hudson River; Jersey City finally had access to its own water line. Later in 1834 the first railroad cars from Newark rolled over the Meadows to forge a bond between Jersey City and the West.

John Stevens of Hoboken took Hudson County and New Jersey into the railroad era. His fascination with steam power led him to establish the world's first steam ferry line on the Hudson River, although the New York monopoly forced him to abandon that. In 1815 he secured the first railroad charter in the United States and in 1825 he built and ran on a circular track at Hoboken this country's first steam locomotive. His sons, Robert and Edwin, built the state's first railroad, linking Bordentown and South Amboy in 1832. Three of the line's first four locomotives were built in Hoboken.

The Hudson River waterfront had to be railroad country, thanks to the nation's greatest city being across the river. Thus, in 1834, the Paterson & Hudson River Railroad and the New Jersey Railroad both reached Bergen Hill and took passengers into Jersey City by horsecar. Locomotives chugged on both lines the following year. When a deep cut through Bergen Hill was finished in 1838, locomotives could steam directly to the riverfront. Jersey City was on its way.

Concurrently, canalboat enthusiasts hailed the coming of the Morris Canal to Jersey City in 1836. This mountain-climbing canal stretched through northern New Jersey to link Jersey City with the Pennsylvania coal fields and the Morris County iron forges. Soon Jersey City docks were piled high with both anthracite and iron.

Such vitality heightened the long-brewing aggravation at having to go all the way to Hackensack for Bergen County courts and other county business. Finally, in February 1840, the state legislature established the new county of Hudson, to include essentially the same area the county now holds—a mere forty-five square miles, smallest of the counties.

The new county had a solid basis for growth over and above its transportation stature. Jersey City could pridefully claim the American Pottery Company, where the nation's foremost potters learned their trade, and Isaac Edge's fireworks plant, famed as a training center for early American pyrotechnists. Dummer's Jersey City flint glass was widely known. Hoboken's Land & Improvement Company was established in 1838 to encourage growing waterfront business without destroying the city's inland residential charm. On the other side of the meadows Harrison came into being in 1840 by the same legislative act that set up Hudson County. A small trunk factory, opened in 1846, became the forerunner of Harrison's teeming factory region. Down the Neck, in what is now Bayonne, industry dated to the establishment of the Hazard Powder House in 1812.

Explosives on Bergen Neck were somewhat of an irony, for the biggest powder makers of all had been there and gone. These were the du Ponts, who had settled in 1800 at Bergen Point, facing the Kill Van Kull,

after fleeing the French Revolution. They bought a manor house on the Point big enough to house seven adults and six children. Hopefully, they called it Good Stay. Two years later, one of them, son Irénée, went to Delaware to found the great enterprise that bears the name of DuPont.

Much of Hudson County remained a playland until the Civil War. Hoboken's beer gardens, river walks, and pleasant groves brought thousands over on the ferries from New York every weekend. The Stevens family home on Castle Point dominated the scene and Sybil's Cave, hewn into the Point's rocky base, became a lovers'

Alexander Hamilton's bust stands on the dueling ground at Weehawken where Hamilton, a brilliant young political leader, fell fatally wounded in a duel with Aaron Burr on July 11, 1804. (*Walter Choroszewski*)

Currier & Ives lithograph shows a baseball game at Elysian Fields, where regular play started in 1845. (*Library of Congress*)

rendezvous. The magnificence of Elysian Fields, shaded by stately trees, helped make Hoboken the playground of the East. Major cricket matches were often held between American and English teams. There, on a cricket field laid out by John Cox Stevens (son of Colonel John), the Knickerbockers faced another New York team on October 6, 1845, in the world's first organized baseball game. Nearby, the Hoboken Turtle Club met regularly to enjoy the mingling in their stomachs of turtle soup and good Hoboken beer.

Many of the visitors decided to remain in Hoboken, the most prominent being fur trader and millionaire John Jacob Astor, who built a villa there in 1829. Many others tarried long, with vacationists including Washington Irving, Edgar Allan Poe, Martin Van Buren, and William Cullen Bryant. Most visitors came to relax only briefly, however, and the fickle sporting set switched to Jersey City from 1837 to 1845 to watch the horse races at the old hilltop Beacon Race Course.

New York aristocrats spurned all such plebeian pursuits, however, and went in dignity to Bayonne, "The Newport of New York." The oldest and wealthiest of New York's families acquired huge estates overlooking beautiful (and then sweet-smelling) Newark Bay. Some boarded expensively and expansively at the Mansion House that David La Tourette started after he bought the old du Pont house in 1845. By 1860, La Tourette had expanded the mansion to accommodate four hundred guests.

Hudson County came fully of age in the Civil War. In donning a mantle of transportation supremacy and industrial vigor it laid aside its adolescent playgrounds. County abolitionists assumed responsibilities in shepherding more than sixty thousand fugitive slaves through Hoboken, Bayonne, and Jersey City and on to freedom by way of the Underground Railroad, a system with no advertised stations, no known timetable, and no visible tracks.

Traditional railroad systems moved into riverfront dominance, too, and this served well a nation at war. Rail passengers streamed through Hudson, proof of which is found in an 1855 report showing that seven million passengers used Jersey City ferries annually—at a time when the city's population was only twenty-two thousand.

The Morris & Essex (today's Erie-Lackawanna) stretched its tracks into Hoboken in 1856, in time to feast on the Civil War prosperity that struck all railroads. Then, in 1864, the Jersey Central Railroad built an unprecedentedly long bridge over Newark Bay to Bayonne and extended its tracks into Jersey City, where the forerunner of the Pennsylvania Railroad already had a strong base.

Hudson County terminals were a Civil War bridge between North and South. Troops from the north and east streamed across the river and boarded trains that carried them toward Confederate strongholds. Industry poured its goods onto the Jersey City and Hoboken docks for shipment south.

The greatest Hudson Civil War memory is in the name of General Philip Kearny. He built "Kearny's Castle" on his lovely West Hudson estate, Belgrove, in 1855. Only ten weeks before his death at Chantilly, Virginia, in the summer of 1862, he wrote: "How beautiful Belgrove must look! If I were there, I would never leave. . . ." The soldier's funeral was held at Belgrove, and when the region broke away from Harrison in 1867 it memorialized Kearny by taking his name.

Railroad growth changed forever the shape of the Hudson River banks. The Jersey Central Railroad dumped untold thousands of tons of New York garbage into Jersey City's South Cove to create ground for its terminal built in 1864. That and subsequent dumpings, which became less odoriferous after Greenville residents violently protested garbage dumping by the Pennsylvania Railroad in 1875, eventually built the entire county riverfront out into the Hudson River as much as four thousand feet from the original line. Limited waterfront footage left Hudson County no alternative—it had to build out into the river.

Hudson grew phenomenally after it became a county. Starting with a population of 9,483 in 1840, it listed 163,000 by 1875 and 386,048 in 1900. Industrialists came across the river from New York, attracted by the excellent transportation facilities and the zooming labor market. Jersey City, for example, was still young when it gained three of its basic industries: William Colgate brought his soap kettles over from New York in 1847; Jo-

seph Dixon moved his expanding crucible plant from Salem, Massachusetts, at about the same time; and the P. Lorillard Tobacco Company moved its snuff factory to the city in 1870.

Transportation stepped up to worldwide proportions with the coming of major steamship companies to Hudson. The Cunard Company built a dock at Jersey City in 1847 and the sailing of Cunard's *Hibernia* on January 1, 1848, merited a hundred-gun salute. Upstream, four major German or Dutch steamboat companies adopted Hoboken as their American port.

Out in the western meadowlands along the Passaic River, Harrison and Kearny moved ahead industrially. Starting with the establishment of Thomas A. Edison's

Ellis Island, famed after 1892 as America's welcoming place for immigrants, is tucked neatly into the Jersey City waterfront. (*Walter Choroszewski*)

first incandescent lamp factory in Harrison in 1881, that area of the meadows also attracted William Hyatt's roller bearing factory in 1903, and soon the region made way for Crucible Steel, Otis Elevator, Worthington Pump, Western Electric, and dozens of other industries. William Howard Taft, stumping for reelection in 1912, exclaimed: "Why, this is a hive of industry!"—and that Republican exclamation became Democratic Harrison's slogan.

Huge population increases forced realignments of municipalities, but Hudson County partially reversed one popular statewide trend in the latter years of the nineteenth century when it consolidated towns and townships rather than creating numerous new municipalities (as in Bergen County). Jersey City absorbed Van Vorst Township in 1859, Hudson City and 210-year-old Bergen town in 1870, and the Township of Greenville in 1873. Bayonne consolidated Constable Hook, Bergen Point, Centerville, and Saltersville into one city in 1869.

Bayonne's aristocratic New Yorkers left town after the Prentice Oil Company established the first of Bayonne's many oil refineries in 1875. Others followed soon after—Standard Oil, Tidewater, and Gulf—and the shad fishermen, hotel proprietors, and bathing beach operators sadly moved elsewhere. Tidewater Oil Company, founded in 1878, brought the refinery business to a new peak of efficiency when it planned the first pipeline to tap interior oil fields, but it took eight years of fighting the competition, the railroads, and mountains to the west before the line stretched completely from Pennsylvania oil fields to Tidewater's Bayonne refinery in 1887. Standard Oil's power permitted it to start late but finish sooner. John D. Rockefeller's company completed its four-hundred-mile pipeline in a year. In 1880 it boasted the first pipeline to reach the waterfront.

Nineteenth-century immigration altered Hudson County's character and speech just as transportation changed its face. The Germans and Irish started to come in the 1840s, with most of the Germans gravitating to Hoboken and North Hudson and most of the Irish heading for railroad or canal work in Jersey City. Later the Scots came to work in the mills in Harrison and Kearny, and the Swiss arrived to work in West New York and Union City's embroidery industry. All of the Old World

immigrants were joined at the turn of the century by increasing numbers of Italians, Hungarians, and Poles, lured by industry within the very shadows of the Statue of Liberty and Ellis Island, both of which are within the territorial boundaries of Hudson County.

German traditions completely dominated Hoboken and North Hudson until World War I, when a wave of intense partisan feeling suppressed the Schuetzen societies, the beer halls, and the German parks. Hoboken's importance as the World War I port of embarkation for American troops boomed its industries, but also destroyed many of its Old World traditions.

Immigration altered Hudson County in another way, by adding the voting strength needed to make the political machine all-powerful. Wave after wave of new arrivals eagerly listened to waterfront politicians, particularly the Irish who found themselves bewildered, alone, and in perilous straits when the railroads, which brought many of them over, hired them and fired them at will.

Hudson County politics have prompted millions of written and spoken words since the 1870s, without satisfying either Hudson County residents or out-of-county critics. Nevertheless, two facts emerge: first, the waterfront situation, with its continuing waves of immigration and its periodic booms and busts, made the political machine a possibility—maybe even a necessity. Second, it took two-party interplay to bring the Hudson County machine to maturity.

The Republicans, for example, first forced a viciously gerrymandered district on Hudson in the 1870s when they devised the infamous Jersey City "Horseshoe" voting district to include nearly all Democrats (and thus leave the rest of the city and all the county free for Republican control). Frank Hague, significantly, was born in that "Horseshoe"; he learned politics there and became the master of them all.

Actually, Democrats might never have gained Hudson County had the Republicans endorsed their own Mark Fagan and his "New Idea." Fagan served as a ruggedly independent and scrupulously honest Jersey City mayor from 1901 to 1907. On his reelection for a third time as mayor in 1905, he took all Hudson County Republican Assembly candidates into office on his coattails. Jealous GOP bosses decided to derail Fagan in

Pulaski Skyway, named for the Polish nobleman who died in the American Revolution, won accolades as "history's outstanding highway engineering achievement" when completed in 1932. (*Walter Choroszewski*)

1907. They succeeded, but when his political juggernaut jumped the tracks, the Republican manipulators went with it.

The Democrats promptly took over the "New Idea," with moderately few changes at first; they put Frank Hague in the driver's seat and by various devices, alterations, and hidden assets steamrollered Hudson County and much of New Jersey for four decades. Hague, Hudson, and power became synonyms. John Kenny and his associates shouldered their way aboard the machine in 1949, forcing Hague out of office, but Republicans gained slight solace, if any, from that. The Democratic faithful merely switched to hats of another Democratic hue.

This is no place to judge Hudson County politics, but the polling place rules supreme in Hudson as in no other New Jersey county (partially because party machines elsewhere have always been much, much more discreet, even if just as smoothly oiled). Since the Land of the Peacock was transformed from the garden spot of the West to the transportation center of the East, politics has been a way of life. No one denies it, is ashamed of anything, or admits that not all people wait to see what politicians say.

Hudson County population has been eroding since 1940, when 652,040 people lived in the county. Steel tracks then glistened throughout the tiny county, bring-

Entrance to the Lincoln Tunnel which, with the Holland Tunnel, makes Hudson County the gateway to New York. (*P.N.Y.A.*)

ing eight major railroads to riverfront terminals ranged from Weehawken to Bayonne. Ocean liners shuttled hundreds of thousands of passengers annually between Europe and Hoboken and Jersey City. Huge railroad yards abounded in the county's meadowlands, fringed by heavy smokestack industries. This was blue-collar, workaday Hudson County.

Change began with the opening of the Holland Tunnel in 1927, luring automobiles off the ferryboats and sending them rolling under the Hudson River to and from New York. Three tubes of the Lincoln Tunnel, completed in 1937, 1945, and 1957, heightened the pace of automobiles moving through the county. Opening of the Bayonne Bridge to Staten Island in 1931 added another means of entering or escaping the county.

Completion of the New Jersey Turnpike extension through Bayonne to Jersey City and the Holland Tunnel

in 1956 ended any lingering doubts that automobiles and trucks had all but replaced passenger and freight trains in Hudson County preeminence. The difference was that railroads brought business and jobs to the county; gasoline-powered vehicles contributed relatively little to the county economy.

Still, even in 1960, no one sensed that the railroads were all but doomed. By 1970, only the Lackawanna-Erie terminal remained open. State and county governmental officials stood placidly by while workers ripped out in months the tracks and intricate switches that had taken decades to construct. Shippers deserted the Hudson County piers, except for the huge military Ocean Terminal in Bayonne, the largest military shipping center in the world.

Huge areas of former railroad yards fronting on the river stood vacant, the cinder-covered terrain reclaimed by weeds and the ubiquitous foxtails that thrive where nothing else will grow. The largest of all, the former Central Railroad of New Jersey property in Jersey City, lay deserted. Just offshore stood two symbols of American greatness: the Statue of Liberty and Ellis Island, both within Jersey City limits. The fine old Central Railroad terminal stood vacant and vandalized, a sad reminder of days when the building hummed with immigrants headed west and commuters headed east.

Spurred by a persistent Jersey City resident named Morris Pesin, interest grew in converting the railroad yard and terminal into a huge urban park. The State of New Jersey acquired the property in 1970 and began work on Liberty State Park, one of the major surprises of Hudson County and the state. Its uniqueness lies in large measure on the towering skyscrapers of New York City across the Hudson River.

Liberty State Park is a New Jersey treasure, from the reception center on the south to the acclaimed Science Center on the north. The railroad terminal has been completely refurbished and serves again as a berth for small ferries shuttling back and forth from New York. Boats leave a park dock several times during each day to carry visitors to Ellis Island and the Statue of Liberty.

Hudson County's renaissance seems based on the park success and a gradual awareness that there is no place quite like the shoreline that faces New York. Fast train service on PATH, the Port of New York's dependable rapid transit, makes Manhattan only ten to fifteen minutes away from Hoboken and Jersey City. Riverfront businesses and condominiums have risen to take advantage of the nearness of New York. New docks have been built. Promotion-minded leaders call the waterfront a "Gold Coast" and might well be right.

Today, trucks and automobiles clatter and bang over the maze of old waterfront streets in Hoboken and Jersey City or stand in long lines of traffic at the tunnels. Millions of automobile passengers say "hello" and "good-bye" to New Jersey by way of the Holland and Lincoln tunnels, Bayonne Bridge, and the Turnpike.

The lure beyond question is New York. Most of the crowds pouring aboard boats headed for Ellis Island or the Statue of Liberty (including hundreds of thousands of New Jerseyans each year) neither know nor care that

both are in New Jersey. Many of the new people settling in Hoboken or Jersey City do so because both are far closer in time to Manhattan that either the Bronx or Queens. Jersey City loves it; population increased in 1990 to 228,537, the first rise in decades. Somehow, nothing seems to have changed. The mecca lies to the east. Getting people there has been Hudson County's lot. Crossing the river has progressed from small private boats to commercial ferries; from stagecoaches to trains; from passenger cars to automobiles; from ferries to tunnels. Does it really matter, as long as the urge to reach New York is satisfied?

New Jersey's "trilogy of immigration" lines up the Statue of Liberty to the south, Ellis Island in the center, and the state-owned former station of the Central Railroad of New Jersey. All are within the boundaries of Jersey City. (*Walter Choroszewski*)

Since completion in 1906, Essex County's marble courthouse has dominated the low slope rising westward from Newark. The beautifully proportioned work was designed by celebrated architect Cass Gilbert in modified Renaissance style. Interior walls feature murals by such a noted early twentieth century artist as Howard Pyle. Outside is the famous seated statue of Abraham Lincoln by the sculptor of Mount Rushmore, Gutzon Borglum.

ESSEX

ROBERT TREAT'S BARGAIN

Robert Treat, just off the boat from Milford, Connecticut, spoke angrily in the warmth of a mid-May afternoon in 1666. He expressed himself flatly as being all for going back to Connecticut and leaving these New Jersey meadows on the shores of the beautiful Passaic River to the Indians. According to Treat's bitter argument, Governor Philip Carteret of Elizabethtown had indicated the land already had been bought from the Indians. Now, the Indians ordered the Connecticut colonists back to their boats with a clear mandate: "No wampum, no land."

Treat decided to stay, despite his initial anger. The New Englanders settled down to found what they believed would be an enduring theocracy, where church and town were one. Purchase of the land from the Indians became official in July 1667, the transaction ranking high among all-time real estate bargains. The Indians exchanged most of what is now Essex and Union counties for what seems today more like a collection of assorted trinkets to satisfy the personal whims of the sellers rather than a calculated selling price.

Apparently the Indians went off in high glee with their receipts, which included, in addition to 850 fathoms of wampum, this miscellany: "50 double hands of powder, one hundred bars of lead, 20 axes, 20 coats, 10 guns, 20 pistols, 10 kettles, 10 swords, four blankets, four barrels of beer, 10 pair of breeches, 50 knives, 20 hoes, two an-

kers of liquor [about 20 gallons] or something equivalent, and three trooper's coats." Eleven years later, by the additional payment of "two guns, three coats, and 13 kans of rum" the settlers secured an Indian deed to land all the way to the top of Orange Mountain.

By then the town on the Passaic had changed its name from Milford to Newark, for Newark-on-Trent, England. Its growth quickened with the arrival of the Reverend Abram Pierson and his flock from Branford, Connecticut. Mr. Pierson demanded, and got, an agreement that only members of "some or other of the Congregational churches" could vote, hold office, or attain chief military trust.

Newark was a compact town by 1682, when the East Jersey legislature established Essex County, centered on Treat's settlement. Laid out around Broad and Market streets, both 132 feet wide—unusually spacious for a colonial town—the village had a church, "an ordinary [inn] for the entertainment of travelers," a ferryman, a town drummer, a corn mill, and a sawmill (which Thomas Davis built after agreeing that "he shall let any of the inhabitants have boards as cheap as others and before strangers"). Still, Newark life was primitive; the killing of wolves and bears within the village was encouraged and rewarded by bounty payments.

The few second-generation families that pushed beyond the village limits by 1700 found that the Dutch had already come over from Bergen County to settle along Second River (Belleville) and in West Essex, particularly in the sprawling meadowland where the Passaic River looped in a broad arc through marshy meadows to form the "Horse Neck." Newarkers bought 18,500 acres in this area in 1702, adding all of today's Caldwell, Roseland, and Livingston to Newark township. Nearly all of modern Essex County was part of one town.

Newarkers slowly spread outward to the Orange Mountains and to the meadows of West Essex. Sons of original colonists led the movement up the mountains, where settlement centered around individual farms—proof of which lies in early crossroad names: Speertown (Upper Montclair), Wardesson (Bloomfield), Morehousetown (Livingston), Doddtown (East Orange), Camptown (Irvington), and Williamstown and Freemantown (both West Orange).

So many had gathered on the Orange Mountain slopes that "The Mountain Society" established itself in 1719 to build a church. Farmers prospered, particularly because their apple orchards produced top-grade cider and vinegar (and if a goodly bit of the cider ripened into wonderful "Jersey Lightning," so much the merrier).

Essex County had little industry, but discovery of copper on John Dod's land atop Orange Mountain in 1721 sent prospectors digging. They succeeded reasonably well, for Dod's mine operated thirty-five years.

When the East Jersey Proprietors in 1745 challenged the land claims of farmers living in "Big Piece" and "Little Piece" meadows, all of emerging West Essex stiff-

Woodcut of 1844 shows the Bloomfield Presbyterian Church on the village green. (*Barber and Howe*)

ened. As a lesson to others, the law clapped one of the farmers, Samuel Baldwin, into Newark jail in 1745, but 150 rioting relatives, friends, and neighbors from the "back settlement" smashed into the jail and freed him. A similar riot early in 1746 convinced the Proprietors that they were in the wrong territory. Horse Neck people continued on the land, even though the Proprietors held legal claims.

Newarkers smiled genteelly at the impetuous farmers. The town had grown and acquired some dignity by 1746, despite bitterness generated in 1733. That year Colonel Josiah Ogden broke away from Old First Church because Old First members objected when, rather than let his wheat be ruined by rain, he harvested it on a Sunday. Ogden and several followers founded Trinity Church soon after.

The controversy split the village, and to help soothe wounded spirits Old First brought twenty-one-year-old Reverend Aaron Burr to Newark in January 1737. He succeeded admirably, and his leadership among Presbyterians was responsible for the choice of Newark in 1747 as the location of the College of New Jersey. Founded in Elizabeth in 1746, the college needed a new home after the death of its first president, the Reverend Jonathan Dickinson. Mr. Burr became the second president and led the college through pioneer days until it moved permanently to Princeton in 1756 and eventually became Princeton University. Burr's son Aaron Burr, Jr. (later vice president of the United States) was born in Newark. Burr, Jr., is most remembered in history for fatally wounding Alexander Hamilton in a duel at Weehawken in 1804.

Essex County had prosperity enough in 1776 to provoke serious internal dissension over the American Revolution. Wealthy farmers like Caleb Hetfield, a large landowner in West Essex (in the region now marking his memory as "Hetfield Swamp"), openly supported the British. Newark had considerable Tory spirit among its one thousand inhabitants, particularly those who attended Episcopal services at Trinity Church. Discord split neighbors and friends—even families. Presbyterians favored the war; Episcopalians opposed it.

When General Washington led his bewildered army of about thirty-five hundred men into Newark from Hackensack on November 22, 1776, the mixed reception failed to cheer the soldiers. Thomas Paine began to write *The Crisis* while sitting in a Newark park, saddened by the knowledge that the "summer soldier and sunshine patriot" had already begun to desert the American cause. He could begin in truth: "These are the times that try men's souls. . . ."

Lord Cornwallis took his time pursuing Washington. He leisurely entered North Newark on November 28, at almost precisely the same time that Washington left the southern limits. Cornwallis, presuming victory, paused in Newark while Washington slipped across the state to regroup his riddled legions in Pennsylvania. Loyalists welcomed the invaders, only to see their homes looted.

Essex County's well-ordered farms received merciless attention from foraging parties and punitive sorties by the British. On the night of January 25, 1780, a group of British soldiers and Tory allies swooped into Newark. They burned Newark Academy, killing seven or eight defenders. Returning to New York, they stopped by the house of Justice Joseph Hedden, confiscator of Tory estates. They routed him from bed and forced him to accompany them across the frozen meadows clad only in his nightclothes. Judge Hedden died within a few months, from illness brought on by that night's walk.

Foundations for industrial Essex developed quickly after the Revolution. In about 1785 James Condit set up Orange's first hat factory and soon after was joined by Cyrus Jones. Moses N. Combs started producing shoes commercially in Newark in about 1790. Tanning had been important in Newark almost from the start. The clear water in streams gushing down the hill to the swamp west of Broad Street proved ideal for the process. Many leathermakers located in "The Swamp," but it took Combs to change Newark shoemaking from a strictly local enterprise to a far-flung commercial proposition. Others emulated Combs, and within twenty years the town became celebrated for fine shoes, which were sent by the wagonload to New York, Philadelphia, and Savannah.

Newark's industry did not make it a city. Indeed, Essex County's total population of twenty thousand in 1800 lagged behind that of Sussex County. West Essex was sparsely settled; cattle and sheep on their way to Newark market stirred the dust in the narrow mountain passes and met swine being driven up the hills from

Newark to summer rooting along the Passaic River at West Caldwell.

Dutch traditions lingered in Bloomfield and Speertown, where storekeepers spoke both Dutch and English. In the fall, wagons rolled constantly over county roads, bringing farm products eastward from Morris and Sussex counties and taking winter supplies westward to the farms.

Essex County needed better communication between villages. That need began to be met in the "turnpike era" of the early 1800s. Charters granted in 1806 opened the way for turnpikes to Elizabeth, Belleville, New Brunswick, Springfield, Morristown, and Pompton. Bloomfield Pike, forerunner of today's Bloomfield Avenue, was the personal promotion of Israel "King" Crane, a highpowered Bloomfield entrepreneur whose wide-traveling fleet of wagons brought him power and wealth. The "King" was directly descended from Newark's founders. He represented the westward trend away from the city.

Old Newark Township lost its grip. One section departed in 1793 to help found the new municipality of Springfield. A very large parcel was lost when the Caldwell region broke away. Newarkers recognized the needs and desires of mountain people for self-government when Newark Township split into Newark, Orange, and Bloomfield wards in 1806 to facilitate tax collections and elections.

Scandal swept through Essex County in 1807 as citizens voted on whether a new courthouse should be built in Newark or Elizabethtown (all today's Union County was then part of Essex). Newark won because its individual citizens voted far more often than Elizabethtown's. Newark women were as unscrupulous as the men, for women could vote in New Jersey then. The legislature ruled the result fraudulent and as punishment took voting privileges away from women. Newark got the new courthouse anyway, and finished it in 1812.

Rumblings of discontent continued in the outlands. Orange declared its independence in 1806. Bloomfield Township broke away in 1812, taking an area comprising all of modern Montclair, Bloomfield, Glen Ridge, Nutley, and Belleville. A year later the state legislature created Livingston Township in the far western section of the county. Both Bloomfield and Livingston honored New Jersey governors in their names: William

Looking north on historic Broad Street, widest street in the colonies when laid out in 1666. Old Trinity Church, on the right, is on the edge of Military Park, town militia grounds in colonial days. (*Walter Choroszewski*)

thousand citizens, whom an observer called "a remarkably industrious people, pounding away at their trades from 5 A.M. to 10 or 12 at night." The city already had a wide reputation for its leather, shoes, fine carriages, and jewelry.

Railroads spelled change for the "back settlements," too. The Morris & Essex gave new life to Millburn's many papermills and added markets for Orange's thirty-two booming hat factories in the late 1830s. More important, the M. & E. enticed the first of a new breed known as commuters to the Essex hills. Essex County grew rapidly along the thin line of the Morris & Essex, snaking its way through the mountains to Morristown.

The Panic of 1837 prostrated the infant city of Newark and struck the Orange hatters hard, but the return of good times in the 1840s gave new life to the resurgent industries. Newark's post-Revolutionary character as a "genteel neighborhood where there is much tea drinking" crumbled before progress. The original New England descendants were augmented by steady streams of Irish and Germans. The Irish built the canal and the railroads, while the Germans worked in the breweries. Interestingly enough, despite the influx of German beer drinkers and beermakers, it was a Scot, Peter Ballantine, who established the city's first large-scale brewery in 1840 after he bought the small brewery General John Cummings had started in 1803.

Progress in the city accelerated dissatisfaction in the hinterlands. Farmers felt that city people who discussed such things as gaslights in the streets and watchmen "by day and by night" were peculiar enough without expecting farmers to pay taxes for such extravagances. Caldwell, Orange, Livingston, and Bloomfield were independent of Newark by 1813 and Clinton Township broke away in 1835. Then, like a cell dividing as life develops, the townships in turn split up. Belleville seceded from Bloomfield in 1839, Irvington from Clinton in 1852, and Millburn from Springfield in 1857 (when all of Union County was separated from Essex). Later, in 1868, Montclair split from Bloomfield when the latter refused to bond a railroad venture that would benefit Montclair.

Division proceeded briskly in Orange Township after Orange incorporated as a town in 1860, thus gaining the right to spend money for such "frills" as a police depart-

Livingston was the first governor after New Jersey became a state; Bloomfield was the fourth, and the first Democrat.

Newark's industrial pattern became set in the 1830s. Improved transportation provided the impetus—first with the completion of the Morris Canal in 1832, then through the building of the New Jersey Railroad and the Morris & Essex Railroad in the middle 1830s. The dramatically improved transportation systems joined the riverbank factories with the iron and coal to the west and the markets to the east and south. In addition, enough sailing vessels moved in and out of the bay to make Newark a port of entry in 1834. Imports that year totaled $2 million, while exports reached $8 million. Included were products brought in by whaling vessels that berthed at Newark from about 1832 to 1840.

Newark finally became a city in 1836, amid the thundering of cannon and the vigorous stirring of its nineteen

ment, street improvement, school development, and other municipal departments. Orange's outlying regions wanted no part of the inevitable taxes. South Orange became a separate village in 1861, and East Orange and West Orange both incorporated in 1863, satisfied that they had frustrated modernization and had saved money at the same time.

South Orange had a very modest claim to attention: Seton Hall College, founded in 1856 at Madison, had moved to South Orange in 1860. One student comprised the entire first graduating class in 1862. The tiny college survived small enrollments and two disastrous fires in 1866 and 1909 to become today's Seton Hall University, one of the largest Catholic institutions in the United States.

The Civil War shattered the tremendous markets that Newark industrialists had built up with the South in boots and shoes, carriages, clothing, saddles, and harness. Leather men in "The Swamp" vehemently blamed Abraham Lincoln in their bitterness for the loss of markets below the Mason-Dixon line. But the city and county soon rallied to the cause when the Swamp people found Union war contracts every bit as lucrative as Southern peacetime contracts. President-elect Lincoln received a tremendous welcome when he passed through Newark in February 1861; a crowd of twenty-five thousand jammed the streets to greet him, despite a lively snowstorm.

The first fully outfitted soldiers to reach the Capital were three thousand armed New Jersey troops, led into Washington by Brigadier General Theodore Runyon of Newark, who later became mayor and state chancellor. Back home, the Hewes and Phillips Iron Works gave each of its men who entered the service a blanket and revolver, paid full salaries to volunteers, and kept their jobs open. Dr. Marcus L. Ward, acclaimed as "The Soldier's Friend," led a successful movement to have a fourteen-hundred-bed army hospital opened in the city. His popularity with soldiers did not help Ward win when he ran for the New Jersey governorship in 1863, but he won that honor three years later.

The 1870 census showed 143,839 people in Essex County, with 105,000 of those living in the bustling city of Newark. The city began to assume diversified character as increasing numbers of Italian, Russian, Polish,

and Hungarian immigrants streamed in to join the Irish, the Germans, and the descendants of "first families." More than forty-five thousand people worked in Newark that year, including an estimated fifteen thousand people sewing garments in their homes. Shoes, carriages and buggies, beer, and jewelry paced the industrial life. Newark manufacturers staged a memorable 1872 industrial exhibit in the skating rink to show off the city's "Made in Newark" might.

Most Newarkers knew that unassuming Seth Boyden would have enjoyed the exhibit most, but he had died in 1870 after spending fifty-five productive years in or near Newark. Boyden came to Newark from New England in 1815 as a young man, and in 1818 he produced the first patent leather in the United States. He announced this country's first manufacture of malleable iron in 1826 and in the 1830s built locomotives and steam machinery. Newark's "Uncommercial Inventor" profited little from his discoveries, however, and in 1855 he moved to Hilton (near Maplewood) where he lived as a poor farmer. There he perfected the amazing Hilton strawberry, which brought a dollar a quart, but not to Boyden, since he gave away his plants.

Other inventors found a fertile atmosphere in Essex County. Thomas Alva Edison moved from Menlo Park to open a research laboratory in West Orange in 1887, and built a phonograph works there between 1887 and 1890. His movie pioneering was carried on in West Orange. John Wesley Hyatt, inventor of celluloid in 1870, gave Newark an important industry overnight when he built a five-story factory in the city in 1873. Dr. Edward Weston's pioneering in electrical instruments in the 1870s led to another important Newark firm. Weston developed the first volt standards, installed the carbon electric lights on the Brooklyn Bridge in 1883, and invented the photoelectric cell.

Newark's industrial growth was accompanied by the growth of its banking and insurance companies. Banking dated from 1804, when the Newark Banking & Insurance Company was founded in a private house on a shaky capital of only forty thousand dollars. Major insurance companies had equally small beginnings; Mutual Benefit started in 1845 without even having the three hundred dollars to pay for its charter. Thirty years later John F. Dryden's pioneering in industrial insurance met with little financial support; yet he founded the Prudential Insurance Company in 1875 and watched it grow rapidly.

Industry had more limited growth in the suburbs. Orange's hatters celebrated a hundred years of their enterprise in 1892 by turning out nearly five million hats in twenty-one firms. The Stetson family, famed for the big "ten gallon" hats claimed by Texans, operated in the Orange valley for a century after founding their company in 1790. A 1909 strike over the use of union labels doomed the hat industry in Orange. Some hatters moved to Millburn after the Civil War; eight firms prospered there in the 1880s, only to suffer eventually the same fate as the Orange plants. Millburn's paper plants, numerous and prosperous in the 1890s, gradually died from cheaper competition elsewhere. One of those factories is now the Paper Mill Playhouse, the premier New Jersey theater.

The suburbs saw a greater destiny: to be developed as residential areas. Several noted early real estate ventures prospered and attracted prosperous clients: Llewellyn S. Haskell's Llewellyn Park grew rapidly after its establishment in 1875, and Stewart Hartshorn's exclusive Short Hills property was immediately successful after he announced the project in 1877. Other wealthy newcomers bought homes in Benjamin Small's summer colony at St. Cloud, and such noted people as General George B. McClellan lived in Dr. Edgar Marcy's development on "The Ridge" in West Orange.

Culture came to western Essex through these newcomers. Mrs. Louise Lord Riley, who moved to Orange from Brooklyn, called fifteen women together at her home in 1872 to organize the Woman's Club of Orange, the first woman's club in New Jersey and the fourth in the United States. When the General Federation of Women's Clubs was founded in 1890 to coordinate club work nationally, the first president was Charlotte Emerson Brown of the Orange Club.

Growth of the suburbs heightened Newark's economic welfare, since the people in outlying towns continued to shop in the city or work in its insurance companies and factories. Perfection of a street railway system made it easy to live in a suburb, yet visit Newark for work and pleasure.

First came the horse-drawn streetcars, starting in the 1860s. By 1880, some million and a half people paid fares annually. Horses left the rails after 1890, when the first electric streetcars ran from Newark to Irvington. Within ten years, trolleys ran outward from Newark to every Essex suburb, across the Passaic River to Hudson County towns, and southward to Elizabeth, New Brunswick, Trenton, and Camden, as well as to the Jersey Shore at Long Branch.

Trolleys were not a matter of mundane transportation alone. For thirty years they offered as well a chief means of recreation. Trolleys opened the Orange mountaintops to Sunday excursionists at Eagle Rock and Cable Lake. Thousands of Newarkers rode streetcars out to Vailsburg for picnics in the 1890s. Other thousands of trolley excursionists joined in German songfests at Becker's Grove in Irvington (where even "My Old Kentucky Home" was sung in German).

Significantly, the Essex County Park Commission was formed in 1895 as the nation's first county park system to preserve for the public some natural beauty spots—Eagle Rock, South Mountain, Branch Brook, and Weequahic Park, for example. Forming the commission was an exceptionally progressive step, since at the time the only other place in the nation that had any vital public parks of the sort was cultured Boston, and that was only a city system.

The automobile—rather than inflexible railroad and trolley lines—finally metamorphosed Essex County farmland into homeland. At the turn of the century only Newark, Orange, and East Orange had more than 10,000 inhabitants, with industrial Orange's 15,000 population the largest outside of Newark. More than two-thirds of Essex County's 359,000 people still lived in Newark in 1900; it was just too hard to get even as far out as Vailsburg on the western edge of the city via trolley.

Automobiles brought demands for improved roads—and also brought more suburban dispute. In widespread Caldwell Township, for example, arguments over the disposition of road funds between 1898 and 1908 dissolved the once-huge township into the six small municipalities of Caldwell Borough, North Caldwell, West Caldwell, Verona, Cedar Grove, and Essex Fells. In the division the house where President Grover Cleveland had been born in 1837, and where he had lived for four years, stayed within Caldwell Borough limits.

After Thomas Edison moved his research laboratory to West Orange in 1887, he bought this estate, called "Glenmont," in fashionable Llewellyn Park.

Through its first 240 years Newark had struggled along without a real port, despite its strategic location on broad Newark Bay. The Board of Trade's long-standing prediction of port development began to assume reality in 1915 when a mile-long channel was dredged in the Meadows. Government money helped the port become an actuality during World War I, when Newark led American cities in shipbuilding tonnage. Nearby, Newark Airport was built in the Meadows in 1928, making the marshland more useful than it had been since cattle of the early settlers roamed freely through the salt hay.

Newark's skyline jutted upward in the late 1920s and

early 1930s, climaxed finally by construction of the thirty-four-story Raymond Commerce Building in 1930 and the thirty-five-story National Newark and Essex Building in 1931. The city embraced new ideas—radio, for example, by welcoming radio station WJZ, second in the nation. Radio's impact on the county and nation became indelible with the first broadcast of a World Series game from Newark's station WJZ in 1921. A year later station WOR began broadcasting from L. Bamberger & Company. Its star was the first of three John Gamblings to host an early morning program.

Everything spurted in Newark in the 1920s. Factories

Branch Brook Park's annual April display of cherry blossoms in Newark and Belleville boasts far more cherry trees and varieties of blossoms than the much-publicized Washington, D.C., festival. (*Walter Choroszewski*)

boomed, banks and insurance companies expanded, great department stores such as Bamberger's, Hahne's, and Kresge's became the mecca of suburban house-wives. That importance made the Depression even more shocking, since more than six hundred factories closed their doors and business lagged. Hard times hit all of the county, but Newark suffered most cruelly. Yet those Depression days of the 1930s were Newark's golden hours; an economic and political decay already had set in. The results would become startlingly clear in the years after World War II.

Suburban growth mushroomed on the eve of the war with Germany and Japan. In 1940, half of Essex County's population now lived outside Newark. Five towns had populations in excess of 30,000: East Orange, 68,945; Irvington, 55,328; Bloomfield, 41,623; Mont-clair, 39,807; and Orange, 35,717.

Essex County's population growth has been nearly

stabilized. There is little room for growth. Much of the eastern part surrounding Newark blends into one big city, with strangers hard put to know where one municipality ends and the next begins. Major population increases since World War II have been in the western part of the county—near the Caldwells, in and near Livingston, Cedar Grove, and Millburn.

The postwar blows that have struck all American cities hit Newark with particular force. As thousands of descendants of immigrant families fled the tenements, black families from Southern farms took their place. The city's population is more than 60 percent black, plus a large Hispanic community. The Newark slums are an indictment of twentieth-century America. Bitter riots in Newark in 1967 underscored the miserable economic and social conditions offered the newest group of people hoping for elevation and equality in an urban prosperity.

Despite its apparent inability to eradicate its slums (an impotency shared with all cities), Newark remains New Jersey's foremost city in every way—financially, commercially, industrially, and as a center for transportation. The national home office of the Prudential Insurance Company remains in the city, housed in a handsome downtown skyscraper. New Jersey Bell Tele-

Port Newark, originating in 1914, became a vital East Coast shipping destination when the Port of New York and New Jersey Authority leased it in 1946 and expanded the facility to include a new port in Elizabeth. (*Walter Choroszewski*)

phone Company (now part of Bell Atlantic) and Public Service Corporation have home offices in the city. New Jersey's financial strength is based in Newark.

More than anything, Newark is the transportation hub of New Jersey. It keeps New Jersey in touch with the world through the Port Newark–Newark Airport complex.

Newark correctly boasts that it is the only city in the world where seaport, railroads, highways, and airport runways are side by side, so close that an outfielder with a strong arm could stand on a runway at Newark International Airport and throw a baseball over the New Jersey Turnpike and the Jersey Central Railroad into Port Newark. The Port Authority of New York and New Jersey as-

Newark International Airport, growing steadily for the past forty years, is now one of the leading airports in the nation. (*Walter Choroszewski*)

sumed control of both Newark Airport and Port Newark in 1948. Changes since then have been phenomenal. Some fifteen hundred vessels are handled at the port annually, a tripling since 1948. About five thousand workers annually earn more than $25 million, a similar tripling of statistics. Eventually some eighty-five hundred people will work at the Port. The Newark International Airport area has been increased from fourteen hundred to twenty-three hundred acres under Port Authority control, roughly four times the size of LaGuardia Airport. New runways and terminals have been built. Today Newark International Airport is one of the best-equipped air terminals in the world.

No Newark undertaking matches its higher educational story, however. When Rutgers University acquired old Newark University in 1946, its main building was the one-time Ballantine brewery, converted to college use. By 1965, some eighty-five hundred students sat in classrooms scattered through a miscellany of old buildings, none of them built for college use. Nearby, Newark College of Engineering, a respected engineering school with a long history, struggled along in a series of old buildings better fitted for nineteenth-century factories than twentieth-century education.

Rutgers and the New Jersey Institute of Technology (the new name for the old Newark College of Engineering) have seen startling physical changes on contiguous campuses on the hill in the western part of Newark. N.J.I.T. has doubled its campus area to accommodate twelve thousand students. Rutgers has built high-rise college buildings to permit the education of some twenty-five thousand students on a vibrant urban campus of less than thirty acres. Close by are Essex County Community College and Seton Hall law school. If the future of America truly is tied to higher education, that future looks bright for Newark. Adding to the bright academic aura is the imaginative and daring new $150 million cultural center rising on property running from near Military Park to the Passaic River. When completed, it will be the second largest such center, topped only by New York City's Lincoln Center.

Essex County is intensely urban, but there are major patches of open public lands, thanks to the long-range wisdom of the Essex County Park Commission. The Eagle Rock and Southern Mountain reservations offer

Verona Lake, a vibrant patch of blue in suburbia, is another part of the historic Essex County Park system, the nation's first county park plan when started in 1895. (*Walter Choroszewski*)

shade and scenery in the midst of suburban towns; Branch Brook and Weequahic parks provide shade and recreation on the northern and southern edges of Newark.

The Essex County park saga is an important lesson for any region in the beginning stages of urbanization. It has proved that beauty is possible, even in densely packed regions of humanity. As only one example, Branch Brook Park, shared by Newark and Belleville, has more varieties and numbers of flowering cherry trees than Washington, D.C., despite the glowing press coverage accorded the latter's cherry festival.

Colleges, parks, cultural facilities, and other public amenities are mixed blessings since they pay no taxes to cities hard pressed to make budgets balance. Newark is Exhibit A. The higher educational complex, the county parks, the excellent Newark Library and Newark Museum, and the arts center, all extensively utilized by non-Newarkers, impose financial problems for the city providing them both space and essential services.

Perhaps some might wonder what Robert Treat would think of modern Essex County. He undoubtedly would not like the cinder-stained Meadows or the industrial smells that have replaced the delicate scent of apple blossoms. Yet he was an adventurer, in tune with his times; he likely would be a leader in today's growth and change. Unquestionably, too, he would agree that he had made a bit of a real estate bargain in 1667.

Union County's courthouse is dwarfed by a fifteen-story annex that dates from 1913, but this white granite building completed in 1905 merits close attention. It was built in the form of a Maltese cross, with the front portico upheld by Corinthian columns. A long flight of stone steps leads to a portico bearing the carved proclamation: *Vox Populi, Vox Dei* ("The voice of the people is the voice of God"). (*Irving Tuttle*)

UNION

HOUSE DIVIDED

Persistent national talk about secession in the 1850s found understanding along the Elizabeth River, where residents for years had discussed splitting from Essex County. Slavery and states' rights had nothing to do with the secession sentiment in Elizabeth; local citizens simply chafed under Newark domination. They broke away on March 18, 1857, and in a twist of semantics called their seceded county Union.

The Essex-Union schism was predominantly an Elizabeth-Newark affair, since life in the two county regions pivoted on the sister cities that had grown in rivalry for nearly two hundred years. The House of Essex was not big enough to hold both, particularly with slightly younger sister Newark taking most of the cake and leaving the crumbs for Elizabeth.

The divided house in time benefited both Union and Essex, but in 1857 Union County took comfort mainly in faded memories. Boundaries of the new county roughly coincided with the old boundaries of Elizabethtown, the first English-speaking settlement in New Jersey. Oddly enough, this first-settled land became the last of New Jersey's twenty-one counties to be established.

Trouble with Lenape Indian raiders initially prevented New Amsterdam's Dutchmen from using the regions by the Achter Kol (Arthur Kill). Surely they regretted this: they knew good land when they saw it. Bolder Englishmen living on Long Island unsuccess-

fully negotiated with the Dutch in 1660 for permission to settle near what is now Elizabeth. Three years later, New Amsterdam guns drove off a party of twenty Long Islanders seeking to buy a plantation near the Raritan River from the Indians without first consulting the Dutch.

English guns had the final say in late August of 1664, however, when New Amsterdam capitulated to an English fleet. Colonel Richard Nicolls, sent to govern the region, changed New Amsterdam to New York and let it be known that he welcomed colonists. Within a month six Long Islanders—John Bailey, Nathaniel and Daniel Denton, Luke Watson, John Foster, and Thomas Benedick—obtained Nicolls's permission to dicker with the Indians for a tract along the Achter Kol.

The Indians accepted the usual English offer of wampum, coats, gunpowder, and miscellany. On October 28, 1664, they deeded to the Long Islanders a plot of ground including all of present-day Union County and pieces of Essex, Middlesex, Somerset, and Morris counties, about five thousand acres, for which the Lenape received goods worth about £154. Settlement started in November 1664, after Benedick and the Dentons sold their shares to John Baker and John Ogden, Sr. The latter, with five grown sons, was a powerful addition to the original property holders.

Meanwhile, the Duke of York sat down in England on

Howard Pyle's mural in the Essex County Courthouse depicts the landing of Philip Carteret at Elizabethtown in August 1665.

June 23, 1664, and had given all the land of Nova Caesaria (New Jersey) to a couple of his court friends, Lord John Berkeley and Sir George Carteret. Governor Nicolls obviously had no knowledge of this blithe gift when he permitted the Elizabethtown colonizers to bargain with the Indians. This strange royal maneuver would bring trouble in years to come.

Philip Carteret, cousin of George, sailed from England early in the summer of 1665 to become governor of Nova Caesaria in the name of Berkeley and Carteret, completely unaware that Englishmen already lived there. His surprise arrival on the Achter Kol in August 1665 excited and distressed the few families already there, for naturally they wondered how his presence might affect them. Carteret's ship *Philip* anchored offshore and the twenty-six-year-old new governor came ashore along with thirty immigrants, including eighteen servants.

Carteret made the best of a difficult situation. He greeted the established settlers, and in a politician's show of husbandry shouldered a hoe as he marched up from the wharf. At the same time he named the settlement "Elizabeth Town" in honor of cousin George Carteret's wife. The young governor amiably sought to be one of the Associates; within a month he purchased the rights of John Bailey, who had decided not to settle in Elizabethtown.

Robert Treat and his Connecticut followers dealt with Carteret when they founded Newark in the spring of 1666. They accepted Elizabethtown's preeminence when Governor Carteret designated the town the capital of New Jersey and summoned the state's first General Assembly to meet there in 1668. Laws enacted by the Assembly covered everything from tippling in "tapphouses" after nine o'clock at night to putting disobedient children or witches to death. But, as one authority has written, "Puritan austerity was so tempered by Dutch indifference that mercy itself could not have dictated a milder system." The harsh laws, in short, were not strictly enforced.

Rivalry between Elizabethtown and Newark began early. Leaders in both towns met on Divident Hill (in what is now Weequahic Park) on May 20, 1668, to settle boundary differences. In the fall of that year little whal-

Washington's Headquarters, Morristown, 1779–80

"Old Barney," Barnegat Lighthouse

Walter Choroszewski, whose skills are demonstrated on these eight pages (and elsewhere in the book), has become the best-known photographer dealing with the entire state of New Jersey. His four books, the latest being *Garden State in Bloom*, show the state at its best and Choroszewski calendars are an annual sellout.

Peaceful meandering in the Oswego River

Cranberry harvesting, Burlington County

Washington Park, Newark

Skylands Botanical Garden, Ringwood

Great Falls of the Passaic, Paterson

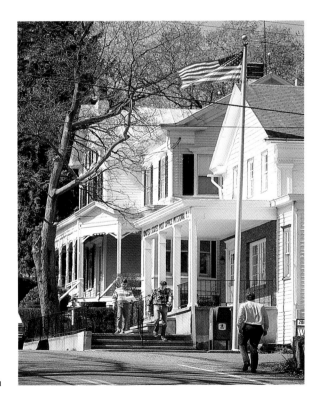

General store, Pittstown

The green fields of Sussex

Perth Amboy on Raritan Bay

Golden dome of the State House

Gingerbread in Cape May

The Palisades of the Hudson River

ing vessels began to set out from the Elizabeth River. Soon Elizabethtown tanners began to cure leather, and the village quickly became a center of the leather industry in colonial America. Many leather enterprises in other New Jersey towns and other colonies were started by migrating "Betsytowners," including the first tannery in Newark. Elizabethtown leathermakers exported their products as early as 1678.

Farming necessarily occupied all male settlers, even those engaged in whaling or leathermaking. Quite simply, the numerous cattle in the settlement logically led to the early leather curing. As families increased and demands for farmland increased, settlers pushed outward through the fertile valley south of the heavily forested Watchung Mountains.

Agriculture-minded newcomers from Connecticut moved down in the summer of 1667 and established Connecticut Farms (now Union). Scottish families from Perth Amboy came overland and stopped in 1684 in the fields on the plain south of the Watchungs; their villages became known as Scotch Plains and Plainfield. Quakers from Woodbridge built sawmills on the Rahway River in 1683 and 1684 and named their place Rahway after the river. Then, in 1699, Elizabethtown settlers divided the pasturelands well to the west of their town—and called it simply the West fields (now the town of Westfield).

A family named Briant stopped in 1717 to occupy the fields where a spring gushed forth into the headwaters of the Rahway River. The village name? It had to be Springfield! Isaac Sayre built his house in about 1710 on top of the plateau that naturally came to be called Summit. Just to the west, the preponderance of wild turkeys led new arrivals to call their area Turkey, and in about 1758, when the gallery in the Presbyterian Church collapsed without injuring any worshipers, the grateful congregation celebrated their good fortune by changing Turkey's name to New Providence. No region has ever been settled more easily or named more naturally than Union County.

Trouble brewed throughout the area, dating to the understandable belief of early settlers that their purchase of the land directly from the Indians took precedence over arbitrary distribution of the region to East New Jersey Proprietors, a group of real estate speculators who

bought the land from Sir George Carteret's estate in 1682. The Proprietors tried to collect annual quitrents but the settlers stood firm and ready to fight, even against royal authority. They persistently refused to pay.

Rioting erupted as early as 1670, when Elizabethtown residents refused to pay rents to Carteret. They formed a posse in 1699, rode to Newark, and released a prisoner jailed by the Proprietors. These and constant lesser protests merely paved the way for major troubles in 1745 and 1746 when Elizabethans were in the center of vigorous anti-Proprietor riots that swept all of East New Jersey. The approach of the French and Indian War, plus the fact that Governor Jonathan Belcher chose Elizabethtown rather than Perth Amboy as his capital when he arrived from England in 1751, helped ease the tension.

Elizabethtown claimed to be the leading settlement

Springfield's Presbyterian Church replaced the church burned when British troops attacked the town in June, 1780. (*Earl Horter drawing, The State Library*)

119

in New Jersey. The location of the original provincial capital in town attracted men of substance and culture and gave the population a more cosmopolitan tone than found in other colonial towns. Village life centered in the Presbyterian and Episcopal churches, particularly after two notable leaders, the Reverend Jonathan Dickinson (Presbyterian) and the Reverend Edward Vaughan (Episcopalian) came to the village in 1708.

Mr. Dickinson and Mr. Vaughan had remarkably parallel careers. Both came to Elizabethtown at about

Commemorating June 23, 1780, a lone Minuteman stands vigil where Parson James Caldwell distributed Watt's Hymnals from his Presbyterian Church to use as gun wadding in the Battle of Springfield. (*Walter Choroszewski*)

the same time, both advanced their churches greatly, and both died within a few days of each other in October 1747. Mr. Dickinson gained particular attention as a preacher, teacher, farmer, and practicing physician of note. He was an obvious choice to become the first president of the College of New Jersey (now Princeton University) when it was founded in Elizabethtown in 1746. He held classes in the parsonage, but after his death in 1747 the college moved to Newark, which heightened the growing jealousy between Elizabethtown and Newark residents.

Rent battles with the Proprietors helped to prepare the region for the quickening opposition to King George III. In February 1775, an Elizabethtown resolution cut off trade with Staten Island merchants because the Island inhabitants "have manifested an unfriendly disposition towards the liberties of America." Tory sentiment pervaded the area, particularly among Episcopalians, and became especially strong in 1776 after the defeat of American troops in the Battle of Long Island and the subsequent November retreat of Washington's army across New Jersey.

Despite sympathies for the Crown, the region that is now Union County had Revolutionary leaders aplenty. These included William Livingston of Elizabethtown, elected the first governor of the state of New Jersey on August 31, 1776, and reelected continuously until he died in office in 1790; Abraham Clark of Elizabethtown and Rahway, one of New Jersey's five signers of the Declaration of Independence; Jonathan Dayton, an officer on Washington's staff and subsequently a leader in Congress; Aaron Ogden, distinguished field officer; and Elias Boudinot, outstanding member of the Continental Congress, who as president of Congress signed the peace treaty with Great Britain in 1783.

Tories forced many Elizabethtown patriots to take to the hills. British sympathizers struck often from Staten Island in the winter of 1779–80, making one particularly damaging foray on January 25, 1780, when Cornelius Hatfield, Jr., led royal sympathizers into Elizabethtown and burned the courthouse and Presbyterian church. Proof of the divided sentiment in the settlement, however, is the fact that Elizabethtown resident Cornelius Hatfield, Sr., father of the raider, immediately opened the doors of his "large red storehouse" as a temporary church.

The British made two desperate efforts in June 1780 to drive west from Elizabethtown to get at Washington's troops quartered in Morristown, but each time furiously fighting militia combined with badly outnumbered Continental regulars to turn back the King's men.

On June 6, 1780, General Wilhelm von Knyphausen swung ashore at Elizabeth Point with six thousand brilliantly uniformed troops and headed for the gap through the Short Hills. Colonel Dayton established twelve men at the eastern end of Elizabethtown with instructions to delay the march. The dozen gave ground doggedly while "Old Sow," the eighteen-pound cannon atop Beacon Hill above Springfield, called out the militia and summoned Washington's brigades from Morristown.

General William Maxwell and his New Jersey Brigade mauled von Knyphausen's massive force at Connecticut Farms, then fell back to Springfield to join aroused militiamen. As the invaders left Connecticut Farms they torched the village. One of the British soldiers shot through an open window and killed Mrs. James Caldwell, wife of the Reverend James Caldwell, nicknamed "The Fighting Parson" (or "The High Priest of the Revolution," in British eyes). The drive on Springfield failed; von Knypausen withdrew wearily.

Sixteen days later, five thousand British troops again headed toward the Short Hills, only to meet a militia savagely aroused by the burning of Connecticut Farms and the wanton murder of Mrs. Caldwell. Some twenty-five hundred Continentals, including the New Jersey Line, were spread east of Springfield along with nearly five thousand militiamen. Parson Caldwell inspired the fighting Americans at Springfield, passing out Watts's hymnals for use as wadding in the Americans' guns. His ringing shout, "Now give them Watts, boys!" has rolled down through the years.

English troops burned the church and most of the houses, then fell back from Springfield to conclude the last battle of consequence on New Jersey soil. The tide of battle shifted to Virginia and the nation moved toward peace. War's end meant disaster for many old Tory families, forcing them to leave their homeland for exile in Nova Scotia or New Brunswick, Canada. General

State-owned Boxwood Hall in Elizabeth was the home of Elias Boudinot, a Revolutionary War leader. (*Earl Horter drawing, The State Library*)

Washington paid a visit to Elizabethtown's Boxwood Hall, the residence of Elias Boudinot, on April 30, 1789, while on his way to New York to take the oath of office as President.

Essex County, including all of modern Union, had about seventeen thousand residents after the war, with Newark and Elizabeth almost of a size, each having a population of nearly one thousand. The towns vied for leadership although Elizabethtown people became increasingly filled with envy because of Newark's growing prosperity. Even Elizabethtown's long-established leather leadership gravitated to Newark. William Rankin, Elizabethtown hatter, went to Newark in 1811 to escape what he called "a depressing aristocratic atmosphere."

Elizabethtown's fall can be traced to 1790, when the state legislature approved a new sixty-four-foot-wide roadway from Newark Court House to Paulus Hook (Jersey City), with long wooden drawbridges across the Passaic and Hackensack rivers. Completion of the bridges in 1795 drew most of Elizabethtown's trade to the new route.

Westfield's Miller-Cory House, built by Samuel Miller in 1740, is a living museum of family farm life and work. The clapboard farmhouse has been restored to the way it was during the Revolutionary War. (*Walter Choroszewski*)

The smoldering battle between the towns broke into flame in February 1807 when Essex County voted for the location of a new courthouse. Citizens of both Elizabethtown and Newark voted often, if not wisely, with so many votes being cast that it was evident a glaring fraud had been perpetrated. Nevertheless, Newark won the battle and got the new courthouse—but in their stubbornness, the Elizabethans kept their old courthouse anyway! They kept it only a year, when it was burned down by accident. Ever optimistic, townspeople erected a new courthouse in 1810.

A more personal and more important struggle in-volved the New York steamboat monopoly of Aaron Ogden and Thomas Gibbons, who fought for control of the Elizabethtown waterfront. Ferries had been running to New York for a century until Robert R. Livingston and Robert Fulton of New York gained monopoly rights to New York waters from the New York legislature. The latter judged "New York waters" to extend to the New Jersey shoreline.

Ogden received permission from the New York monopoly in 1815 to run the steamboat *Sea Horse* between Elizabeth Point and New York. Gibbons entered the fray in 1817 by running his steamboat, the *Mouse of the*

Mountain, from Elizabeth Point to New York. Protracted legal maneuvering finally ended in 1824 when the U.S. Supreme Court, in a case involving the New York–Elizabethtown struggle, voided monopolistic steamboat practices in interstate commerce and opened the waters to all comers.

That set the stage for growth. Turnpikes radiated from Elizabethtown to outlying villages, but the real key to the future lay in railroads. Visions of riches danced in speculators' minds when the state legislature chartered the Elizabethtown & Somerville Railroad on February 9, 1831. It took five years to lay tracks from the ferry docks to Broad Street in Elizabethtown, and the first "train" on August 13, 1836, was pulled by four horses. Steam locomotives pulled a train through Westfield to Plainfield on January 1, 1839, and three years later the Elizabethtown & Somerville finally was a reality, after eleven years of building. The railroad changed its name to the Central Railroad of New Jersey in 1849.

Up in the mountains the Morris & Essex Railroad (Lackawanna) chose to make the eighty-foot climb to Summit, not because Summit was a place of beauty or a symbol of progress, but because the land was free. Trains climbed the mountain to Summit in the summer of 1837. The mountain village put aside its frontier days and began to grow.

The most important and most successful of the county's railroads was the New Jersey Railroad, chartered on March 7, 1832, to run from Jersey City to New Brunswick by way of Newark, Elizabethtown, and Rahway. Tracks reached Elizabethtown in 1834, Rahway late in 1835, and New Brunswick in 1838. On January 1, 1839, a link was made with the Camden & Amboy Railroad, providing service between the Jersey City ferries and the Camden ferries. This became the Pennsylvania Railroad through New Jersey.

Change was inevitable. In 1854, old Elizabethtown gained state approval to be the City of Elizabeth. Three years later, on April 13, 1857, Union County was officially freed from Essex. The old county finally was split after exactly 175 years of coexistence that had been increasingly less congenial.

Union County had only about twenty-five thousand residents when it became a separate entity, compared with about ninety-five thousand in Essex County. But in spite of this inferiority in numbers, Union residents were so happy to be free that the Republicans and Democrats agreed to split new county offices equally, a spirit of harmony that had not been seen before and has not prevailed since.

Industry of widely varied sorts came to the region in the first half of the nineteenth century, following the railroads. Plainfield, for example, found pre–Civil War prosperity from the many hat factories and clothes-making establishments started in the first years of the nineteenth century. Rahway had twelve carriage factories in the 1830s and became famed as a center of fine carriages until the Civil War ruined its Southern trade.

Elizabethport was spoken of in 1844 as a "new and thriving place" because of its railroad connections. Elizabeth City boasted a population somewhat in excess of five thousand in 1857 and had several small machine manufacturers. Many Union County towns had papermills in the 1840s, most of them concentrated in Springfield Township, which then included Millburn (now a township in Essex County).

David Felt came from New York in 1845 to buy the old mill that Peter Willcoxie had built a century before on Blue Brook on the south slope of Watchung Mountain. Felt, a printer and stationer in the city, decided to build a self-contained manufacturing village. He built homes, a school, a church, and a country store. Things went along well until the Civil War, when markets collapsed and Feltville became a deserted village. (Feltville endures as "The Deserted Village" in Watchung Reservation of the Union County Park System.)

Easily the most significant industrial happening in all Union County history took place in 1873, when the Singer Manufacturing Company of New York City consolidated its several separate sewing machine manufacturing plants into one huge plant in Elizabethport beside the Jersey Central Railroad. Singer put $3 million into a thirty-two-acre plant that employed three thousand workers. Few industries in the nation exceeded the plant in size. Singer's success focused instant attention on the wide-open Union County meadowland available for big industry.

Industrial development was paralleled by the growth

Part of the Bayway refinery of Humble Oil & Refining Company, known as Standard Oil when the refinery was opened in 1909. (*Humble Oil & Refining Company*)

of residential towns along the railroads. The beautifully shaded streets of Westfield, Plainfield, and Scotch Plains appealed to settlers, many of them men of wealth drawn to the county by good railroad schedules. The Jersey Central Railroad itself started to develop Fanwood in 1867, and in 1878 a luxurious summer hotel was built at Netherwood at a cost of $175,000.

In the mountains, the Lackawanna Railroad transformed Summit. First it became a resort town, but by the 1880s wealthy commuters came to stay permanently. The Lackawanna's Passaic & Delaware branch rolled out through New Providence and Berkeley

Heights in the early 1870s to link that region with the cities.

Just as county leaders wanted freedom, so towns sought independence. Linden was created from Elizabeth and Rahway in 1861. Clark split from Rahway in 1864. Summit broke away from Springfield and New Providence townships in 1869. Cranford was created in 1871, taking pieces of Westfield, Springfield, Union, Linden, and Clark in the process. Fanwood was created in 1878 from parts of Westfield and Plainfield. Hillside broke away from Union Township in 1913.

Strangely enough, in view of the excellent railroad

connections, the land south of Elizabeth developed slowly. As late as 1890 Linden was an area of truck farms, while Rahway's carriage factories still claimed industrial leadership in that town. Within the next two decades, however, this entire section of eastern Union burst forth into industrial prominence. This portion of Union County's die was cast: it would be urban and industrial.

Among the first to found an important industry in the area was J. Noah H. Slee, who developed his Three-in-One Oil in a Rahway shack and sold his first three dozen bottles there in 1894. George Merck purchased 150 acres of land on the Rahway-Linden boundary line in 1900 and by 1903 had completed construction of a three-story brick building, forerunner of today's tremendous Merck chemical and drug enterprise. Soon after, the Wheatena Company started to make cereals in Rahway.

At the same time Standard Oil Company, seeking to escape the congested conditions hemming in its refin-

Opened in 1942, the Murray Hill facility of Bell Telephone Laboratories has become one of the world's foremost research centers. (*Bell Telephone Laboratories*)

The three-tiered waterfall on the Raritan River in Cranford, built to provide power for the Williams-Droescher Mill in the background, is a pleasant historical site in the Union County Park system. (*Walter Choroszewski*)

Industrial expansion swept through Union County between 1930 and 1950, with a major emphasis being on research facilities and very modern plants. Ciba Pharmaceutical pioneered in moving into a major suburban town by building a well-landscaped plant in Summit in 1937, proving the point that industry can employ large numbers of people and also be aesthetically acceptable. That same year, General Motors finished its sprawling automobile assembly plant in Linden.

Union County has an ability to attract impressive research facilities. Merck & Company started the trend in 1933, building its first important research facility at Rahway despite the Depression. Standard Oil Company followed suit, completing its handsome Esso Research Center at Linden just before World War II. Most impressive is the Bell Telephone Laboratories at Murray Hill, finished in 1942 and now acclaimed as one of the most important electronics research centers in the world. The transistor, the tiny device that has revolutionized the science and electronics industries, was wholly developed at Murray Hill and perfected in 1947.

Recurrent real estate booms swept over nearly all the county before World War I, with Hillside and Union townships being prime examples of what happened. Hillside parted from Union in 1913 to set up its own township. Each municipality took about half the then-total population of 3,500. Today, Union Township has 50,000 residents and Hillside about 21,000.

The tremendous industrial growth since the turn of the century increased Union County's population from 99,353 in 1900 to 328,344 in 1940 on the eve of World War II. That total soared to 504,255 in 1960, rose to 543,116 in 1970, then started a slow decline, reaching 493,819 in 1990. This number must be considered in relation to Union County's limited area: only Hudson is smaller.

Hidden within the county population figures is a singular fact: nineteen of the county's twenty-one counties lost people between 1980 and 1990. Most of the losses were small, probably attributable more to a lowered birth rate than to disaffection with the home towns. The two municipalities with gains, Elizabeth and Plainfield, might seem surprising in light of the American legend that population is draining outward from all cities. Eliz-

eries in Bayonne and Jersey City, built a pumping station in Linden and on January 2, 1909, the first battery of Linden stills was fired, principally to make kerosene. The Bayway Refinery grew into one of the world's largest refineries.

Industry has spread throughout Union County from those beginnings—to Garwood, Clark, Plainfield, Hillside, Kenilworth, and to many new locations in Elizabeth, Linden, and Rahway. Today Union is the third most important industrial county in the state, despite the fact that it is the second smallest in land area.

abeth's population has remained steady for more than thirty years, reaching 110,002 in 1990, about the same as it was in 1950 before the panicky flight from the cities erupted across America.

It is no secret that people and corporations have been fleeing the eastern Union County's industrial and heavily-urban area for thirty years, heading outward toward Somerset, Morris, and Hunterdon counties. The major research facilities have been moved to the pasturelands in the belief that heavy thinking is possible only on broad acres. One exception is the Bell Laboratories in Murray Hill—but it has been in "the country" since the first part was completed in 1942.

Union's open space is found mainly in its county parks and reservations, inaugurated in 1913 when the Union County Park Commission was started as the second county system in New Jersey. One park commission reservation covers much of the Watchung Mountain top, conserving a rare bit of wild land in the face of frenzied urbanization.

Highways and railroads crisscross Union County, ranging from older and traffic-jammed Routes 1, 22, and 28 to such newer (but often equally jammed) roads as the Garden State Parkway, the New Jersey Turnpike, and Interstate Highway 78, finished through the county after settlement of a drawn-out clash between conserva-

tionists and highway planners on whether a portion of the Watchung Reservation should be taken for the road. Railroads roar through the county, still viable as rapid transit. The transportation web that men began to spin in the 1830s covers Union County completely.

Union County's most amazing transportation facility is the city's port. Completion of the Elizabeth channel and construction of thirty-seven deep-sea berths, thanks to the Port of New York and New Jersey, made Elizabeth one of the world's major seaports.

Rapid growth has wiped out many of Union County's old landmarks, burying some of old-time Elizabeth, in particular, under modern advances. Although islands of antiquity linger, the oldest part of the original historic center has been almost completely rebuilt.

Union County is now well past its century mark in years, but it retains its memories—and certainly has a bright present. Above all, Union has its pride—something that residents felt had been completely lost before they took that bold step away from Newark domination in 1857.

Thus, the house divided did not fall. The sisters who went their separate ways grew and prospered in different fashion. They are on much friendlier terms than they were in 1857, when those who seceded chose the name Union to finalize the act of division.

When Middlesex County dedicated its new glass-walled, ultra-modern courthouse in New Brunswick on September 1, 1960, it simultaneously announced plans for demolition of the 119-year-old classic courthouse that had served the county since 1841. As the six Greek-style redwood columns of the original two-story courthouse fell a month later, Middlesex County was serving notice that traditional had succumbed to functional.

MIDDLESEX

THE VITAL BRIDGE

John Inian's vision probably did not extend much beyond linking the east and west banks of the Raritan River when he established a ferry at what is now New Brunswick in 1686. Nevertheless, his ferry was the first exploitation of Middlesex County's ever-vital role as the connecting bridge between East and West Jersey, between cities and the Jersey Shore, between New York and Philadelphia, between New England and the South.

Twentieth-century trains that thunder over Middlesex on one of the busiest stretches of railroad tracks in the world and today's principal highways stretched over the county owe their status to the same simple reason that prompted Inian's Ferry. The theory is easily demonstrated: trace a straight line between New York and Philadelphia; astride the line is Middlesex County, the necessary link.

Indians journeying from the northern hills to the Jersey Shore in their summertime quest for fish and clamshells crossed the Raritan River not far from modern New Brunswick. Dutch messengers traveling between New Amsterdam and Holland's settlements along the Delaware River forded at the same spot, possibly as early as 1640. Other colonists preceded Inian, too. When he arrived in 1681, the place already was known as "Pridmore's Swamp."

By 1681, English settlers had lived in the region for nearly fifteen years. Agents from the Piscataqua River valley in New Hampshire and from Newbury, Massachusetts, both bought land from the Elizabethtown Associates late in 1666. The New Hampshire settlers thought of home and named their village Piscataqua (time has slurred that to Piscataway). The Massachusetts group founded Woodbridge, named for the Reverend John Woodbridge, a favorite back home in Newbury.

When the Assembly formed New Jersey's first four counties in 1675, one of them was loosely composed of Woodbridge and Piscataway. Seven years later, Middlesex was officially established, with its boundaries including most of modern Somerset County. Far-flung Woodbridge had six hundred residents at the time, but the East New Jersey Proprietors ignored the evident merits of the big township when they looked for a headquarters. They chose instead "sweet, wholesome, and delightful" (as well as unpopulated) Ambo Point. The Proprietors propagandized their unbuilt town as the "London of the Western Hemisphere" because of its "commodious situation upon a safe harbor."

Three substantial houses graced Ambo Point by August 1683, but real growth began two years later when the Earl of Perth permitted two hundred oppressed Scots to emigrate to the Point. The Scots gratefully dubbed the village New Perth; in time, Ambo Point gave way to the compromise name of Perth Amboy. Either way, the Proprietors publicized their "convenient town for merchandise, trade, and fishery." They were more interested in real estate sales than a name.

Middlesex County's "bridge" character began to emerge in 1686, when Perth Amboy became the provincial capital of East New Jersey. That necessitated communication with Burlington, capital of West New Jersey, and led to the gradual widening of the Indian paths into rough roads across the narrow waist of New Jersey. Two roads traversed the length of Middlesex, the "upper" road going to Princeton and Trenton via Inian's Ferry, the "lower" road extending from South Amboy to Burlington via Cranbury.

Meanwhile the rich Raritan River valley beckoned Dutch settlers. Some of them stopped off at Inian's Ferry early in the eighteenth century, and named their main street Albany in memory of the New York town whence they came. The proud little river town became New Brunswick officially in 1730, ending years of casual designations that had ranged from Pridmore's Swamp to Inian's Ferry to "The River," and occasionally Onion's Ferry. The new name honored the House of Brunswick, then occupying the throne of England.

New Brunswick enjoyed an enviable position. James Alexander wrote in 1730: "As to New Brunswick at Inian's Ferry, it grows very fast, and the reason is that the county grows very fast back of that place; for when I came to this place in 1715, there were but four or five houses in the thirty miles between Inian's Falls and the Falls of the Delaware, but now the whole way it is almost a continued lane of fences and good farmer houses." Alexander wrote that New Brunswick was the storehouse and shipping point for wheat and flour produced inland. Consequently, land was worth "near as great a price as so much ground in the heart of New York."

Perth Amboy also grew steadily, but its pride suffered a severe setback in 1747 when Governor Jonathan Belcher arrived in town, apparently to dwell there as most royal governors had before him. Governor Belcher delivered himself movingly: " . . . and you may depend on everything on my part to render it a flourishing town . . ." Then he went to live in Elizabethtown.

However, as the colonies moved toward an open split with England in 1776, Governor William Franklin established his residence at Perth Amboy and dedicated himself to avoiding a split between New Jersey and the Crown. On the night of June 15, 1776, Colonel Nathaniel Heard of the Continental Army knocked on Franklin's door to offer him his choice: either sign a parole and sit out the impending war in a town which Franklin could choose, or submit to arrest. The governor scorned the parole; Heard arrested him.

Washington's dispirited army crossed the Raritan at New Brunswick on November 30, 1776, on the retreat across New Jersey that led finally to the Battle of Trenton. The troops burned the long wooden bridge, then headed south. British and Hessian troops occupied the town from December 2 to the following June, building hatred by robbing Tories and Patriots alike. Fear spread; as many as two to three hundred adults streamed into New Brunswick during that December to accept Lord Howe's offer of amnesty in return for a renunciation of revolutionary sentiments.

Howe found his riverbank position untenable in the late spring of 1777 after Washington moved his troops from Morristown to the southern slope of the Watchung Mountains, overlooking the Raritan valley. Howe tried to lure Washington out of the hills on June 22 with attacks in the direction of Millstone and Middlebush, but the Americans did not budge. When Howe turned back to New Brunswick, Washington sent Continentals to harass his rear, only to chase back to the slopes when Howe turned.

Tiring of the cat-and-mouse game, Howe marched his troops off to Staten Island and from there shipped them to Philadelphia. The British burned and pillaged as they went to Staten Island, adding to the suffering Middlesex County had already endured. No savage battles raged over the country, yet more than 100 buildings were burned and the British ransacked at least 650 other homes.

The county saw little direct warfare after 1777, but Washington led troops through the lower part of the county in late June 1778 on the way to the Battle of Monmouth, then brought his army to New Brunswick after the battle. Much later, on August 20, 1781, the

Old Queens, started in 1809 when Rutgers University was Queens College, shown in this 1862 photograph. It is still the symbolic heart of the State University. (*Rutgers*)

general dramatically and unexpectedly revealed in New Brunswick the plans to take his army to Virginia for the decisive showdown with Cornwallis at Yorktown.

Middlesex County's most heralded Revolutionary hero was Captain Adam Hyler, a seagoing man of about forty when war broke out. Hyler owned a little gunboat, the *Defiance*, and manned it with whaleboatmen for raids against British ships anchored in Sandy Hook Bay. On one occasion in October 1781, Hyler and his daring crew destroyed four British ships in the bay in fifteen minutes.

New Brunswick edged to the fore as the county's prime town and met only token opposition when Middlesex courts were transferred there in 1778. Elsewhere in Middlesex in the waning days of the eighteenth century, a few potteries began to utilize the rich clay beds underlying Middlesex County soil in a wide arc from Woodbridge to Cheesequake. Most of southern Middlesex depended on huge lumber and timber shipments, although farmers along the Manalapan Creek knew that the Indian name for the creek—meaning "good country producing good bread"—correctly characterized their region.

Prosperity did not extend to Queens College, chartered first in 1766 and rechartered in 1770 when the first document produced no results. The Dutch Reformed Church nominally backed the college and chose New Brunswick over Hackensack as its location by a narrow margin of one vote. Trustees named Frederick Frelinghuysen as their lone faculty member and acquired a former tavern, the Sign of the Red Lion, as their college building. One faculty member was enough: the first graduating class in 1774 had only one graduate. He was Matthew Leydt, son of a trustee.

Such a college at least had the advantage of mobility. British troops drove the college out of New Brunswick, first to Millstone in 1777, then to North Branch in 1780. Just barely alive, the college returned to New Brunswick in May 1781. There were no graduates in 1784, '85, or '86, and Queens closed its doors in 1795, apparently unlamented and unloved, and definitely unsupported. Even an attempt in 1793 to merge with the College of New Jersey in Princeton failed.

Classes resumed in 1807 and optimistic trustees finished a substantial brownstone college building in 1809. This was "Old Queens," still the sentimental heart of Rutgers University. That helped, but not much. Queens College closed its doors again in 1821, dead for a second time.

Finally the trustees announced in 1825 that the institution would reopen on November 14, 1825, happy that thirty students had signed up for classes. The college had a new name: Rutgers. Trustees pointed out that "Queens" had become unpatriotic as a result of the Revolution—but anyone who believed that the re-christening had been induced more by the generosity of a New York philanthropist named Colonel Henry Rutgers than by patriotism would not have been far wrong. The name change came cheap; Rutgers gave only $5,000 and a bell for the new cupola on the college building. To the long-suffering trustees, that was largess of the highest order.

The financial plight of poor Rutgers College had failed to loosen the bulging purses in thriving New Brunswick, where more than five thousand people lived by 1830. Life surged vividly about the town's twenty taverns and hotels. Down on the waterfront a dozen fast sloops stood by, awaiting grain from Hunterdon, Somerset, and Warren counties. Twice a week long lines of massive grain wagons, drawn by as many as six horses, rolled to shipside over the New Jersey Turnpike between Easton and New Brunswick. Often as many as fifty wagons lined up in Water Street overnight while the waterfront erupted with the sound and strife in the taverns and rough hotels for traders. An early historian said the difference between New Brunswick's trader hotels and its hotels for overland travelers was that "travelers wanted rest."

Quantities of peaches from the uplands also cleared through New Brunswick, but that trade centered in Washington (now South River) under the leadership of Samuel Whitehead, Sr. Whitehead first set out peach trees in the early 1820s, and became so successful that farmers for miles around emulated him. In season, four to six peach-laden steamers left Washington daily for New York before declining crops ruined the business in the 1850s.

Even more important to all Middlesex, however, were the streams of people crossing between New York and Philadelphia. Perth Amboy, South Amboy, New Brunswick, Woodbridge, and Washington all vied for the trade. Competition between steamship companies connecting New York and Middlesex County became fierce; stagecoach companies battled without quarter at county ports for passengers leaving the boats.

South Amboy had a dramatic battle for the travel business from 1806 to 1833, when Samuel Gordon and Daniel Wilmurt "kept things hot between Amboy and Bordentown" with their rival stage routes. Intense rivalry flared in New Brunswick, where the "Citizens" and "Union" steamship lines scrapped for business. Whistling inbound steamers rammed into New Brunswick docks. Passengers, who took unto themselves the rivalries of the steamboat owners, risked life and limb by leaping ashore and sprinting for competing stagecoaches. Off went the coaches, up Burnet Street in the swirling dust, with as many as twenty-two coaches jockeying for positions on the narrow street.

New Brunswick gloried in its midway prominence.

Built in 1770 "to provide a convenient house" for New Jersey's royal governor, the Proprietary House in Perth Amboy has been restored to the way it looked during the tenure of Governor William Franklin, 1774 to 1776. (*Walter Choroszewski*)

The docks were busy enough, but stagecoaches also trundled across the long, low-level wooden bridge that spanned the Raritan at the foot of Albany Street. It opened to traffic on November 2, 1795, and by 1830 was filled with coaches dashing north and south to satisfy a world gone mad for speed.

Downcounty Middlesex towns cared little who got the upcounty trade first because they shared in the fortune eventually. Inns in Dayton, Rhode Hall, Cranbury, and Kingston catered splendidly to the cross-state transients. The pre-Revolutionary Kingston House, for example, boasted of having as many as forty-nine stages waiting out front at once, while more than four hundred passengers dined or rested inside.

Even greater trade lay ahead, for the railroad and canal era had begun. Railroads in time ruined the grain trade with inland counties, but the Delaware & Raritan Canal and the Camden & Amboy Railroad made up for wheat losses, and then some.

The D. & R. Canal reached New Brunswick in 1834, uniting the Delaware and Raritan rivers over a fine low-level route that would inspire profits for decades. Great numbers of barges passed through the canal locks, carrying Pennsylvania coal eastward to industry and carrying finished goods westward to opening markets in the West. New Brunswick was twice blessed. Not only did the canal bring a booming trade that gave the Raritan River the third largest tonnage of any river in the country, but a fall of fourteen feet of water from the last lock before the Raritan River offered marvelous water power for emerging industries. Scores of boats tied up at the great basin at New Brunswick and their crews and families came ashore to buy and to trade.

Railroads were a bit slow in coming to New Brunswick, although New Jersey's first railroad—the Camden & Amboy—was completed to South Amboy in December 1832. Two years later steam locomotives roared between Camden and South Amboy, cutting the New York–Philadelphia trip to seven hours. Within five

years the Camden & Amboy was carrying 165,000 passengers a year. Hightstown and Jamestown benefited from the railroad, but in 1839 the line was shifted to Trenton, Princeton, and New Brunswick to link with the New Jersey Railroad at the Raritan River. The first Camden to Jersey City train steamed through New Brunswick in 1840 and over the long, new wooden railroad bridge toward Newark and Jersey City—later the route of the Pennsylvania Railroad.

Power afforded by the canal lock's waterfall and quick movement offered by the railroad led to the rapid rise of New Brunswick industry. Young Martin Howell opened a wallpaper factory on Water Street in 1837, using canal water for power; Horace H. Day founded a rubber plant in 1839, and other companies took advantage of the

This 1882 engraving of the Excelsior Fire Brick Works in Perth Amboy shows that ceramics have long been a Middlesex specialty. (*The Newark Library*)

Boynton Beach, circa 1890, when Perth Amboy retained its "sweet and wholesome" character. (*Rutgers Special Collections*)

ready supply of power and the ease of importing raw materials, including anthracite coal unloaded from canal barges.

Rubber became a prime industry in Middlesex County, mainly because of Christopher Meyer, who came from Newark in 1839 to set up Horace Day's machinery. While Day continuously poured his money into the courts in a vain attempt to protect himself during a protracted suit for alleged infringements of Charles Goodyear's vulcanizing patents, Meyer struck out on his own in Milltown in 1844.

Eventually Meyer controlled Day's plant, as well as the Milltown factory and a New Brunswick hard rubber manufactory. Millions of boots, rubbers, and the patented "arctic" overshoes flowed from his Middlesex rubber works in the Civil War era and immediately after.

The big North Middlesex clay industry, long one of the county's chief economic bellwethers, edged into the industrial picture at the same time. Some use of the fine Raritan clay had been made in the eighteenth century in small potteries, but two Frenchmen finally made clay into big business in Woodbridge in 1825. That year Michael Lefoulon and Henry De Casse started the Salamander Works, which in twenty years became the state's largest clay manufactory.

John R. Watson set up a firebrick plant in Perth Amboy in 1836, and James Wood build brick kilns at Sayreville in 1851, although the important "big" names in those communities were Alfred Hall in Perth Amboy and Peter Fisher and James Sayre in Sayreville.

Hall located in Perth Amboy in 1845 to make firebrick, but his greatest contribution to the ceramic industry came in 1849 when he started an extensive terra-cotta plant. Others followed Hall's example. Perth

Amboy and the nearby area became the terra-cotta center of the world, and Middlesex terra cotta is today found around the globe.

Fisher and Sayre started their brick plant in 1851 and within twenty years made more than twenty-two million bricks annually. That, plus the eight million manufactured each year by the James Wood Company, made Sayreville one of the nation's biggest brick producers. By 1878, eight Raritan River brickyards combined to turn out fifty-four million bricks yearly, with Fisher and Sayre far out in the lead.

The Civil War stirred the Raritan Valley. The local militia, the "National Rifles," left town for federal duty immediately after Fort Sumter was bombarded. Soon the railroads bore carloads of cheering soldiers southward through New Brunswick. Trains roared through,

day and night. Coal barges unloaded hastily and hurried back for more fuel to stoke the war machine.

Industry's gain was Rutgers's loss. Once again the college faced collapse. Students left to join the armies, including J. Greeville McNeel and his brother Pleasant, who departed to join the Confederate Army in their home state of Texas. Both died for the South. Enrollments went down—to 105 in 1862, to 77 in 1863, and to 64 in 1864. The Class of 1862 had 38 graduates, and that number fell to 11 by 1864.

Rutgers was nearly a hundred years old, but was far closer to collapse than to good health. Three significant occurrences on the eve of its centennial boosted Rutgers toward both academic and economic solidity.

First, the state in 1864 gave Rutgers the Land Grant funds—sought also by the College of New Jersey in Princeton and Trenton Teachers College—to establish the College of Agriculture and Mechanics, first called "The Scientific School." Secondly, Rutgers in 1865 threw off its Dutch Reformed cloak and became nonsectarian. Finally, an intensive scholarship and endowment campaign by the Reverend Dr. William H. Campbell, the college's president, raised $144,758 in the closing days of the Civil War. By the 1870s Rutgers began to attract some large endowments, and its reputation was further enhanced by the establishment of the State Agricultural Experiment Station at the college in 1880.

In fact, the school had shucked enough of its academic rigidity and its economic problems to encourage some campus lightheartedness. One result was the nation's first intercollegiate football game, played on the Rutgers campus on November 6, 1869. Visiting Princeton obligingly dropped a 6–4 decision after the rival schoolboys (twenty-five on a side) trampled over one another. Four years later Howard N. Fuller (Rutgers '74) wrote the words to "On the Banks of the Old Raritan," the college alma mater. He set his words to the tune "On the Banks of the Old Dundee," and the result still makes loyal Rutgers men (and women) rise to sing the words, slightly revised to accommodate the women on campus.

Middlesex remained distinctly rural in the 1870s, even in the larger towns. Perth Amboy, despite its brick-

This 129-foot tower at Menlo Park indicates the site of Thomas A. Edison's research laboratory. (*N.J.D.C.E.D.*)

Johnson & Johnson headquarters in New Brunswick is the nerve center for a world-wide enterprise. (*Johnson & Johnson*)

yards, continued as a quaint village, where visitors came to enjoy the "salubrious sea air." Woodbridge had a reputation as a summer resort. Hundreds of men sought livings in the big oyster beds in the healthful Raritan Bay off Perth Amboy. Then the Lehigh Valley Railroad, built from Easton to Perth Amboy in the 1870s, brought huge coal shipments into Perth Amboy and overnight changed "sweet, wholesome" Amboy into a bustling in-

dustrial town. Population jumped from about twenty-eight hundred in 1870 to more than seven thousand in 1880.

When Thomas Alva Edison sought rural solitude in 1876, he found it at Menlo Park, where he set up the first American laboratory devoted entirely to research and invention. Edison promptly devised a "talking machine," which in the fall of 1877 repeated in Edison's own voice four lines of "Mary Had a Little Lamb." He put it aside as a toy; he had bigger things on his mind.

Edison and his staff turned to the development of a practical incandescent bulb. The search for a long-lasting filament focused, after hundreds of experiments, on ordinary cotton thread, burned and shaped to form a carbon filament. Edison turned on the current early in the evening of October 19, 1879, and the cotton filament glowed. It burned steadily for forty hours until Edison stepped up the current and the lamp expired in "a dazzle of brightness."

On New Year's Eve, 1879, three thousand visitors came to Menlo Park on a special excursion train to watch a public demonstration of the light. Before Edison left Menlo Park for West Orange in 1887, the hilltop laboratory was the site of many other inventions—including an electric locomotive, which Edison operated at Menlo Park. Some three hundred separate patents resulted from the teamwork at Menlo Park.

The rubber and wallpaper industries that had buoyed New Brunswick through several decades began to slip as the twentieth century dawned, but New Brunswick had in the meantime welcomed Robert W. and James W. Johnson, who came in 1885 to establish their pioneer gauze and adhesive tape plant. Within two years, J. & J. introduced absorbent cotton in the familiar blue box and used its "red cross" trademark for the first time. The Johnsons started in the old Parsons Mill by the river at a time when antiseptic standards were virtually unknown. Soon they had much of America reaching in emergencies for a red cross bandage rather than a torn-up old sheet or towel.

Perth Amboy's industrial character was set in 1899 when the Raritan Copper Works started to refine ore in the city. Within a few years it became the world's largest copper refinery. Middlesex County had two more copper refineries before 1903: a second in Perth Amboy and one in Carteret.

Milltown enjoyed a spurt of a different sort when the Michelin Tire Company of France bought the old Christopher Meyer rubber works in 1907 to make automobile tires. Michelin hired as many as three thousand people before it moved out of the Meyer plant in 1931.

If anyone needed convincing that industry was the way of the Middlesex future, World War I did the trick. The three copper plants combined to turn out more than half of all United States refined copper. The Wright-Martin Aircraft Corporation made $50 million worth of airplane engines in New Brunswick in 1918. Manufacturers of chemicals made the first stumbling steps toward replacing dyes and other chemicals cut off from Germany.

Munitions makers swarmed into Middlesex County. With E. I. DuPont supplying most of the know-how from its Parlin plant, shell-loading operations were set up in Parlin, Morgan, Old Bridge, and Maurer. New Jersey had 75 percent of the nation's shell-loading capacity, most of it located in Middlesex County near Raritan Arsenal.

The happy feeling engendered by war-swollen paychecks ended suddenly on October 5, 1918. A small blast at the T. A. Gillespie plant in Morgan that evening was followed by explosions that lasted for fourteen hours. Windows were broken within a thirty-mile area and residents fled in terror. Property damage exceeded $25 million and at least one hundred known dead were counted; exact totals were never known, since company records also disappeared in the searing tragedy.

Meanwhile, old Rutgers moved through its 150th anniversary in 1916 with modest celebration because of the approaching involvement in the war. Quiet excitement tinged the banks of the Old Raritan. For one thing, women were on the way, not on the staid downtown all-male campus, of course, but across town near the Agricultural College. The State Federation of Women's Clubs, spurred by a dynamic young widow named Mabel Smith Douglass, pressed the Rutgers trustees for a state college for women at the east end of New Brunswick. The trustees established the New Jersey College for Women in 1918 with Mrs. Douglass as the first dean. She badgered the state legislature into erecting three buildings before 1926—but another thirty years passed before state funds built another structure. Mrs. Douglass fought for the college before and after founding until her death in 1933. Fittingly, the institution's name was changed to Douglass College in 1955.

Less dynamic but equally persistent, Dr. William H. Demarest, Rutgers president from 1905 to 1924, steered the college through the transformation that made it ready to be a true state university. It was a slow process. In addition to the Land Grant funds initially given to Rutgers by the state in 1864, the New Jersey legislature established state scholarships at Rutgers in 1890. The college had to sue to get the money, finally getting $107,000 in 1905, the first year of Demarest's presidency.

Demarest successfully urged trustees to sever remaining ties with the Dutch Reformed Church by eliminating in 1920 the requirement of the 1766 charter that a Rutgers president must belong to that church. He built three new buildings on campus and acquired funds for another four on the College of Agriculture campus. When Dr. Demarest took office in 1905, he could count only 235 students. When he stepped aside in 1924, enrollment had reached 734. More important, Rutgers College became Rutgers University during his last year at the helm.

Middesex emerged from World War I with a heady feeling of growth. Its population edged above 160,000 in 1920 but nearly half of those people lived in either New Brunswick or Perth Amboy. Elsewhere, the fields stretched wide and far, filled with potatoes in the southern sections and with little or nothing north of the Raritan River.

Swift transformation was on the way. By 1930, State Routes 1, 9, and 27 rolled across the county. Completion of the Outerbridge Crossing to Staten Island in 1928 poured more thousands of motorists into Middlesex County, forcing construction of the Edison and Victory bridges over the Raritan. Trains continued to race through, making the New Brunswick-to-Elizabeth corridor the busiest railroad stretch in the world.

Since then the story has been an intensification of highway building. When New Jersey's first two toll roads—the New Jersey Turnpike and the Garden State Parkway—were completed in the early 1950s, naturally they crossed in Middlesex County. More specifically, they crossed in Woodbridge Township, and there the last farewell to open land was properly said.

Middlesex County had a population of 264,872 in 1950, seventh in New Jersey. By 1990 that had soared to 667,761, third in the state behind Bergen and Essex.

Commencement ceremonies at Cook College, originally a land-grant institution and one of the several units within Rutgers University. (*Walter Choroszewski*)

Woodbridge became the true crossroads, not only of the county and state but of the East. It is the gateway to the Jersey Shore, takeoff point for Philadelphia and Washington or New York and Boston.

Population grew rapidly everywhere—well, nearly everywhere. Places such as Jamesburg and Spotswood scarcely changed. Cranbury stood as a shining symbol of old-fashioned non-growth charm in the midst of the frenzied quests for ratables. Bypassed by the Camden and Amboy Railroad in 1833 and by Route 1 about a century later, Cranbury is a place where it is said people enjoy "seeing nothing happen." On the other hand,

Jamesburg's Buckelew Mansion commemorates James Buckelew, who in 1833 purchased much of the area called Gordon's Mills. He renamed it Jamesburg in 1847. (*Walter Choroszewski*)

Woodbridge population reached 93,086 in 1990, followed by Edison's 88,680, making them the fifth and sixth largest municipalities in New Jersey, replacing Elizabeth and Trenton among the state's so-called "big six" cities. (Woodbridge and Edison technically are not cities. Each has a township form of government.)

Such growth brings joy to real estate developers and county publicists, but it has not been accomplished without pain. There have been scores of schools to build, roads to maintain, traffic jams to fight, and problems of policing, garbage collection, and soaring tax rates to face. This is suburbia, rapidly shifted to city status.

The Rutgers-state relationship reached firm ground in 1945, when the state legislature officially made Rutgers the State University and agreed to appropriate "just and reasonable sums" for its support. Since then the growth has been meteoric. New buildings have sprouted yearly since 1956 on the downtown campus, at Douglass College, on the agricultural complex, and on Busch and Livingston campuses on the north bank of the Raritan River. Rutgers campuses at Newark and Camden are expanding. Rutgers University has indeed become the state university, complex, far-flung, and vital to every corner of the state.

New buildings have been augmented by enlarged faculties. Student enrollment has swelled tremendously. And, as a matter of pride, the athletic teams have been winning national attention (both the football and basketball teams were undefeated in regular season play in 1976). The women's basketball teams have won national recognition.

Rutgers has witnessed three great stages: its founding as a pre-Revolutionary church-affiliated college, emergence as a Land Grant institution, and full acceptance as the state university. It is the only state university in America to combine colonial heritage with Land Grant and state support. Change continues. The College of Agriculture has been renamed the George Cook College of Agriculture and Environmental Science, in recognition that New Jersey's agricultural acres are decreasing even as such problems as air and water pollution increase. The Cook name commemorates the nineteenth-century deeds of Professor Cook in making Rutgers the state's center of agricultural thought and inspiration.

Thus Rutgers bridges the long years from colonial beginnings to the sophisticated, bewildering, trying years of today. The choice of New Brunswick as a college site in 1771 was a happy and logical one, for even then the roads between New York and Philadelphia were clogged with young America on the move. The place for intellectual stimulation is always where the action and excitement are.

Middlesex County is far more the bridge between North and South, between East and West, than it was when John Inian opened his ferry in 1686. Today's highways are more numerous, wider, and far more costly, but the reasons for crossing the Raritan are the same as when Indians forded the river on their way to the Jersey Shore, when stagecoaches rattled between East and West Jersey, or the decades when railroads monopolized the New York-to-Philadelphia corridor. Often, on summer days, traffic stalls completely on either bank of the Raritan River. Only a rare driver fuming at the delays would blame history for this twentieth-century phenomenon.

But history is at fault—for placing New York to the east, Philadelphia to the west, with Middlesex County between.

Mercer County's courthouse is easily recognizable, yet it is almost lost in Trenton, where county government must vie with state government for attention. The cornerstone for this sandstone courthouse was laid in 1902; it was finished two years later. The new building replaced an earlier courthouse at the same site. Its only bow to construction in government traditions are the six Corinthian columns set one story above the street.

MERCER

SEAT OF GOVERNMENT

Long before its official birthday in 1838, Mercer County had a heritage upwards of 150 years long. Its early settlers came from the finest families; prestige and culture and heroics lodged firmly in their backgrounds. The wonder was not that Mercer finally was set off as a county, but rather that the process took so long.

Little bliss accompanied Mercer's actual birth, mainly because it occurred in the "smoke-filled" atmosphere so typical of state capitals. Burlington, Middlesex, and Hunterdon counties, on the one hand, and Somerset, on the other, all grudgingly contributed land to form Mercer. Somerset, given assurances that none of its own territory would go to the new county, sanctimoniously joined the majority of the legislature in severing parts of Burlington, Middlesex, and Hunterdon on February 22, 1838, to form the "original" Mercer County.

Five days later Burlington, Middlesex, and Hunterdon, with understandable relish, endorsed a second legislative act—this time cutting off a bit of Somerset to be joined to brand-new Mercer County. Thus, with extended unpleasant maneuverings and two birthdays, Mercer came to be. It should have been much easier.

The region surrounding the state capital had long been unnaturally divided. Residents on the north side of Assunpink Creek, which cuts through the heart of Trenton, went to Flemington for county business.

Neighbors across the creek journeyed to Mount Holly for their county affairs. Princeton people were even worse off, for Somerset and Middlesex counties split along Nassau Street. Those on the north side of Nassau traveled eighteen miles to Somerville to the county seat; their Middlesex County friends across the street had to go twenty miles to New Brunswick on courthouse matters.

Despite the ignominious forming from the tail ends of four counties, no section of the state had a more homogeneous past. No area had more reason for being united. Start, for instance, with the colonial heritage. The first settlers had much in common, coming either from Burlington or across state from Long Island. Most of them were Quakers. Most of them were well-off when they arrived or quickly became land-rich through the purchase of large tracts at very low prices.

Mahlon Stacy of Burlington came first, sailing up the river to "the falls of the Delaware" to build one of the state's first mills in 1679 at what is now Trenton. He prospered quickly—evidence that others also had found space nearby, where they could grow corn for Stacy's grinding.

Jonathan, James, and David Stout, of the big and notable Monmouth County Stout clan, all settled in Hopewell Valley soon after a hunting trip there in 1686. Two years later one Andrew Smith bought land nearby and received a deed that called the area Hopewell. Ralph Hunt and Theophilus Phillips of Long Island bought land in 1694 at what became a formal township named Maidenhead in 1697. This is today's Lawrenceville, renamed in 1816 for Captain James Lawrence, a hero of the War of 1812.

More Long Islanders trekked westward in about 1695 to buy large estates in Stony Brook. Chief among them was John Stockton, who settled in 1696 to found the illustrious Stockton family. Five years later he bought five thousand acres of land from William Penn for £900, and in 1724 there were enough new Stocktons and others to make the settlement worth calling Prince Town. Soon

after, Queens Town was started north of Stacy's Mills, but that quickly became Penny Town (Pennington), probably because of its small area.

Colonel William Trent, a wealthy Philadelphia merchant, bought an eight-hundred-acre farm from Mahlon Stacy's estate in 1714, and built a fine brick home in 1719. This house still stands in Trenton. He acquired more land at the falls, and, by donating some of it in 1720, induced the Hunterdon County freeholders to keep county government in town. Grateful villagers agreed in about 1720 to call the settlement Trent's Town, although many of the conservative older inhabitants grumbled that Stacy's Town would have been more appropriate. Trent was named New Jersey's first chief

When this 1875 lithograph was published, the College of New Jersey in Princeton already was impressive. (*Library of Congress*)

justice in 1723. He died of apoplexy on Christmas Day, 1724.

Population still centered in Maidenhead and Hopewell Township, but the gradual widening of the King's Highway between New Brunswick and Trenton shifted development there. James Trent, William's son and heir, opened a ferry in 1726 to capitalize on the traffic to and from Philadelphia. Along the King's Highway, taverns at Kingston, Princeton, and Trenton all knew the turbulence of racing carriages and boisterous activity in the taprooms. More newcomers followed the road— New England Presbyterians, Huguenots, Scots, and others—and stayed to lend variety to the predominantly Quaker population.

The decision by the College of New Jersey's board of trustees to move their young college out of Newark in 1754 had more to do with the area's early growth than roads, mills, taverns, or the trickle of immigrants. The trustees first approached New Brunswick. They bargained: the college would move to the banks of the Raritan if local people would raise £1,000, and donate ten acres of land in town and two hundred acres of woodland within three miles of town.

New Brunswick residents weighed the bargain too long. Progressive Princeton neighbors stepped forward with an offer to meet the college's terms. Immediately the offer was accepted and work started two years later on a college building. Imposing three-story Nassau Hall was ready in 1756. Called "the largest stone building in all the colonies," Old Nassau's 60 rooms had a capacity of 147 students, although the college had only 70 students when it transferred from Newark in 1756.

The college naturally intensified cultural feelings throughout the region. Six miles away in Hopewell, the Reverend Isaac Eaton opened his Baptist Academy the same year that the college came to Princeton. Mr. Eaton's academy could claim that it was the birthplace of Brown University, since the academy's first pupil, James Manning of Piscataway, founded what is now Brown University and became its first president in 1764.

Even more vital to the future of the region and of the nation, the College of New Jersey became the center of intense anti-British feeling, particularly after the fiery Reverend John Witherspoon arrived from Scotland in 1768 to head the Presbyterian college. Students in 1774

William Trent house, build in 1719, is Trenton's oldest home. It was restored in 1934. (*N.J.D.C.E.D.*)

burned tea on the campus after word came of the Boston Tea Party. Witherspoon and Princeton lawyer Richard Stockton gave outspoken support of revolution and their voices found an echo in Hopewell, where John Hart bitterly denounced the British.

Small wonder, then, that Witherspoon, Stockton, and Hart became three of New Jersey's five signers of the Declaration of Independence (Francis Hopkinson of Bordentown and Abraham Clark of Union County were the others). No wonder either that the first state legislature met in Nassau Hall in August 1776, or that New Jersey's first governor, William Livingston, took his inaugural oath in Princeton.

The fires of revolution flickered low early in December 1776, when General Washington's sadly disorganized army limped through Mercer County and disconsolately crossed the Delaware to Pennsylvania. British and Hessian troops swarmed through Princeton, Trenton, Hopewell, and Lawrenceville, showing scorn for the ragged revolutionists and displaying an eagerness to punish the area for its rebellious leadership. Outspoken John Hart fled from his home in Hopewell and hid

N. Currier's 1846 lithograph of Washington at Princeton is noted more for its spirit than its accuracy. (*Library of Congress*)

in the Sourland Mountains. Witherspoon closed the college and left town, along with Stockton and other rebels. (Stockton was captured and imprisoned in the notorious "hulks" in New York Harbor.) The state legislature hastened away to Haddonfield.

But even as the gloom deepened, Washington plotted the boldest stroke of the Revolution. On Christmas Day, 1776, scouts brought word from Trenton that the Hessians had dropped their guard in holiday spirit. The Continental Army moved quietly from Pennsylvania, across the ice-choked river from McKonkey's Ferry, eight miles north of Trenton. Nine hours passed in the ferrying before twenty-four hundred nearly frozen, ill-equipped men gathered about Washington on the New

Jersey side to hear him order the attack on Trenton. Southward they turned, moving through a sleetstorm.

Meanwhile, the Hessians dozed lazily in the Trenton barracks, completely unable to believe the word brought at 8 A.M. that American soldiers had pierced the city's outskirts. Minutes later Washington's army smashed into the rattled defenders, killing or wounding 106 Hessians and capturing 23 officers and 895 enlisted men. Up the river road raced Washington's victorious men, headed back across the menacing Delaware to Pennsylvania. Washington reported to Congress that he suffered only four wounded men, one of them being Lieutenant James Monroe, future fifth President of the United States.

Washington and the colonial troops recrossed the Delaware on December 30, this time walking over on the ice. They dug in on the south side of Assunpink Creek to face the now-furious enemy. Three times on January 2, 1777, the British attacked the bridge over the creek; three times they fell back. As darkness fell, Lord Cornwallis called off his redcoats with the offhand comment that "we'll bag the fox in the morning."

Next morning the fox was gone up the slippery back road toward Princeton, leaving behind about five hundred men, brightly burning campfires, and a few wooden cannons to befuddle the British. The startled Cornwallis heard musketfire far off in the distance near Princeton early on January 3, but before he could move his cumbersome army into action the fox had swept on. Nassau Hall changed hands three times in bloody battling, with the British finally holding the building as Washington withdrew his weary forces and hastened up the Millstone River valley toward winter headquarters at Morristown. Behind in Princeton lay thirty dead or wounded Americans, including General Hugh Mercer, for whom the county is named.

Princeton served as the temporary capital of the infant nation from June 26 to November 4, 1783, when the Continental Congress convened in Nassau Hall. There news was received of the signing of the peace treaty and there Washington received the official thanks of the nation. Nearby, at Rocky Hill, the general waited for the official end of the war.

Strong sentiment in New England and elsewhere favored Trenton as the permanent capital of the United States. Congress convened in Trenton in 1784, and a three-man commission actually met to fix a spot "not more than six miles from Trenton." But Southern states favored a location at Georgetown on the Potomac River, and when Washington expressed mild disapproval of the Trenton location in February 1785, selection of the Potomac site became inevitable. Nevertheless, yellow fever epidemics in Philadelphia three times drove federal departments to Trenton in the 1790s, and in 1799 President John Adams and his wife lived temporarily in the town.

Trenton's reverence for Washington continued, of course, despite his disapproval of the place for a national capital. As he passed through town on April 21, 1789, headed for New York to accept the Presidency, white-robed "virgins fair and matrons grave" (they so described themselves in song) greeted him at Assunpink Creek beneath a flower-festooned arch which proclaimed in gilt letters: THE DEFENDER OF THE MOTHERS WILL BE THE PROTECTOR OF THE DAUGHTERS.

The following year the state legislature permanently fixed the New Jersey capital in Trenton. Work started on the first quaint State House in 1791. Parts of the original building still exist somewhere in the vastly enlarged and much-altered State House of today.

Johnson House in Washington Crossing State Park, once mistakenly known as the McKonkey Ferry House, is said to be where the final phase of the December 26, 1776, assault on Trenton was planned. (*Walter Choroszewski*)

Trenton was little more than a village in 1790, with a town pump, a pillory, and a whipping post on its streets. Its location astride the New York–Philadelphia stage route aided its growth, and completion in 1806 of an eleven-hundred-foot wooden covered bridge over the Delaware sped travelers on the way to and from Philadelphia. Life for the discriminating traveler centered at Princeton's Nassau Hall Inn, where from 1812 to 1836 innkeeper John Joline had more than a hundred horses standing in the immense stables to serve the thirty stages that each day started from the hotel. Inside the old pre-Revolutionary inn, high-living college students downed their grog, carved their initials in the rough furniture, and occasionally brawled in the barroom.

College students became exceedingly troublesome in Princeton from 1800 to 1820. The burning of Nassau Hall in 1802 was believed to be the work of undergraduates. In an effort to bring discipline to the campus, college president Dr. Samuel Stanhope Smith insisted that students should remove their caps and stand silently when within ten rods of the president or within five rods of any faculty member. Students became ever more rebellious, and about 125 of them were expelled in 1807.

Dr. Smith's successor, Reverend Ashbel Green, proved to be an even sterner disciplinarian, and violence flared in January into what has been called "the worst student rebellion in history." Students locked up the entire faculty on January 19, 1817, and set fire to outbuildings, then held Old North Hall for a full day with cutlasses and pistols before the rebellion died. Only twenty-one students were graduated that year and by 1827 enrollment had dropped to seventy-one students.

Development of water power by the Delaware Falls Company, completion of the Delaware & Raritan Canal, and construction of the Camden & Amboy Railroad in the 1830s hastened Trenton's change from a charming colonial village to a busy metropolis. The city on the Falls of the Delaware had four thousand inhabitants and was on the eve of an industrial spurt that blossomed at the time of the Civil War and came into full flower in the 1880s.

Trenton leaders naturally led the call for the new county in 1838. They then welded together the intellect and heritage of Princeton, the burgeoning industry of Trenton, and leaders from the hillsides of Hopewell, the plains of Windsor, and the wide open stretches of Nottingham Township (now Hamilton Township) in Burlington County. The canal cut through the center east and west, railroads brought north and south together. Running north and south through the county was the old East-West Jersey Line, once the boundary between Middlesex and Burlington and between Somerset and Hunterdon.

The canal and the C. & A. Railroad shaped the course of all Mercer. Just as important as the fact that they brought industrial and commercial power was the fact that both carefully kept out of the center of Princeton, thus preserving the college town's exclusive residential character. The canal ran south of Stony Brook and east of the Millstone River, well out of the college view. Until 1840 the railroad ran through the southern part of the county, via Yardville and Hightstown, which meant passengers bound for Trenton had to transfer to stagecoaches at Yardville. Hightstown, long a prosperous agricultural center, tripled in size within a decade after the coming of the Camden & Amboy—then settled back to the quiet life beneath its towering Baptist Church steeple after the main line of what is now the Pennsylvania Railroad switched northward to include Trenton.

Mercer County necessarily played an important role in the Civil War. The presence of the legislature in town heightened the drama of war. Abraham Lincoln paused on February 21, 1861, to speak to a hostile legislature as he headed to his inauguration in Washington. Thereafter Senate and Assembly halls often rang with bitter debate. Soldiers gathered in town for shipment south. Industries hummed, supplying both iron and India rubber to feed the Union war machine.

The College of New Jersey, generally known by then as Princeton College, faced another problem. Princeton long had been favored by Southern plantation owners as the place for educating their sons. The college often was called "the northernmost of the Southern colleges," and in 1860 about one-third of Princeton's three hundred students came from the Confederacy. The war divided the campus, and when the college closed for summer recess in 1861 most students left for war. Princeton lost about eighty men in the war, equally divided between Blue and Gray.

Trenton's Old Barracks, built in 1758 for British troops, served both sides during the Revolution and is now a museum. (*N.J.D.C.E.D.*)

Mercer's character was fixed by 1870. State official-dom kept the capital city in constant turmoil—particularly through forty years of strife when the Camden & Amboy Railroad held unbridled and undisguised sway in the State House and nearby hotels. Trenton's industry formed a sharp contrast with the extensive oat fields in nearby Ewing Township, the broad dairy farms near the Sourland Mountains, and the fertile potato fields surrounding Hightstown.

Princeton's college air continued to exert a profound influence. The educational atmosphere reached out early to surrounding communities and encouraged the start of preparatory schools, such as Lawrenceville Classical and Commercial High School, founded 1810; Pennington Seminary, founded 1839; and Hightstown's Peddie Institute, founded 1860. All still exist, under slightly changed names.

Mercer gained additional higher educational dimension in 1855 when the state legislature voted $10,000 to start the state's first teacher-training school. It was a "normal school," from the French term *école normale*, where teachers were trained to teach in the lower grades. Several towns, including Princeton, Orange, New Brunswick, and Pennington, sought the school but Trenton won by offering free land and $14,000 for buildings. Today the normal school has become Trenton State College, set on a broad campus in Ewing Township.

Post–Civil War days brought Southern sons back to the Princeton campus, and also brought the much-loved Dr. James McCosh, who started a twenty-year term as college president in 1868. He found the college provincial and more than ever dominated by Presbyterian influence. Before he stepped down in 1888 he had

The Woodrow Wilson School of Public and International Affairs at Princeton memorializes the university man who became Governor of New Jersey and President of the United States. (*Princeton University*)

introduced a system of broad elective studies, upsetting the rigid theory of church-oriented education. He doubled the student body and moved Princeton toward campus liberality and the university status it assumed in 1896.

One of the students under Dr. McCosh was young "Tommy" Wilson, Class of 1879, who returned in 1890 as Professor T. Woodrow Wilson and then became university president in 1902. Wilson's campus presidency found him fighting three bitter battles. He won only one—the battle to introduce the preceptor system at Princeton.

He lost in an attempt to rid the campus of its exclusive eating societies, and was defeated in 1910 in his fight to have the graduate school as an integral part of the university rather than a separate campus. His university

losses had much to do with his entry into politics. He was elected governor of New Jersey in 1910 and President of the United States in 1912, but continued to call Princeton home.

While Princeton moved from a small college to a major university, industry boomed in Trenton. A Trenton editor wrote in 1882: "The city has indeed, been fairly transformed in 20 years from a sleepy, old-fashioned town into a live, wideawake, and growing city."

He correctly credited iron, steel, rubber, pottery, and wire rope for the transformation. Trenton potteries, started in the eighteenth century, got into full swing between 1850 and 1870. Dozens of potteries operated in Trenton by 1880, making products ranging from white graniteware to the finest china. From Trenton came, in

1873, the first sanitary porcelain (commodes, sinks, and bathtubs) in the United States. Trenton potters boastfully called their city the "Staffordshire of America," and some even went so far as to call Staffordshire the "Trenton of England."

Trenton-born Walter Scott Lenox, who learned the ceramics industry as an apprentice in his home town, resolved in the late 1880s to perfect a fine American china. His efforts led to the creamy, richly lustrous ware known throughout the world as Lenox china. Stricken blind and paralyzed with his dream about to be realized, Lenox lived until 1920, long enough to know that President Wilson bought seventeen hundred pieces of Lenox china for the White House, the first American china ever used there. The original set was replaced three times with new sets of Lenox china, first by Franklin D. Roosevelt in 1934, then by Harry S. Truman when the White House was redecorated in 1952, and most recently by Ronald Reagan in 1981.

Iron joined clay as a stable Trenton product. Extensive ironworks had started in Trenton in the 1830s, and Peter Cooper and Abram S. Hewitt founded the Trenton Iron Works in 1847. By 1885 the Cooper-Hewitt plant

covered eleven acres of ground and had pioneered America's first use of the "open hearth" system of steel production. Trenton's several iron industries employed a total of three thousand men and produced an annual volume exceeding $5 million in value in the 1880s.

John A. Roebling, founder of the Roebling wire rope company and foremost exponent of the use of wire rope in suspension bridges, transferred his operations to Trenton in 1849. Roebling, who built the suspension bridge over Niagara in the early 1850s, received fatal injuries in July 1869 while inspecting the site of Brooklyn Bridge. The Roebling sons completed Brooklyn Bridge, and put the company on the solid footing that saw it become internationally famed—for the George Washington and Golden Gate bridges, among many spans.

Rubber was the third of Trenton's industrial "big three." Rubber had first been manufactured in the town in 1850, and within thirty years Trenton was one of the country's foremost rubber centers. Charles V. Mead, Frank A. Magowan, and the Cook brothers, George and Edmund, paced the rubber advance until the northeastern part of the city was redolent with the smells of rubber making. It was big business, and became even

Lenox China Company, founded in Trenton in 1888, has relocated its headquarters to nearby Lawrenceville. Manufacturing is at Pomona, in Atlantic County. (*Lenox*)

bigger when the automobile age brought undreamed-of needs for the product.

Industry naturally pushed residential areas outward from the center, out to the western part of Trenton and north to Ewing Township and Pennington. Colonel John Kunkel of New York started to develop pastureland in Pennington in 1894, and William P. Howe, Sr., developed nearby fields after 1910. Pennington's muddy streets offered little inducement to newcomers. In 1908 Mayor William Radcliffe had to ask the council to set aside "one place where ladies can get on and off trolley cars without wearing boots." However, a Board of Trade began to "boost Pennington" in 1911, and when town officials paved the streets the Board of Trade found its promotional task easier.

Princeton's shady streets and handsome estates off the beaten track lured wealthy retired men there at the turn of the century, including ex-President Grover Cleveland. The university campus sprouted new buildings in profusion in the 1920s, all of them in the showy and expensive collegiate Gothic so favored by Ivy League colleges six to seven decades ago. Ten new dormitories were included, thus enabling Princeton to remain residential despite a rise to twenty-five hundred students in 1930. The Hobey Baker hockey rink and Palmer Stadium reflected the increased emphasis on Princeton Tiger athletics, but overbalancing that was the completion of six new classroom or laboratory buildings between 1922 and 1931.

While Trenton took pride in its booming industries and its rising population—up to 119,289 in 1920—Princeton Borough discreetly found satisfaction that it grew scarcely at all. Not much of Mercer County had grown, for that matter. Trenton had an astonishing 75 percent of all county inhabitants in 1920.

The great estates surrounding Princeton began to be split up, particularly after the Depression embarrassed some of the owners financially, or when old family heads died away and their heirs failed to share the sentimental attachment for the Princeton heritage. Not that the university sentiment diminished; indeed, more and more old graduates returned, not just for reunions but to buy property where they might live out their years in what they deemed to be America's heartland.

Others came, too. A $19 million gift in 1930 from Louis Bamberger, Newark department store owner, and his sister, Mrs. Felix Fuld, started the Institute for Advanced Study in Princeton. World-famous scholars have studied and worked there, most notably the great physicist, Albert Einstein, professor in residence at the Institute from 1932 until his death in 1955. Westminster Choir College, founded in Dayton, Ohio, in 1920, moved to Princeton in 1933 and its nationally acclaimed choir added a new cultural dimension.

An intellectual atmosphere kept attracting people with new ideas. George Gallup started his American Institute of Public Opinion in 1935 to test the prevoting opinions of Americans in his Gallup Poll. The Educational Testing Service, deviser of the College Board Examination, the familiar SAT, and numerous other tests, chose Princeton in 1948.

Research pervades the Princeton area today, on campus and on the edges. RCA finished a giant research plant in 1942 and many varied research firms have moved in close by. Princeton University established the James Forrestal Research Center along Route 1 in 1951, occupying 850 acres and 15 buildings formerly owned by the Rockefeller Institute for Medical Research. Researchers on the streets of Princeton are nearly as common as undergraduates.

All of Mercer County is changing, albeit slowly. The pace differs in various municipalities, but county population has jumped from 266,392 in 1960 to 325,824 in 1990. Even Princeton Borough and Princeton Township (which surrounds the Borough like a huge doughnut) are gaining new people. Between 1950 and 1960 the population of Princeton Township doubled, and in the peak year of 1956, one thousand buildings of various types were erected. Growth has leveled off; the Borough and Township now share about 26,000 people equally with a slight edge to the Borough.

The big population thrust is southeast of Trenton in adjacent Hamilton Township, the once-rural Nottingham Township. Hamilton's 1950 population of 41,156 had doubled by 1990, and now the township is New Jersey's ninth largest municipality in population. That status as the ninth "city" is hard for visitors to accept; Hamilton's 82,000-plus people are spread through forty square miles without any genuine town center.

Hamilton Township's gain is Trenton's loss, for people are fleeing the capital city, out to Hamilton and Ewing

Ranging north along the Delaware River, this complex of new buildings surrounds the much-rebuilt
State Capitol in Trenton. (*N.J.D.C.E.D.*)

townships especially and more slowly into all surrounding communities or across the Delaware River into Pennsylvania. Trenton suffers from all of the modern city woes, perhaps the saddest commentary on a state government so dominated by farmland votes and suburban pressures that it scarcely addresses the plight of cities.

Trenton's governmental facade at least has gone through a pleasant renewal. Starting in 1960, a continuing program added several gleaming white and severely "modern" new structures for various branches of New Jersey government. The complex enhances the riverbank and offers hope that the capital city also may be on

its way to transformation in the areas of housing and business.

State House activity always has been vital in Mercer, yet it has always seemed superimposed rather than an integral part of the county. That is because the state legislature meets on a part-time basis. Rapid transportation facilities in and out of the city speed legislators homeward after each session. Trenton, accordingly, has not become the social or even the total political center of the state in the manner of most state capitals.

Once governors joined the quick return to their own counties. That changed in 1951, when former Governor and Mrs. Walter E. Edge donated their storied Princeton home to New Jersey for use as a governor's mansion. That home was Morven, a lovely Georgian house built by Richard Stockton sometime in the late 1750s and occupied continuously by a series of distinguished Stocktons until the late 1920s. As the governor's mansion from 1954 to 1982, Morven became a logical social center, bringing together groups interested in business, industry, history, music, art, education, and politics.

The New Jersey Historical Society refurbished another, larger, Princeton mansion called "Drumthwacket" (said to be Celtic for "wooded hill") as the home of future governors. Morven, also refurbished, would become the society's new headquarters. Unfortunately, Governor and Mrs. Thomas Kean decided not to live in Drumthwacket and the Historical Society relinquished its hopes for Morven. Governor and Mrs. James

J. Florio moved into Drumthwacket in 1990, becoming the first to occupy the chief executive's mansion.

Morven and Drumthwacket typify both Princeton and Mercer County. In Princeton, they are just two of the scores of splendid houses of varying ages and periods of architecture; few American towns surpass this college town in appearance or aesthetic appeal. But Morven and Drumthwacket also typify Mercer County, where a long heritage and the surge to the twenty-first century are intermingled.

The blight and pollution that accompanies too much of the urban landscape between New York and Philadelphia has touched Mercer chiefly in the state capital. Today the fields surrounding old Hightstown are rich and green and the wooded slopes near Hopewell are bright and unsullied. Mercer County belies the tiresome cliché that New Jersey is just a part of a megalopolis: ac-

Morven, built by Richard Stockton shortly before the Revolution, was the New Jersey governor's residence from 1957 to 1982.

The Hall of Science in the New Jersey State Museum is a favorite with the thousands of schoolchildren who visit Trenton every year. (*State Museum*)

cording to the 1990 census, only about 3,311 people live in Washington Township's twenty square miles; only 6,431 in West Windsor's twenty-seven square miles. Even 82,801 people spread over Hamilton Township's forty miles do not give the impression of crowding.

Mercer County is New Jersey's focal point. People from High Point to Cape May look to Trenton for government. Schoolchildren from all points of the state come each year to visit Washington's Crossing and the Johnson House; the Old Barracks in Trenton, where Hessians slept on Christmas night in 1776; the State Library and State Museum, both finally housed in modern surroundings; and the State Capitol, where sometimes the governor comes out to say hello and to shake hands.

No New Jersey county has a more notable colonial heritage and it is unlikely that any comparable region in the nation played a more vital and active part in keeping alive the hopes of independence. Mercer's educational assets are well known, and not alone because of Princeton University. Rider College, relocated in 1964 on a new campus in Lawrenceville after a century in downtown Trenton, has grown rapidly. Trenton State College is regarded as one of the top state colleges in the nation. Mercer County College has also relocated from downtown Trenton to a suburban site.

Most of Mercer's personality existed long before the county was created—then re-created—in 1838. The proof of Mercer's right to county status has been found in the easy way that the parts of four other counties have fitted together ever since. They are compatible. They are one. To repeat: the wonder is not that Mercer became a county, but rather that it took so long to bring together the needed components.

Built in 1931, Camden County's courthouse is New Jersey's tallest and most costly county seat of government; the edifice at Federal and Market streets, Camden, cost $10 million. The county's original courthouse, built in 1853, housed both the city and county offices, but a second courthouse, erected in 1906, separated county and city functions. The two governments were reunited in the 22-story, 310-foot-high structure.

CAMDEN

OUT OF THE SHADOW

Camden County's Quaker beginnings were subdued enough, yet highlights twinkled—in the bold romance of remarkable eighteen-year-old Elizabeth Haddon and in the Celtic enterprise of Mark Newbie's "Patrick's Pence." Eventually Philadelphians crossed the Delaware River to frolic and gamble in the county, but, just as highlights had brightened the earlier Quaker somberness, the less volatile residents in the region insisted firmly that their towns must not be painted permanently red by such interlopers. Walt Whitman came to give poetic contrast after the Civil War; at the same time industrial giants added vigor.

Always, however, history shaped the Camden story within the deep shadow cast from across the river by Philadelphia.

So all-pervading was the Philadelphia influence, in fact, that Camden town was known merely as Cooper's Ferry for its first century. Right from the time that William Roydon was granted a license in 1688 to run a "very needful and much wanted" ferry across to Philadelphia, the ferries seemed to run "to" Philadelphia rather than "between" towns. Roydon had taken up land on the New Jersey side in 1681, a year before William Penn founded Philadelphia.

William Cooper also settled in what is now Camden in 1681. A Burlington Quaker, he came upriver and built a home on land he called Pyne Poynt. Soon after Roydon established the ferries, Cooper bought them and built up the cross-river trade, although few others had chosen to settle on the New Jersey side of the river. Exceptions were the Irish Quakers, who ventured inland on Newton Creek in 1682, to found towns now known as Collingswood, Woodlynne, and South Camden.

One of these was fiscal-minded Mark Newbie, who before sailing from Ireland had filled his sea chests with quantities of halfpence struck in Dublin forty years earlier to commemorate a religious war. The coins, known as Patrick's Pence because of a likeness of St. Patrick on one side, were not legal tender in Ireland, but in America they were a valuable currency. Soon after his arrival Newbie secured a bank charter from the New Jersey Assembly and issued the coins, making him this country's first banker.

Other colonists settled Gloucester Point at the mouth of Big Timber Creek, close to where a Dutch colony had mysteriously vanished in the 1620s. The disappearance of sixteen Dutchmen set ashore by Captain Cornelius Jacobsen Mey in 1623 rivals the story of Roanoke's Lost Colony. Mey built Fort Nassau for the tiny settlement before he left behind "four couples married at sea on their voyage from Holland, together with eight seamen." When another Dutch ship sailed to the spot in 1631, nothing remained, not even a clue to the cause of Fort Nassau's demise. Undaunted, the Dutch left another thirty-four colonists, but that group was withdrawn after about twenty years.

Determination marked all early Quakers, but gracious, courageous Elizabeth Haddon was the most determined of all. Elizabeth, a mere eighteen years old, came alone to America in 1701 to develop the five-hundred-acre plantation purchased in 1698 by her London Quaker father, John Haddon. She rode on horseback through the woods to the Haddon acreage on Cooper's Creek and started housekeeping in a hut in a forest clearing. Her zeal was not alone indomitable pioneer spirit; her heart belonged in America, to the young Quaker missionary John Estaugh, who had emigrated to this country a few months before.

Eventually John arrived in New Jersey from a Virginia preaching tour and Elizabeth met him. John showed great reluctance in coming to the point of proposing marriage, so Elizabeth (in words written by Longfellow in *Tales of a Wayside Inn*) finally whispered to the missionary on the way to Quaker meeting: "I have received from the Lord a charge to love thee, John Estaugh!"

John spoke for himself soon after, of course, and they were married in her wilderness home in 1702. Three times the Estaughs traveled back to London, yet always they returned to New Jersey. John died on a preaching trip in the West Indies in 1742; Elizabeth lived on to the age of eighty, pleased that her town had become known as Haddonfield.

Romance also brought twenty-one-year-old Betsy Griscom across the Delaware River. Betsy, demure and proper in a Quaker bonnet, slipped over to Gloucester Point in 1773. In famous old Hugg's Tavern she stood side by side with John Ross, a serious harness maker's apprentice, and heard a justice of the peace marry her "out of meeting"—and to the son of an Episcopal rector at that!

The marriage was kept secret for a year, but in 1774 the Quakers heard of the union and read the young wife out of the faith. Three years later, tradition declares, Betsy Griscom Ross sewed thirteen stars on America's first flag.

All West Jersey roads led to Cooper's Ferry long before the Revolution. Farmers brought their garden harvests to sell in the "Jersey Market" in Philadelphia. On the ferries they joined the oystermen and the charcoal makers, also on the way to sell in the City of Brotherly Love. The ferries ran both ways; by 1700 Philadelphians had begun to ride westward to enjoy a day in the wilds surrounding Cooper's Ferry.

One of William Cooper's sons, Jacob, had migrated to Philadelphia to seek his fortune as a merchant. He watched the Pennsylvania town grow, keenly aware that the crowded streets and high real estate prices forced businessmen to live ever farther from their stores and offices. Why not, he mused, work in Philadelphia and live in New Jersey, a pleasant ferry ride away?

Cooper widely advertised part of the family holdings in 1769, emphasizing the "dry and wholesome" air, the soil "fitted for gardening," and "the conveniency of being near the city of Philadelphia for distilleries, breweries, lumberyards, stores, and other offices." He had no takers in 1769 and none in 1771 when he again pushed the advantages of his real estate. Discouraged by the prospect of selling in bulk, Jacob cut 40 acres up into 167 lots. He named the town plot Camden, in honor of the powerful English champion of American liberty, Charles Pratt, Earl of Camden. Cooper visualized six streets running north and south, intersected by Cooper and Market Streets, but no one paid much attention. Cooper's Ferry remained the town name.

Present-day Camden County was then a part of Gloucester County with county courts at Gloucester Point. The Revolution found the area surrounding Cooper's Ferry playing a legislative rather than an aggressive role. There were a few minor skirmishes, because Cooper's Ferry and Haddonfield were important outposts of Philadelphia. British soldiers streamed across on the ferries in June 1778 as the enemy broke camp in Philadelphia and headed east for the Battle of Monmouth. During the war, Mad Anthony Wayne, Count Pulaski, and Lafayette strode the streets of Haddonfield with their troops.

However, Haddonfield will be best remembered as the meeting place early in 1777 of the New Jersey legislature, driven out of Trenton by the Hessians. Meeting in Hugh Creighton's tavern (built in 1750 and now called the Indian King), the legislature approved the powerful Council on Safety, endorsed bills involved in the design and preparation of the Great Seal of the State of New Jersey, and enacted a bill substituting "state" for the word "colony" in certain official documents.

Cooper's Ferry had distinguished visitors on May 20, 1777, when the trustees of the College of New Jersey were driven out of Princeton by the British. Governor William Livingston and a dozen other college trustees convened on the Delaware banks to award degrees to twenty-seven members of the graduating class.

Philadelphia really discovered its little New Jersey neighbor after the war. Excellent ferry service lured thousands across the river, among them winsome Miss Dorothea (Dolley) Payne, who frequently visited her uncle Hugh Creighton, proprietor of the Indian King Tavern in Haddonfield. A Quaker with charm, beauty, and vivacity, Dolley married John Todd in 1790, and became a twenty-four-year-old widow in 1793 when Philadelphia's yellow fever plague took her husband. The next year she met and married James Madison and went on to renown in the White House as Dolley Madison, wife of the President.

Many wealthy Philadelphians headed for Gloucester Point, particularly the aristocratic Fox Hunting Club, which gathered there from 1766 to 1818 to chase foxes through Jersey meadows. Later the well-remembered Fish House Club met in a riverfront cottage at Delair, north of Camden. For many years, too, farmers from all over the state gathered at Gloucester Point for a tremendous picnic and a day-long fishing expedition. They were not aristocrats, but they had just as much fun.

Cooper's Ferry and Gloucester Point both suffered diminished importance when the Gloucester County seat was moved to Woodbury following a fire that destroyed the Gloucester Point courthouse in 1786. Out in the eastern regions of present Camden County, several important stage stops became popular: Blue Anchor, where the 1740 inn was a favorite stopping place; Winslow, with its noted Sailor Boy Tavern; Mountain Ephraim, where Ephraim Albertson kept a top-notch place on the King's Highway; Chew's Landing, where travelers stopped in the two-and-a-half-story pre-Revolutionary War hotel and heard tales of John Chew, war hero;

Haddonfield's Indian King Tavern, now state-owned, welcomed the New Jersey Legislature during the Revolution. (*Earl Horter drawing, The State Library*)

Blackwood, where Uriah Norcross centered his big stagecoach business; and Stratford, where a white horse pictured on a swinging sign gave the road to Absecon its familiar name of White Horse Pike.

Most noted, however, was Long-a-Coming, fifteen miles from the Delaware and astride the pike from Camden to Mays Landing and Somers Point. Good-natured disagreements among natives arose concerning the origin of the name. Some attributed it to a group of sailors who struggled through the forests on their way from the Jersey Shore to Philadelphia. Hungry and thirsty, they found a spring in the forest. One drank deeply, then turned and exclaimed, "Wonderful, but sure long-a-coming!" More prosaically, others insisted the town name described the slowness of the stagecoaches.

The spring story has good possibilities because Long-a-Coming (now Berlin) is near a low ridge known to geologists as "The Divide." Here four of South Jersey's most important streams rise. Water from springs on the eastern slopes flows eastward to the Atlantic Ocean in the Mullica and Great Egg Harbor rivers. Other springs feed streams that flow westward to the Delaware River in the Pennsauken and Big Timber creeks. All four streams are parts of Camden County's borders.

Two buildings dominated the skyline of Camden as the 1990s began—Campbell Soup, with can on its company headquarters, and the multistory courthouse in the background. (*Walter Choroszewski*)

Transferring the courts to Woodbury inevitably made the ferry owners and real estate hopefuls of Cooper's Ferry restless. An attempt to shift the county government back to Gloucester Point failed in 1820. If the courts had returned, there is strong likelihood that Camden County might never have separated from Old Gloucester County. Woodbury's gain in 1820 would be Gloucester County's loss.

Cooper's Ferry took the first stride to independence in 1828 when town leaders cut themselves off from Newton Township and officially adopted the name Camden, which Jacob Cooper had given his real estate dream in 1773. It wasn't much of a town—only 1,143 inhabitants—but its proximity to Philadelphia gave the promoters hope, even though one "segar-box" was enough to hold all the mail that newly created Camden received in a day.

Engagingly enough, the noisy Philadelphia sporting set was partially responsible for the incorporation of the town. First those pleasure-seekers from William Penn's Quaker city flocked over to use floating bathhouses anchored near Camden's Windmill Island. Bathers undressed in unscreened accommodations, much to the consternation of modest passengers aboard the ferryboats. Then the gay crowd frolicked in John Johnson's Vauxhall Gardens (where John's rum toddies were often too strong for weak heads), Gottlieb Zimmerman's Columbia Gardens, and various other wide-open "gardens" surrounding Camden. All-night reveling made the sterner folk resolve to set up their own government—and their own police department. Scornful Philadelphians called the new town "Pluck-'em-in," claiming that Camden's purveyors of amusement bled the unwary visitors.

Camden seemed to have more bustle and prosperity than it actually enjoyed. Except for the amusement centers and the legitimate taverns where stagecoaches deposited or picked up ferry passengers, there was little commerce. The town was noted primarily for its several sausage makers, who trundled wheelbarrows loaded with links onto Philadelphia-bound ferries. Camden had more future than present in 1828, but it wanted law and order, and by 1835 had rid itself of the notorious floating bathhouses.

Sterner laws failed to squelch the Philadelphia sporting set; they simply went to more understanding places on the edge of town. The Philadelphia and Camden Race Course, built in 1835 on the White Horse Pike near Haddon Heights, welcomed those who claimed interest in "improving the breed." Spring and fall meets drew the best horses in the land—and some of the worst people. Betting on the horses cleaned out many a once-steady neighborhood farmer, and what the horses didn't take the crowds of confidence men did. It was said that "ladies were never scarce and entered into the sport and the betting with as much zeal as their escorts."

Drunkenness, gambling, and debauchery hastened the track's demise. Despite the usual pleas of the promoters that they existed only to make horses better, opposition persisted. Finally, after a great crowd gathered in 1845 to watch Fashion ("The Queen of the Turf") defeat Peytona in a nationally heralded match, the track closed in 1847—much to the improvement of humans.

Agitation of a more important nature swept through the area at the same time. Secession talk stirred Camden when the coming of the Camden & Amboy Railroad to town in January 1834 ensured growth for the river town. Meetings in February 1837 called for a new county to be called Delaware, but the time was not yet ripe. Many opposed a break from Gloucester County as "altogether useless and unnecessary," but on March 13, 1844, Camden County was created by the state legislature.

Formation of the new county enraged residents in the eastern section. They determined that they would frustrate Camden town's ferry barons and emerging politicians by putting the county seat anywhere but in the river town. On the third election to name a county seat, Long-a-Coming held a clear majority, and the Board of Freeholders awarded a contract for county buildings. Camden's Democratic leaders forced through a fourth vote in 1848 and this time swung enough votes to choose Camden. Bitter charges of voting irregularities followed, and it was not until 1854 that legal battles ended in a Supreme Court order to the freeholders that they must build in Camden. Long-a-Coming lapsed back into an obscurity that lasted until 1872, when the name was changed to Berlin. Many disgruntled old-timers showed their displeasure by refusing any letters addressed to them at Berlin.

Camden grew even during the court battles. New homes were built on streets sliced through cornfields; hundreds of wagons loaded with South Jersey produce, South Jersey bog iron, and Philadelphia-bound shoppers rumbled through town headed for the bustling steam ferries. Camden's principal business continued to be ferrying, with big boats constantly shuttling back and forth, carrying produce to Philadelphia or bringing passengers back to the railroad terminals. There was increased hope that Philadelphia families might see the advantages of living in rural Camden County, now that transportation was so good.

Suddenly, on the night of March 15, 1856, that hope died. More than a hundred persons were crowded aboard the ferry *New Jersey* that night when the boat eased out into the ice-clogged Delaware River and headed slowly for Camden. If the passengers knew that the boat had neither life preservers nor fire-fighting equipment, they paid no heed. Fire broke out near the smokestack when the laboring ferry reached midstream. Billowing smoke drove the pilot and engineer from the bridge, leaving the flaming ferry to drift helplessly in the river. Ice hampered rescuers, and the next morning Camden counted more than sixty dead aboard the *New Jersey* or in the freezing water. Philadelphians temporarily lost their enthusiasm for visiting, much less living in, Camden County.

The Civil War years found the county well established. The Camden & Atlantic Railroad was founded in 1852 to cut through to Absecon Island (now Atlantic City) from Camden by way of Haddonfield, Ashland, Kirkwood, Berlin, and Atco. The new route encouraged glass manufacturers to start or expand businesses in Atco, Waterford, and Clementon. Near Winslow, J. L. Mason made his famous fruit jar from 1856 to 1862. Real estate men laid out paper cities along the tracks in efforts to lure city people into the salubrious country, only to have the war check their promotions.

A "railroad" of a far different nature focused a secretive attention on Camden before the Civil War: the

Benjamin Franklin Bridge, built in 1926, looms over the cupola of the Thomas H. Kean State Aquarium, one of New Jersey's newest and finest attractions. (*Walter Choroszewski*)

Underground Railroad used to help Southern slaves escape across the state to freedom. Camden was an important Underground point because of the ferries, and tradition says that escaping slaves sometimes hid in the cellar of Haddonfield's Indian King Tavern. Some freed slaves eventually found their way to Snow Hill (now Lawnside), a town set up by abolitionists in 1840. Most of the fugitives headed for New England or Canada as quickly as possible.

The middle of the nineteenth century marked Camden's beginnings as a notable manufacturing city. Richard Esterbrook came from England in 1858 to establish in town the Esterbrook steel pen factory, the first of its kind in the United States and forerunner of a Camden business that produced 200 million steel pens annually by the year 1900. Nearby, Joseph Campbell and Abram A. Anderson started to pack fancy peas and tomatoes in 1869. The name "Campbell" became nationally known, but it remained for John T. Dorrance, who joined the company in 1897, to introduce the line of condensed soups for which Campbell's is today universally recognized. Campbell's condensed soup, offered at "10-1/2 ounces for a dime" created a sensation, and it made a multimillionaire out of Dorrance. When he died in 1930, he left an estate of $130 million.

Other businesses and industries came to the river town before 1880: lumberyards, tanneries, worsted mills, hatmakers, ironworks, machine works, chemical and dye plants, silver-platers, and porcelain teeth makers. Joseph Wharton, pioneer in the manufacture of refined nickel, established the nation's first nickel works at Camden in 1862. This was America's only producer of nickel in all the nineteenth century.

As Philadelphia prepared to celebrate the centennial of the Revolution in 1876, Camden newspapers carried complaints that cattle ran at large in the Second Ward, that the absence of horse-drawn streetcars on Sundays ruined business, and that streetlights were doused on nights "when the moon was supposed to shine," whether nature cooperated or not.

Across Newton Creek to the south, Gloucester town experienced an economic resurgence in 1844 when David S. Bowen, Philadelphia dry goods merchant, started textile manufacturing in the big four-story Washington Mills. Population of Gloucester town jumped from 200 in 1840 to 5,347 in 1880. The town enjoyed that prosperity, but the views of the populace were split on William J. (Billy) Thompson, shad fisherman, hotel owner, politician, and sporting man, who arrived in 1869 to revive flamboyant times that had seemed to die in the 1850s.

Billy made his start in shad fishing, then opened a hotel specializing in shad toasted on a white oak plank. Spirited advertising lured people from all over the world to eat Gloucester planked shad and to enjoy Billy's genial acceptance of the unofficial title of "Duke of Gloucester." Attempting to make certain that transportation was convenient for his customers, Thompson tried to buy the ferryboats but the owners refused. To add insult to injury they stopped running boats after midnight.

Thompson retaliated by importing the steamboats *Sylvan Dell* and *Sylvan Glen* and running them twenty-four hours a day. He built a racetrack in 1890 and became enmeshed in a statewide controversy that led to strong antiracing movements in the 1890s. Racing was outlawed in New Jersey; the downfall of the "Duke" was swift. First Billy's power vanished, then his wealth, and he died in Ireland in wretched poverty.

The hustle and bustle of Camden after the Civil War suited Walt Whitman, the "Good Gray Poet," who came to live with his brother George in Camden in 1873, soon after he had suffered a paralytic stroke. Then fifty-five years old, he already was one of America's best, and most controversial, poets.

Whitman's Camden period was the happiest of his life. He lived to see a transformation of public opinion regarding his writings, from scorn to praise, and his days were productive and pleasant. He revised *Leaves of Grass* for five new editions between 1876 and 1892, and prepared *Specimen Days and Collect* in 1882–83 for publication. When brother George moved to Burlington, the poet chose to stay near congenial acquaintances in Camden. He bought a house at 330 Mickle Street, Camden, in 1884 and enjoyed new-found friends. Facing death in 1892, he described himself as "a little spark of soul dragging a great lummox of a corpse-body to and fro." Friends buried him in a simple rough-cut vault in Harleigh Cemetery. The vault bore an inscription that Whitman wrote himself: "For that of me which is to die."

Whitman died as Camden began to emerge as a great city, described by an 1890 writer as "crystallizing the life of Southern New Jersey and offering a thousand streams of influence and succor to its giant companion on the west side of the Delaware."

Chance brought Camden one of South Jersey's greatest boons in 1894 when a customer stepped into Eldridge R. Johnson's repair shop with one of the crude Edison talking machines of the time. Johnson studied it and recognized its potentialities, although he noted it sounded "like a partially educated parrot with a sore throat." He substituted a flat disk for the round cylinders perfected by Thomas Edison and began manufacturing his own machines. Johnson incorporated Victor Talking Machine Company in 1901, the year that the little fox terrier listening to "His Master's Voice" was created as a trademark. Victor became the largest producer of phonograph records in the world long before Johnson sold out in January 1927 for a reputed $28 million and 240,000 shares of RCA stock.

Camden's "big three"—soup, pens, and talking machines—became the "big four" in 1899. That year the New York Shipbuilding Company, originally planned for Staten Island, started to build its ways on 160 acres of wasteland on the south side of Camden. Shipbuilding started on November 27, 1900. Ships for both world wars slid down the New York ways—including the *Idaho* and the *Saratoga*. The great trans-atlantic liners *Manhattan* and *Washington* were among peacetime vessels built in the plant. During World War II, the yard built $217 million worth of new navy ships between March 1942 and March 1943, a mark never exceeded.

Industrial growth naturally led to the emergence of a large local working class, one of whom was Peter J. McGuire. Fittingly enough he started his earnest quest for an eight-hour day in the 1870s in the city that bore the impress of Walt Whitman's outspoken democracy. McGuire helped Samuel Gompers found the American

The Camden house where Walt Whitman lived and worked in the last years of his life.

Federation of Labor in 1881, and McGuire's insistence on a holiday for labor led Congress to establish Labor Day in 1894. "The Father of Labor Day" is buried near Pennsauken.

Proud city fathers called Camden "The Biggest Little City in the World" in 1915 promotions. If only, they said wistfully, there were a bridge to Philadelphia. Camden County already was the fourth largest New Jersey county in population, but the boosters wanted more.

Actually, Camden leaders had been dreaming of that bridge as far back as 1816, but not until July 5, 1926, did the dream become actuality. That day President Calvin Coolidge dedicated the 8,536-foot Delaware River Bridge linking the Delaware River cities. Four years in the making, the $40 million span was the longest sus-

Launching of the *Savannah* at the New York Shipbuilding Company in July 1959 in the ebbing days of the company's glory. (*N.J.B.*)

pension bridge in the world at the time of its dedication. This bridge, built to carry both automobiles and trolley cars, became the Benjamin Franklin Bridge.

The bridging of the Delaware might well have cast Camden even more sharply into Philadelphia's shadow, yet strangely the bridge seemed to set Camden free and give it a new-found equality. That was partially because

Philadelphia commuters began to come across the bridge to find homesites in Camden County. Industry attained new prosperity. County population increased sharply, to three times in 1950 what it had been in 1900.

Camden city especially prospered, until by 1950 it was the state's fifth city in population. Its industry was strong, diversified, and stable, and achieved worldwide recognition when the nuclear-powered steamship *Savannah* was launched at New York Shipbuilding Company yards in the mid-1950s.

The year 1950 marked a peak for Camden. With a population of 125,000 people, filled with industries and research facilities, alive with intense railroad activities, boasting a fine hotel and proud of its neighborhoods, the aging city by the ferries could shrug off the shadow of the city across the river. The strengths masked the beginnings of a decline that would in thirty years leave Camden but a shell of its former self.

During the 1950s, Camden still took special pleasure each summer when hundreds of tomato-laden trucks, some piled perilously high with the luscious red fruit, rolled into town daily, around the clock, to bring tomatoes to Campbell's. Soon, too soon for thousands of farmers, the firm discontinued processing tomatoes in its Camden plant.

Elsewhere in the county, amazing transformations took place. Aided by the liberal mortgage support afforded veterans of World War II and the building or widening of major highways during the 1950s and 1960s, young families began to move outward to "the country." The most startling case in point was Cherry Hill Township, east of Camden and now so intertwined with it that anyone driving into or out of the city is hard-pressed to know where Camden ends and Cherry Hill begins.

No one could have found Cherry Hill in 1950. It didn't exist. The area kept its old name, Delaware Township, adopted in 1844 (the year Camden became a county). Fewer than six thousand people lived there in 1940 when extremely scarce materials were allotted to build the Garden State Race Track for the edification of war-weary horse-racing fans, most of them well-paid workers in area factories turning out products for the armed services.

A dozen years later, township expansion lagged until the Cherry Hill Inn, then one of the nation's most elaborate hostelries, opened its doors in 1954. At about the same time, the Cherry Hill Mall won acclaim as one of the nation's first enclosed malls. Then, in rapid order, industries and research plants moved in to share the sur-rounding cornfields with apartment buildings, housing developments, and roadside businesses.

In one amazing four-year spurt from 1959 to 1963, township ratables soared from $2.5 million to more than $40 million. Midway in that spurt, voters changed Delaware Township's name to Cherry Hill Township in 1961. Population zoomed to 31,522 in 1960 and 64,195 in 1970 before leveling off to a shade under 70,000 in 1990.

Elsewhere on the periphery of Camden city, places such as Pennsauken and Gloucester townships and Bellmawr Borough experienced steady growth, although Pennsauken had been a solid town of 22,000 people before the expansion began. The gain of other municipalities was Camden's loss. The once-proud city lost its shipyard, its railroad strength, its tomato-canning preeminence, many of its industries, and a huge chunk of its people. Population plummeted from 124,555 in 1950 to 102,551 in 1970, then down to 87,492 in 1990.

Camden struggles to escape both image and reality. As one shining constant, Campbell's retains its national headquarters in the city where the founder began putting tomatoes in cans in 1869. The opening of the new Thomas H. Kean State Aquarium and the building of a riverfront walk in the city have added amenities. The seaport continues to operate. And on Mickle Street, Walt Whitman's tiny, well-preserved home remains to keep his bright flame aglow.

Camden County's old role as the place to enter and leave New Jersey from or to Philadelphia was heightened with the opening of the Walt Whitman Bridge from Gloucester City to downtown Philadelphia in the early 1960s. In summertime, endless lines of vehicles zip through the county on the Atlantic City Expressway, sliced through the southern end of the county. North and south traffic increased on the New Jersey Turnpike, with two exits in Camden County. Route 130 has been widened and Interstate 295 rolls northward parallel to the Turnpike.

Camden County transportation is not just a matter of gasoline-powered vehicles. In 1969 the Port Authority Transit Corporation opened the nation's newest and finest train system, a twenty-two-mile run from Lindenwold to downtown Philadelphia. The system, known familiarly as the "Lindenwold High Speed Line" (but more properly as PATCO), is fully automated, from dispensing tickets to stopping and starting trains at the twelve stations. Nine of these are in the county (Lindenwold, Ashland, Woodcrest, Haddonfield, Westmont, Collingswood, Ferry Avenue, and Broadway and City Hall, both in Camden city). About forty thousand Camden County commuters use the system daily.

People stream steadily outward from Camden and the bridges, almost like lava flowing from a center volcano. This intermingled traffic and population is all that most visitors to Camden County ever see. But casual glances north from the Atlantic City Expressway show great patches of open space in the eastern edge of the county where the farmlands blend with the Pine Barrens. From the Turnpike. motorists can catch glimpses of the green county where horse farms abound.

The old stagecoach stops have disappeared, but the east-west highways bear the old names of former inns: the Black Horse Pike and the White Horse Pike. Near the site of old Long-a-Coming, not far from Route 30, is Pine Valley, the golf course whose sandy fairways and tricky greens have resisted the par-breaking efforts of the world's best golfers. Linksmen agree that this scenic

Rutger's South Jersey campus in Camden is a significant factor in the intellectual and economic life of southern New Jersey as well as a place of quiet in a stricken city. (*Rutgers*)

Settled in 1685, Barclay Farmstead, a typical South Jersey Quaker farm, was donated to Cherry Hill Township in 1974. The brick farmhouse was built in the 1820s. (*Walter Choroszewski*)

course is the most difficult test of golfing skill in the world.

Much of Camden city's past has been covered by its industrial growth, although many narrow streets still attest to its beginnings as a colonial ferry terminal. The county's heritage is rich mainly in Haddonfield, where some of the charm and simplicity of Elizabeth Haddon can still be felt, and where the winsomeness of Dolley Madison seems part of a visit to the state-owned Indian King Tavern. Traces of Camden's Quaker beginnings can be glimpsed occasionally—in typical brick buildings, in meetinghouses, or in the old cemeteries that survive in the midst of frenzied growth elsewhere.

The portrait of Camden is ever being modified. There are those who despair that the Quaker background has been nearly obliterated by highways and industry and railroads. But that's the way of any old canvas: it gives back only those attitudes and opinions that its viewers bring to the judging. All in all, Camden County's portrait is pleasing.

THE GARDEN SPOT

New Jersey is called "The Garden State," usually confounding visitors who know only the concrete strip between New York and Philadelphia. By Garden State, we now mainly mean four South Jersey counties that begin on the lower Delaware River and spread eastward until they blend into the vast Pine Barrens.

They are Cumberland, Salem, Gloucester, and Burlington counties, where the sandy loam grows vegetables at the mere dropping of a seed. Most New Jersey vegetable farms and fruit orchards are in these four counties, and while the Garden Spot spills over into parts of other counties, its principal domain is the lower Delaware River banks.

This is the Garden Spot . . .

Where Burlington County farmers speed their dew-fresh products from field to market; where Salem tomatoes add zest to flavorful summertime meals; where Gloucester County has ever been noted as "The Philadelphia Garden Patch"; and where Cumberland County's vegetable fields reach to the horizon.

This is the Garden Spot . . .

Where early Swedes and Finns and Quakers turned to the soil and found their reward; where intensive use of greensand marl saved the fields a century and a half ago, and where the growing of vegetables has always been THE way of life.

This is the Garden Spot, where a large proportion of all New Jersey vegetables are grown; where well over half of all Jersey tomatoes are picked; where nearly all of the state's asparagus is raised. This is a land where glass manufacturing got its start and where new industries are moving into the lower Delaware River region. This is where today's gardens and tomorrow's industrial progress meet.

But, for now, it is still the Garden Spot . . .

Cumberland County was able to finish its sturdy stone courthouse in Bridgeton in 1909 without the bitter acrimony that long had marked the construction of Cumberland courthouses. Three previous courthouses, all within a stone's throw of the present building, had been possible only after hotly contested votes. By 1909, however, Cumberland peacefully built its handsome courthouse topped by a tower and town clock. (*Walter Choroszewski*)

CUMBERLAND

TIDEWATER LAND

Those who know Cumberland County best insist that it is "tidewater country," closer in topography and pace to Maryland and Delaware than to the rest of New Jersey. Atlantic Ocean tides sweep up and down adjacent Delaware Bay, alternately soaking and draining the extensive bayside marshes. Two of Cumberland's three most vital towns, Bridgeton and Millville, are at the head of navigable creeks, yet both are deep in the county interior. Those creeks have been the keys to unlocking Cumberland's riches and to preserving its "tidewater" character.

Seen from the air, the Maurice and Cohansey rivers both appear as wide, dark green ribbons carelessly tossed on a light green carpet. Both streams have carved devious paths through the low-lying marshes. By water, Delaware Bay is about twenty miles from Bridgeton, about thirty miles from Millville. Overland, in a straight line, Bridgeton is only about ten miles from the bay, Millville about fifteen—except that there is no such thing as "overland" in those bogs.

Streams were the only approaches for early explorers who ventured in off the Atlantic Ocean. The broad mouth of the Maurice enticed Swedish explorers to sail in from Delaware Bay in the 1630s. Tradition says the Swedes named the river after the ship *Prince Maurice*, which burned in the river at a spot known as "No Man's

Friend." Swedes may have settled near present-day Dorchester and Leesburg on the Maurice, but they were gone before Quaker colonizer John Fenwick envisioned a town named Cohansey (Cohanzick) soon after he came to Salem in 1675.

Fenwick's fancy of Cohansey's "Great Streete," a hundred feet wide and two miles long, became reality a year after his death in 1683, when Quakers from Salem and Presbyterians and Baptists from New England acquired sixteen-acre plots along "Ye Great Streete." They named the town Greenwich and opened trade with the outside world, particularly with the village of Philadelphia, founded by William Penn in 1682. Greenwich was made a port of entry in 1687, as testimony to the brisk trade already favoring the docks of the town.

Upstream, Richard Hancock, Fenwick's surveyor general, dammed the Cohansey River and built a sawmill in 1686 where Bridgeton now stands, but his interest was timber, not town founding. Connecticut colonists arrived in the 1690s to establish Fairton, five miles south of Bridgeton on Cohansey River.

Cohansey, as all of the region surrounding the creek came to be known, enjoyed such abundant harvests that in 1695 the provincial legislature authorized annual fairs at Greenwich in April and October. Philadelphia traders and their ladies found the fairs worth visiting. They made the long boat trip to join the local crowd until the twice-yearly event was discontinued in 1762.

As Cohansey River united the interior and the outside world, it also divided settlers on the east and west banks until the few who lived near Hancock's sawmill in 1716 built the bridge that gave their settlement the name Cohansey Bridge, or merely "The Bridge."

"The Bridge" it remained, too, after the legislature sliced away nearly half of Salem County to form Cumberland County on January 19, 1748. About three thousand people lived in the new county, called Cumberland in honor of England's Duke of Cumberland, brother of King George II. The county seat was temporarily set in thriving Greenwich.

Voters decided to move court affairs from Greenwich to "The Bridge" in December 1748, but they kept the

Names of tea burners are inscribed on the monument that recalls Greenwich's revolutionary fire. (*N.J.D.C.E.D.*)

original informal name for the new county seat. The first courthouse had been built and burned and a second courthouse constructed before the hamlet finally became Bridge Town in 1765.

Cumberland prosperity centered in Greenwich as that riverfront town rolled toward a 1774 date with immortality. Largest town in Cumberland and boasting docks good enough to carry on trade from Philadelphia to Boston, Greenwich seemed a logical place for British Captain J. Allen to dock his brig *Greyhound* in the gathering dusk of December 12, 1774. Captain Allen, knowing that his cargo of tea would be unwelcome in Philadelphia, felt certain it would be safe in Greenwich, particularly since leading merchant Dan Bowen willingly stored the cargo in his cellar.

Townspeople, aware that the tea had been unloaded, buzzed angrily but generally agreed to wait on a decision from Bridge Town. Then, on the night of December 22, about thirty anti-tea conspirators met in the home of Richard and Lewis Howell near Shiloh and decided to settle the matter themselves. Disguising themselves as Indians, the plotters headed on horseback for Greenwich, four miles away. They stole through Greenwich's darkened streets, removed the tea from Bowen's cellar to an open place on the Market Square. The hated leaves were destroyed in a roaring fire that lit up the village and burned the name of Greenwich into time.

Strong protests from financially interested nonpatriots rocked Cumberland County, and seven of the tea burners were brought to trial in May 1775. Sheriff Jonathan Elmer, brother of one of the "Indians," summoned a sympathetic jury, foremanned by Daniel Elmer, Jonathan's nephew. Chief Justice Frederick Smyth "gave a very large charge" to the jury, but the burners were found not guilty. The trial involved three men who later became outstanding New Jersey citizens. Richard Howell, one of the burners on trial, became governor of the state in 1792. He was succeeded in 1801 by Joseph Bloomfield, counsel for the seven defendants. Sheriff Elmer was elected one of New Jersey's first two U.S. senators.

Reputedly the tea burners were led by the Reverend Philip Vickers Fithian, just graduated from the college at Princeton, his cousin Joel Fithian, and Andrew

Hunter. Philip kept copious journals—of his Princeton College days, of his travels in Virginia as tutor in a planter's family, as a Presbyterian minister, of his love for Elizabeth Beatty (whom he married in October 1775), and of his life as an army chaplain in the early days of the Revolution. His death of camp fever on October 9, 1776, while with Washington's army in New York, cut short his brilliant existence, but his journals (published by Princeton University Press in 1900 and 1934) make his few years live on.

As the Revolution neared, half of Cumberland's small population lived west of Cohansey River in only one-sixth of the county area. A stage route from Greenwich to Philadelphia began in 1774, via Roadstown and skipping Bridge Town by five miles. Out along the Maurice River, a few settlers established Mattock's Landing (now Mauricetown) in the 1730s, and Lucas Peterson built a solitary house at Shingle Landing (now Millville) in 1750.

Agriculture dominated Cumberland life long before the strife with England. Naturally the county became looked upon as a wartime food supplier. Washington declared that if it hadn't been for the provisions sent by Cumberland and Salem counties to feed his men at Valley Forge in the winter of 1778 he would have had no army to continue the war. Patriotic feeling ran high, even though the war itself scarcely touched the county. The reading of the Declaration of Independence from the courthouse steps in 1776 called for prolonged pealing of Bridge Town's own Liberty Bell.

Bridge Town had special cause for grief in 1780 when word came of the sinking of the schooner *Governor Livingston* off the Capes of the Delaware. Bridge Town's patriots had built the ship and sent her across the seas on only one successful voyage before a British frigate ended her glory.

As the eighteenth century waned Cumberland grew slowly. An "actual count" showed only 8,248 persons living in the county in 1790, with about 300 of those in the county seat. Considerable wheat cleared through Bridge Town and Greenwich for Philadelphia, but local residents had to be content with once-weekly mail service. On the Maurice River, life centered about Port Elizabeth, established in 1785 by Mrs. Elizabeth Clark Bodeley, a Salem widow.

Bridgeton's own Liberty Bell, cast in 1763 and rung in 1776 to celebrate the signing of the Declaration of Independence. (*N.J.D.C.E.D.*)

James Lee, a wandering Irishman whose ability to establish industry exceeded his interest in continuing it, saw a future in the inexhaustible quantities of fine sand surrounding Port Elizabeth. He brought glassmaking to Cumberland County in 1799, setting up the Eagle Glass Works in Port Elizabeth that year. In 1806 he started making window glass in Millville. Nine years later, Lee moved again, this time to Kensington, Pennsylvania, to start still another glass company.

Lee left just as Millville began to be more than another wide place thirty miles up the Maurice River. Growth started in 1803 when Joseph Buck laid out a town and built himself a fine mansion on the corner of Main and High streets. David C. Wood and Edward Smith put a dam across the Maurice River in 1814, creating Union Lake to provide power for their mills. That same year, as proof that James Lee was not the only one

Truckloads of spinach are brought to farm auction in Vineland, where cooperative selling of farm produce has been a tradition since 1931. (*Walter Choroszewski*)

who knew how to make glass, Gideon Scull opened a window-glass factory in Millville.

Downstream on the Maurice, Joseph J. ("Coffee") Jones, son of a wealthy Philadelphia coffee merchant, bought hundreds of acres near Jonathan Dallas's ferry and renamed the village Port Norris, after his son Norris Jones. Coffee tried raising sheep and did well until a wild 1812 storm blew in off Delaware Bay, killing thousands of his animals. He stopped his woolgathering and prospered in the lumber industry, but was discouraged when the British captain who captured his woodship *Plow Boy* in the War of 1812 demanded one thousand dollars ransom. Coffee disposed of his Port Norris real estate in a

lottery and moved away, leaving only his son's name as evidence that the Joneses had been there.

Bridge Town acquired a bank, the first in southern New Jersey below Camden, in 1816. Later that year the "w" was dropped from the town name when the bank issued notes that called the town Bridgeton. Residents either liked the shortened form or felt it would be easier to change a town name than a bank note.

Coincidentally, the bank started just as extremely hard times hit the predominantly agricultural county. The summer of 1816 was the noted "cold summer," when frost often touched the fields during July and August. Farmers wore their "greatcoats" in the fields at harvest time, and shook their heads in dismay when they could not reap enough grain to supply seed for the next spring. Despair swept the county; hundreds of families packed their meager goods and migrated to open lands in Ohio.

Cumberland's fertile soil led the way back. In 1825 a county fair report declared that "it was manifest that increasing agricultural spirit would speedily supersede the toilsome and unprofitable labor of cutting timber." Bridgeton, with a new name, a booming nail works, and a glass factory started in 1836, prospered especially. Hence, Millville's 1837 bold bid for the county seat stunned Bridgeton people.

Bridgeton voters beat back the Millville effort in a public referendum, but an opposite vote by Maurice River dwellers threw the controversy to the Board of Freeholders for final decision. There a four-to-four deadlock prolonged the debate, with voting keyed to the closeness of freeholders to either the Maurice River or Cohansey River. Overnight, without advance warning to Millville, "Columbia Township" was born—and lived only long enough to cast the deciding vote for Bridgeton before lapsing quietly back into Hopewell Township, whence it came.

Regular steamboat service was opened between Bridgeton and Philadelphia in 1845, making Cohansey River busier than ever. Millville took no back seat, for three steamers, six coasting vessels, and a dozen trading schooners used the Maurice River by 1850.

Millville jumped ahead of its county rival when railroad service began in the summer of 1859 on the Millville & Glassboro Railroad. The line ran north from Millville through then unbroken forests and ended at Glassboro. The first locomotive was brought from Philadelphia on a sailing sloop. By 1863 the rails stretched south to Cape May and north to Camden. Bridgeton caught up on July 24, 1861, when the West Jersey Railroad inaugurated service between the Cumberland County seat and Glassboro. A festive crowd on opening day welcomed a railroad official's declaration that Bridgeton was now "on a footing of equality with other parts of the state."

By then Cumberland County had thrown itself wholeheartedly into the Civil War. Long before North and South officially split, Quakers and others waited in the dark marshlands to help fugitive slaves fleeing across Delaware Bay to freedom on the Underground Railroad. Sentiment was far from solidly Union, however.

There were some unusual family splits. Congressman John T. Nixon, a lifetime resident of Cumberland County, was in the House of Representatives when war was declared. He supported the Union. His brother, born near Cedarville, had gone to Louisiana to edit the New Orleans *Crescent* and later became a Confederate colonel. The pastor of Bridgeton's First Presbyterian Church, the Reverend Samuel Brack Jones, was so strongly pro-South that his congregation forced him to retire. As a balance, the minister's brother Paul T. Jones was ardently pro-Union.

The county sent off its famed Cumberland Greys by steamboat in May 1861, after a vigorous flag presentation ceremony in which the principal speaker, Paul T. Jones, punctuated his remarks by thumping the floor with the flagstaff. He thumped so often and so enthusiastically that one of the outspread wings of the handsome golden eagle atop the staff broke off. Later, news of the fall of Richmond sparked a tremendous torchlight parade, led by Professor Dorville's Band and highlighted by the singing of "The Star-Spangled Banner" by young ladies seated on the windowsills of the Female Seminary.

Letters from home to the Cumberland Greys unquestionably carried mention of Charles K. Landis, a Philadelphia lawyer and banker, who saw something in the unpromising woodlands of Millville Township that no one had seen before. Landis bought thirty-two thousand sandy acres of straggling pines and scrub oaks, all well "charcoaled over." About fifty people lived in the vast territory on the morning of August 8, 1861, when Landis drove a stake to found his "town" called Vineland.

Most felt like the native who tradition says sidled up to the twenty-eight-year-old Landis and asked: "What are you doing, friend?" Landis laconically replied: "Founding a town." The native warned nearby workers that Landis was addled. Local people cautiously warned one another to be sure to get paid Saturday night, lest the young visionary be gone by Sunday. Landis allayed that fear by paying each man a gold dollar, the first ever seen by these pineland dwellers. He offered the laborers ten-acre plots on long-term mortgages and advanced money to help them build inexpensive houses.

Landis preached in his brochures of a model way of living in Vineland, frankly admitting this would help him sell his huge real estate holdings. He laid out a central town a mile square, in which would be centered industrial, governmental, and cultural pursuits. Surrounding lands were to be for agricultural use, particularly for vegetables and vineyards. Landis sought New Englanders, used to urban life, for the town. For his farms, he turned to Italy, where farmers knew how to turn any soil into a garden. In the marriage of New England sagacity and thrift with Italian zeal and way-with-the-land, the Landis dream came true.

Landis planned brilliantly, in a time when cities still "just grew." All streets were at right angles to one another, with principal thoroughfares one hundred feet wide and all others sixty feet wide. He sold acreage in five- and ten-acre plots to avoid speculation and to encourage self-ownership. Houses had to be set back seventy-five feet from the street in the country, twenty-five feet in the city. Every property owner was required to plant shade trees and grass beside the roads. Every backyard had to have fruit trees.

An oasis sprang up in the wasteland. On Christmas

Vineland had just begun to sprout in the pinelands when this woodcut was made shortly after the Civil War. (*Barber and Howe*)

Day, 1862, seventy-five settlers hired a fiddler to lead them in celebration. By 1864 more than one thousand acres had been sold, and by 1869, sixty-five hundred persons lived in the Landis tract, which had been divided into Vineland (the central town) and Landis Township (the agricultural belt) in 1864. Interestingly, in this prime grape-growing region, nearly all residents agreed with Landis that liquor should not be sold—and Landis fought through the legislature a bill for local option. Landis was not a teetotaler; he merely felt that liquor was poor business.

One Vineland resident, Dr. T. B. Welch, a dentist and a staunch Methodist, had a strong antipathy to alcohol that led him to fame and fortune. Feeling that it was wrong to use fermented wine for Communion service, he introduced unfermented grape juice in his own church and offered it to others. Demand originated in spiritual use, but soon secular consumption far outstripped church needs. Welch gave up dentistry for full-time grape-squeezing. Before the family moved its business to Westfield, New York, in the 1890s, the Welch grape juice concern was well on the way to its present annual multimillion-dollar income.

At about the same time that Welch's conscience prodded him into his new venture, Captain Edmund Stites of Newport brought Cumberland's oyster beds into prominence by making the first commercial shipment of oysters from Bivalve in 1870. Maurice River fishermen had been harvesting oysters since colonial times but production began in earnest when they transplanted seed oysters from natural beds in 1846 to save the industry, and the mass shipments by Stites gave oyster farming lasting significance.

Bridgeton's glassmakers increased after the Civil War, with a score of glass companies prospering at different times over a twenty-year period until consolidation began in about 1875. Millville's several glass plants were merged into the company that the Whitall family and Edward Tatum founded in 1854. That firm, Whitall, Tatum and Company, continued growing until 1938, when it was purchased by Armstrong Cork Company.

There was plenty of room for glassmen in Cumberland County. Victor Durand started Vineland's first works in the 1880s and his experimentation produced this nation's first successful vacuum thermos jug. Non-blowers thrived too, once they got into glass. Dr. T. C. Wheaton, for example, came to Millville from Cape May to open a medical practice and drugstore in the 1880s. Realizing the need for good pharmaceutical and scientific ware, he started making his own glass in 1888. The firm is today one of America's great glass houses.

Another out-of-towner, Ewan Kimble, chose Vineland as his center. He came from Chicago in 1905, started making scientific glassware; and his firm grew to be the largest maker of scientific glass and laboratory apparatus in the United States. At the same time Kimble began in Vineland, automatic blowing machines became common. Cumberland's workers adapted to the machines; glassmaking became truly big business.

Cumberland's pattern was set by 1900. That year Charles K. Landis died, content that Vineland fulfilled his hopes even if the grape growing had largely given way to truck gardening, glassmaking, and chicken raising. The stamp of industry was such in Millville that the meaning of the town's name was easy to see. Bridgeton had become a bustling county seat, where old houses contrasted with new growth and where the town's three far-famed nineteenth-century private schools (West Jersey Academy, Ivy Hall Seminary, and South Jersey Institute) had just closed their doors in favor of broader public education.

Education in Cumberland also embraced the less fortunate, when the Reverend S. Olin Garrison founded Vineland Training School for the mentally retarded in 1888. His first school served seven children in one small frame dwelling; the institution grew to include 90 buildings and 350 patients. The school has achieved a worldwide reputation for clinical therapeutics and research. Among other advances, the noted Binet intelligence scale was introduced at the school in 1908, and as early as 1914 its representatives had been invited to twenty-six other states to discuss the school. The first army intelligence tests were drafted at the school in 1912.

Another of Cumberland's remarkable young men, Charles F. Seabrook (even then known as "C. F."), was

Mauricetown (pronounced Morristown) on the Maurice River has been a home port for ship captains and their vessels since colonial days. (*Walter Choroszewski*)

nineteen years old in 1900. His fertile mind kept visualizing schemes far beyond the scope of his father's fifty-seven-acre farm. C. F. bought out his father in 1912 and organized Seabrook Farms, Inc. He experimented broadly—overhead irrigation, mechanization, cold storage—and slowly built his farm to three thousand acres by World War I. He induced a New York firm to build a canning plant on his property in 1922 and just eleven years later his experiments with frozen foods resulted in Seabrook's first consumer pack.

Seabrook Farms became the biggest agricultural enterprise in New Jersey and one of the largest in the world. The company owned more than nineteen thousand acres, and nearly a thousand South Jersey farmers leased their lands to Seabrook, selling them products from another forty thousand acres. Seabrook made Cumberland New Jersey's prime agricultural county, particularly in the use of mechanized equipment and modern field methods.

Sharing the phenomenal twentieth-century rise of Seabrook and Cumberland farming in general was Vineland's poultry industry. Farmers in 1900 raised chickens only to supplement their diet of meat and potatoes. Even the establishment in 1905 of the Vineland Co-operative Poultry Association had only minor commercial overtones. That group consisted mainly of sportsmen interested in exhibiting their prize poultry.

However, the founding of the Vineland Co-operative Egg Auction in 1931 focused attention on the chicken farmers in the northeastern section of Cumberland County. The auction sold more than $50 million worth of eggs in its first twenty years and claimed to be the largest egg cooperative in the world. Vineland called itself "the egg basket of the nation." Eggs still are laid in some Cumberland nests, but the poultry industry has declined drastically in all of New Jersey. The "egg basket" is no longer an apt nickname.

Cumberland tops the state in many agricultural categories. It is first in the amount of irrigated land, first in acreage and production of vegetables, first in the amount of farm products sold cooperatively, first in the number and volume of fruit and vegetable processing plants. One-fifth of Cumberland's population is engaged in agriculture on the county's farms, and more than half of the county's acreage is tilled.

Cumberland's economy has been changing for the past twenty years. Agricultural acreage and production has dropped off slowly, typifying farming in all of New Jersey—and all of the nation. The Millville-Vineland-Bridgeton triangle, once one of the world's top glass-producing regions, has declined steadily since the 1960s. Wheaton Industries in Millville is still a major producer of glass (and plastic) bottles and the Kimble Division of the Owens-Illinois Glass Company in Vineland is an important maker of glass tubing and pharmaceutical glassware. The big glass story is the emergence in Vineland of nearly twenty relatively small companies making various forms of chemical, scientific, medical, or laboratory glassware. They range in size from about 10 employees to 150 but their aggregate production is huge.

Old Cumberland is changing—slowly. Nothing ever has happened precipitously in the county, except possibly the sudden drop in chickens and eggs, the loss of many of the glassmakers, and the startling failure of the original Seabrook Farms operation. Farm acres could be available for home or mall developments but Cumberland lies well off the beaten track. No new interstate highway traverses the county and none is on the drawing board. Completion of long-delayed Route 55, a four-lane highway that starts near Exit 3 of the New Jersey Turnpike, is certain to bring an influx of people streaming down from Philadelphia and Camden County. The highway runs from the county's northern border to Port Elizabeth, via Vineland and Millville.

One flaw in Cumberland's bright picture is the demise of its oyster industry, the happy theme of the Maurice River and the Delaware Bay oyster beds until the 1950s. The delectable shellfish had kept more than one hundred boat captains and crews exploiting the bay beds for nearly half a century. Some $6 million in oyster trade came annually to Bivalve, Port Norris, and surrounding villages, with payrolls running more than $70,000 weekly. A mysterious blight struck the beds in the late 1950s. The boats fell idle and their captains ever since have hoped that intensive research and restricted harvesting may someday bring oysters back as Cumberland's valuable pearl.

Cumberland County has achieved the success that nature intended. The extent of its rich green fields always amazes visitors, even those who have come for the hundredth time. Rows of vegetables stretch toward the distant horizon, long irrigation lines sprinkle the fields when nature fails to cooperate, and in harvest time, giant machines pluck the green beans and other vegetables.

Production of green beans and other summer vegetables has declined in Cumberland County, but the vast fields still need low-flying planes to "dust" crops with pesticides and other plant-preserving sprays. (*Seabrook Farms*)

Vineland's 55,000 people comprise about 40 percent of the county's population of 136,513 (1990 census). Landis Township merged with Vineland city on July 1, 1952, creating New Jersey's largest city, in area. The wide, shaded, straight streets of the "old city" are a continuing testament to the planning vision of Charles K. Landis.

Millville has kept pace, growing steadily to a population of about 26,000, about half that of Vineland—but Millville had no surrounding township with which to merge. Millville calls itself "America's Holly City," indirectly honoring the late Clarence Wolf, who more than half a century ago established the world's largest privately owned American holly orchard, with more than 4,000 American holly trees spread among forty varieties.

Millville's valid claim that it is "America's Holly City" is based on harvests from more than 40,000 holly trees in this privately owned holly orchard near the city.

Wheaton Village in Millville offers the chance to see glassmaking as it was in 1888, when Dr. T. C. Wheaton established his glass firm in the town. The eighty-eight-acre village re-creates life in a glass village of the 1880s. The village also has an extensive library for scholars seeking information on southern New Jersey glass.

Bridgeton, the third member of the "triangle," reached a peak in the 1950s, when each year in season the spicy smells from the ketchup and chili sauce makers pervaded the town. The canners moved away, the glass companies shut down, even the old-fashioned Cumberland Hotel felt the wrecker's ball. Unemployment soared to about 20 percent.

Recognizing the decline, Bridgeton boosters fought back. A series of federal grants helped spruce up downtown stores and streets. Municipal leaders established a historic district, the largest in New Jersey and third largest in the nation, to preserve the town's fine examples of colonial, federalist, and Victorian architecture. By looking back, Bridgeton found its future.

Outward from the triangle, today and yesterday merge in Cumberland. This is best typified in Greenwich on Cohansey River. There "Ye Greate Streete" dozes much as it did just before that Tea Party in December 1774. Greenwich citizens are proud of Cumberland County's twentieth-century well-being, yet they also treasure every detail of the only truly exciting moment ever offered the town on the Cohansey. Time has passed Greenwich by. It looks like a village of colonial days. Outward stretch the marshes, clear and unbroken. Far away, in time if not in distance, the rest of the county hums. In Greenwich, New Jersey finds its tidewater heritage.

All Salem County courthouse activity was transferred in October, 1968, to a new and modern $1.5 million building, but sentiment saved this square two-story brick courthouse at Broad and Market streets in the town of Salem. Dating to 1817, the old building was slightly enlarged and remodeled in 1908. The brass Italian-made cannon on the lawn was captured from the British in 1814 at the Battle of Plattsburg, New York.

SALEM

TERRESTRIAL CANAAN

John Fenwick gazed intently inland as the English ship *Griffin* dropped anchor in a pleasant cove off lower Delaware Bay in the autumn of 1675. Across the marshes, wisps of smoke curled through the trees, bespeaking a few earlier arrivals scattered through the vast area that Fenwick had purchased from Lord Berkeley in 1673.

At least Fenwick *thought* the £1,000 he had given Berkeley bought him all the province of West Jersey. Now, after two years of intensive trouble and litigation in England, Fenwick couldn't be sure. He indirectly expressed his troubled thoughts when he stepped ashore to his new land. "Its name shall be Salem," said Fenwick, thinking of the Hebrew word for peace.

For Fenwick, "Salem" was as much a prayer as an expression of the tranquillity of the land. Peace had been Fenwick's desire since his days as a major in the army of the ill-fated Oliver Cromwell. He embraced the Quaker faith after he left the army and listened with quickening interest when travelers spoke of the new lands across the Atlantic Ocean. Thus, when Lord Berkeley offered to sell his half of the province of New Jersey, Fenwick grasped the chance. The price was £1,000 and forty beaverskins annually.

The English courts studied Fenwick's purchase, investigating allegations that Edward Byllynge had used

Fenwick as a front in the transaction. Young William Penn, a Quaker like both Fenwick and Byllynge, sat in arbitration on the dispute and decided in favor of Byllynge and his creditors. Fenwick lost all but an area embraced by the modern Salem and Cumberland counties (not a small piece of real estate, at that).

Fenwick wrote Penn bitterly, but Penn urged him to put aside his rancor. "Away with vain fancies, I entreat thee," Penn advised. "Fall closely to thy business, thy days spend on, and make the best of what thou hast. Thy grandchildren may be in the other world before what land thou hast allotted will be employed."

He could not put rancor aside, but Fenwick fell closely to his business of colonizing. His wife stayed in England, but among the passengers on board the *Griffin* were his two married daughters, Mrs. John Addams and Mrs. Edward Champneys, their husbands and children, a son John and an unmarried daughter Anna, who soon after landing married another ship passenger. Others on the *Griffin* numbered at least fifty and perhaps as many as two hundred. This was a solid colonizing venture, not an adventurer's whim.

Fenwick bought the land from the Indians for the usual guns and shot, rum, and assorted articles of clothing. He laid out a wide street from the wharf on Salem River and saw his family and friends comfortably

A memorable symbol of age is the great oak, one of New Jersey's largest trees, that spreads over the Quaker cemetery in Salem. (*Charles V. Mathis*)

housed. He planned villages at Cohanzick (Greenwich) and Finn's Point.

More English Quakers joined the colony, lured by Fenwick's word pictures of a "happy country." He wrote of pure waters, of unlimited game, of friendly Indians, of people who "never know what sickness is." Fenwick assured prospective buyers that "if there be any terrestrial Canaan, 'tis surely here, where the land floweth with milk and honey."

As settlers pushed outward from the river they learned the story of the Swedes and Finns who had been here since before 1640. They found traces of the New Haven Puritans who had unsuccessfully attempted settlement in 1641 along Salem Creek, twenty-five years before other Connecticut Puritans founded the colony at Newark in Essex County.

By 1675, time already had dimmed memories of the thirty-year struggle the Dutch and Swedes had waged for control of the Delaware River. Governor Johan Printz, bustling, able four-hundred-pound Swedish leader, and the fort that he had built at Elfsborg Point (now Finn's Point) in 1643 were fading into history and legend. The tradition already was firm that mosquitoes swarming over the marshes drove the Swedes from Fort Elfsborg before 1655—something that Dutch guns could not do.

John Fenwick had no time for such tales. Financial troubles continued to plague him. His enemies harassed Fenwick constantly and had him hauled off to New York for short imprisonments in 1676 and 1678. Many of his own followers began to entertain grave doubts concerning Fenwick's right to sell them land. Finally, in 1682, the harassed Quaker conveyed all his land except 150,000 acres to William Penn for ten shillings "and other valuable considerations."

Salem never brought peace to John Fenwick. When he died in December 1683, he must have considered himself a failure. After all, for a man who once thought he owned half of New Jersey, the 150,000 acres he had left seemed like a mere garden patch. His visions of building a great estate for his children evaporated. Fenwick's most lasting memorial is probably the fact that it was he who interested William Penn in America.

Had he not been sickened by his financial difficulties, Fenwick would have been overjoyed by the growth of his "terrestrial Canaan." Mills sprang up along the numerous slow-moving streams in this land of peace. Boats sailed up sinuous Salem Creek in sufficient numbers to enable it to become an official port of entry in 1682, the same year that Penn founded Philadelphia. Being named a port was a real plum for the village.

Farming dominated the "terrestrial Canaan." In May 1682 the first of Salem's famous county fairs was established by the West Jersey Assembly. Solemn Quakers ruled that during the fair, and for two days before and after, all persons were exempt from arrest. But such latitude induced evil, and a 1698 law pointed out that "foreigners do flock in from other parts and do sell liquor by retail." That must stop, said the law. Only local folk could sell liquor and, just to keep everything honest (and the business for local people), the law provided that any Salemite who reported a "foreigner" selling liquor could keep half the confiscated stock. The colonial Quakers

generously allowed distillation of apple whiskey among themselves; there was a whiskey maker in Elsinboro by 1698 and during the next century at least fifteen distilleries flourished in the county.

The land of peace had its violent crime and even more violent punishment. A log jail built soon after settlement was replaced in 1709 with a new and larger prison, complete with a whipping post. Salem, New Jersey, outdid even the cruelest of the notorious Salem, Massachusetts, punishments when, in 1717, a young black slave woman was burned at the stake as an alleged accomplice in the murder of her master. Records indicate that the slave merely knew of the murder in advance, but was not involved in the commission. She was burned, nevertheless.

Otherwise things moved placidly along in the days before the old Fenwick territory lost half its area in the establishment of Cumberland County in 1748. By then Salem County had several scattered villages, mostly located along the winding creeks, which during the county's early days served as the only dependable thoroughfares. Many of Salem County's old houses still face the creeks, commemorating the days when keels rather than wheels linked settlers with other regions.

Most important of all early outposts was Wistarburg, the glassmaking village started in 1738 by Casper Wistar, a button maker from Philadelphia. Wistar bought a large woodland tract in 1738, built a glasshouse, a general store, houses for workmen, and a mansion house. He paid a sea captain £58 to transport four experienced glassworkers from Rotterdam to show him how to convert fine South Jersey sand into splendid Wistar glass, the first successful manufacture of glass in North America.

Wistarware quickly gained fame, and the prominence of the glassworks continued when Casper's son Richard took over after his father's death in 1752. In addition to making exceptional glassware, Wistarburg also trained many glassworkers who then put their knowledge to good use in establishing more glass manufactories in South Jersey and in other states. Today, genuine Wistar glass is a scarce, treasured antique.

The German, Dutch, and Belgian immigrants who came to Wistarburg helped advance religious freedom in Salem County. Catholics who worked for Wistar celebrated mass (probably the first formal mass in New Jersey) in June 1744 in the nearby home of Matthew and Adam Kiger. German Lutherans at the glassworks established their church four years later at Friesburg. Other denominations followed, with all religious groups finding a liberal climate among the Quakers.

Salem's long-accepted reputation as a garden spot attracted the attention of both the American and British armies during all the Revolution. Foraging activity increased sharply in the winter of 1778, when Washington's army was at Valley Forge and the British occupied Philadelphia.

First, General Anthony Wayne landed at Salem on February 19, seeking cattle, which some farmers promptly hid in the swamps. Undaunted by that show of local self-reliance, Wayne and his men collected upward of 150 head in forty-eight hours and started overland to Valley Forge via Haddonfield and Trenton. Wayne marched his troops between the cattle and the river, to "amuse the British."

The British were not easily amused. Alarmed that Salem County beef would help relieve the wretched conditions at Valley Forge, Colonel Charles Mawhood and Major John Graves Simcoe marched their Redcoats over the county in March to "chastise the rascals" (in Mawhood's words). American troops fell back to a thin line along the south side of Alloway's Creek, concentrating men at three bridges in hamlets known as Hancock's, Quinton's, and Thompson's (Alloway).

A bitter, indecisive skirmish at Quinton's Bridge on March 18 delayed the British, but seven Salem men lay dead by the span. Three days later, Major Simcoe led a group of three hundred assorted Hessians, Tories, and disreputable pillagers against the home of Judge William Hancock at Hancock's Bridge, where Salem militiamen had sought safety. Some of Simcoe's three hundred followers knew personally the thirty men sleeping in the house on the morning of March 21 when the British force surrounded it. Precisely at 4 A.M., Simcoe ordered an attack on the darkened house.

Sentries at front and rear doors died quickly and quietly from bayonets thrust into their backs. Then Simcoe's raiders stormed into the house, aroused the sleeping men and chased them into the attic. Blood flowed over the attic boards as the trapped Americans fell under savagely wielded bayonets. Eight men were killed, including Judge Hancock, and about the same number wounded. Simcoe withdrew his troops, satisfied with the night's work. The fortunes of war shifted elsewhere—but darkened bloodstains remained on the boards of the Hancock house to recall the murderous night for generations to come.

Quietude returned to Salem County after the war sooner than to most regions. Wharves along the creeks buzzed with activity; mills spun busily, traffic picked up on the highroad leading to Cooper's Ferry (Camden). Above all, the farmers worked.

How they worked! So much so that without warning the weary soil quit producing in the late 1790s. Bewildered farmers sadly watched wizened crops in the fields. Families fled from heavily mortgaged homes that ancestors had built a century or more before and headed west in the Great Migration. Onward they went, seeking the milk and honey—to western Pennsylvania, western Virginia. Ohio, Indiana, on across the Mississippi River to Kansas and beyond.

Leading the march was Zadock Street of Salem city. In 1803 Zadock founded Salem, Ohio; a dozen years later Zadock and son Aaron founded Salem, Indiana; and in the 1820s Aaron founded Salem, Iowa. The cross-country trail of the Streets finally ended in 1844 at Salem, Oregon. Years later, in 1916, a Salem, Oregon, citizen wrote the mayor of Salem, New Jersey, suggesting that all of the country's other twenty-five Salems change their names in deference to Salem, Oregon, "the most flourishing of all the 26 Salems listed in the postal guide." Salem, New Jersey, people could laugh the laugh of an old, old patriarch.

Discovery of extensive marl beds in the northern part of the county in about 1810 prompted farmers to spread this natural fertilizer extensively on the worn-out fields. Crops grew magically, and the westward migration was checked before the middle 1820s. Salem's men of the soil again ruled supreme, with Colonel Robert Gibbons Johnson of Salem city the leader of them all. Colonel

The Hancock House, scene of an infamous deed on March 21, 1778, when British troops massacred sleeping Americans. (*Newark News*)

The greatest of Salem County's overstuffed livestock specimens was the immense ox that Job Tyler shipped from Salem wharf to Philadelphia in 1823. A special steamer came down from Philadelphia to take the beast upriver, and a brass band led an impromptu parade through Philadelphia streets from dock to market. The ox merited the honors, because when slaughtered and dressed he yielded 2,111 pounds of beef, 365 pounds of tallow, and 176 pounds of hide—2,652 pounds overall!

Job Tyler's water-borne ox also focused attention on Salem County's growing steamship prominence. Steady service, started in the middle 1820s, at first met local opposition, but steamboat lines to Philadelphia, Wilmington, and Baltimore were well established by 1835. The lines prospered for sixty years. Salem, Alloway, Sculltown, Pedricktown, and Quinton's Bridge all grew from increased steamship business. Steamboats from Wilmington brought thousands of visitors in the 1840s to the riverfront amusement areas and the rousing camp meetings in Penns Grove.

Shipbuilding became a major industry, particularly at Alloway, where, in 1824, the Reeves brothers started to cut planks and timber for Philadelphia shipyards. Seven years later they launched their first boat and in 1844 they built their first steamboat. Many canalboats and side-wheel steamers slid down the ways at Alloway before the Civil War. An article in the *National Standard* said in 1844: "Glory to little Alloways [Creek], a mere ditch, but a few rods in width. She has grown upon her banks and borne upon her bosom some of the finest merchantmen that ever floated on the Delaware."

Salem County's proximity to the South, as well as the militant antislavery feelings of its Quaker settlers, gave it a prominent role in the drama leading up to the Civil War. On December 29, 1835, a group of Salem city people forcibly took away from a Philadelphia agent eight naked, nearly frozen slaves who were being led in chains through the city streets at 4 A.M. The agent received rough treatment, much to the indignation of editors in the City of Brotherly Love, whose thoughts lingered on the agent rather than the slaves. From that time until the Civil War broke out, hundreds of fugitive slaves crossed the Delaware River to the shores of Salem

Johnson, wealthiest man in the county, owned many farms but, like many wealthy farmers of the day, lived in town while others worked his acres.

Colonel Johnson became interested in the tomato in 1820, at a time when most farmers considered the rich, red fruit at least worthless and possibly even poisonous. Salem County legend maintains that Colonel Johnson had to eat one of the "love apples" on the courthouse steps to get his fearful fellow farmers to consider the tomato edible. Highly progressive Colonel Johnson helped organize an agricultural society, reintroduced fairs to the county, and in his spare time wrote a credible history of Salem County.

Salem County farmers particularly distinguished themselves throughout the nineteenth century by the immense cattle and pigs that they raised. Judge William Clawson of Woodstown fattened many hogs to over a thousand pounds in the 1850s, while Charles Clark of Pilesgrove in 1860 raised fifty-two hogs averaging over five hundred pounds each. Later, in the 1870s, Clark Pettit of Hedgefield Farm in Salem had the largest herd of breeding hogs in the world.

Fort Delaware on Pea Patch Island off the Salem County shore became a living hell after it was made a Union prison in 1863.

inspector of hospitals and prisons, wrote in 1863 of Fort Delaware: "A thousand ill . . . there are 20 deaths a day from dysentery and the living have more life on them than in them. Thus a Christian nation treats the captives of the sword." Underfed, miserably treated, and given the scantiest of medical attention, Confederate prisoners died horribly. Nearly twenty-five hundred of them found Salem's peace only in the cemetery at Finn's Point. Today a tall obelisk carries the names of 2,436 Southerners known to have been buried at Finn's Point.

The year of 1863 became a year of destiny for Salem County, because, in addition to the heroics of Miss Hancock and the wretchedness of Fort Delaware, it was the year that the Salem Railroad Company finally inched down from Camden to Claysville on the north bank of Salem Creek opposite Salem city. Rails were not laid into the city until 1882. The railroad did two important things: it definitely switched the county's main focal point from Wilmington to Philadelphia, and it brought a resurgence of the nearly forgotten old Salem glass industry.

Salem Glass Works, founded by H. D. Hall, J. D. Pancoast, and J. V. Craven in 1863, became one of the largest hollow glassware manufactories in the world within ten years. Encouraged by that success, John Gayner opened his glassworks in 1874. Other industries came to the county seat at about the same time: an oil-cloth factory, an iron foundry, and two canning companies. Salem city's economy became vigorous. The city population jumped to nearly five thousand, including scores of retired farmers and more than a hundred active farm operators who preferred to live in the city.

Glass also became vital to Quinton where the Quinton Glass Works made its first window glass in 1863, shipping it to markets on Alloway's Creek boats. Quinton's "golden age" of glass lasted until 1908. For forty-five years three million feet of the finest French plate glass in the nation came annually from Quinton Glass Works. Western competition killed the plant eventually, but Quinton had the distinction of being one of the last places in the East to make window glass.

As the nineteenth century waned, farmers in Pilesgrove and Pittstown townships happily applied tons of marl to their fields and reaped their rewards. Shad fish-

County and started northward to freedom on the Underground Railroad.

One of the county's daughters, twenty-two-year-old Cornelia Hancock of Lower Creek, gave Salem County reason for pride at the Battle of Gettysburg, where she was the first woman nurse to arrive on the field of battle. Miss Hancock served with distinction as a nurse throughout the war.

Closer to home, tales of horror seeped back to the Salem mainland from Fort Delaware, the Union prison camp established on Pea Patch Island in the Delaware River to hold Confederate prisoners. In the waning days of 1863, dozens of corpses came to the mainland each day from the fort, where twelve thousand Southern prisoners occupied space intended for four thousand men.

Fort Delaware deserves a place in the annals of infamy. Dr. S. Weir Mitchell of Philadelphia, a federal

ermen pulled thousands of fish from the Delaware River each spring. Tomato growers found increasing public demand for their "love apples." Noted ice cream makers, particularly John Bruna, made Salem County ice cream famous throughout South Jersey and as far away as Washington, D.C. Population edged just over the twenty-five thousand mark in the 1890 census, but Salem County remained rural—and proud of it.

Then, early in October 1890, the E. I. DuPont de Nemours Company announced plans to make smokeless powder at Carney's Point. Salem historians see the DuPont decision as the most important event in the county since the arrival of the Swedes 250 years before or the coming of John Fenwick in 1675. DuPont made its first gunpowder for sportsmen in 1894. The Spanish-American War boosted production modestly, but it took World War I really to make Carney's Point boom.

Allied forces appealed to DuPont to make smokeless powder for the war against Germany. DuPont added two units to the Carney's Point plant, and by 1915 the company's holdings stretched several miles north of the canal at Deepwater Point. Farmers put aside their plows to become carpenters. Shad fishermen dropped their nets to make powder. Skilled workers and laborers from all

Finn's Point Cemetery commemorates the deaths of the nearly 2,400 Confederate soldiers who perished at Fort Delaware. (*N.J.D.C.E.D.*)

The Delaware Memorial Bridge, opened in 1951 to link Salem County and Wilmington, Delaware, has profoundly affected transportation and population shifts in all of southern New Jersey. (*Walter Choroszewski*)

points of the county streamed into Salem County to take some of the twenty thousand jobs available at the Du-Pont explosives plant.

Salem County's 240 years of isolation and peace came to a sudden end. Penns Grove's population jumped from two thousand to ten thousand within a year. Earnest and sober workers mixed with not-so-sober adventurers who brought a new kind of high life to the one-time placid area. The power plant ran around the clock; Salem County was changed forever.

Simultaneously, DuPont was laying the groundwork for a far more permanent effect on Salem Country's economy. The war had cut off German dyes and Du-Pont began to make American dye-stuff at Deepwater in 1917. DuPont sank $43 million into the chemical plant, with no profits for ten years, but in time the plant became the largest general chemical plant in the world.

"Old Salem" gave way before industrialization. The two glass factories in Salem city were joined by a big H. J. Heinz canning house in 1906. Floor-covering plants moved into the county. Population increased. The mud and oystershell roads disappeared under blankets of macadam and cement. Residential areas like Woods-town and Pennsville grew rapidly. Towns surrounding

Penns Grove felt a quickened intellectual pace as chemists and engineers became residents. Intensive farming made the fruitful soil produce wonderfully, and the coming of Seabrook Farms to neighboring Cumberland County opened undreamed-of new markets for Salem farmers.

Despite the changes, Salem County emerged charmingly as the place where John Fenwick's "milk and honey" declarations and his prayer for peace continued to blend nicely with canneries, the glass manufacture in Salem city, and the huge chemical works at Deepwater. About five thousand DuPont employees live in the county. Out along the Delaware River at Deepwater, the generating plant of Atlantic City Electric Company supplies much of the power to counties in South Jersey.

The years since 1950 have changed Salem's outlook markedly. The Delaware Memorial Bridge at Deepwater and the New Jersey Turnpike and Interstate 295 across the western edge returned the county's orientation from Philadelphia to Wilmington, where it was in the beginning. Industry slowly became a major economic factor. Hundreds of new residents are bringing new customers into the county, unlike the days when Salem had the reputation of being land's end, far off the beaten path.

No one would dare link Salem County to the urban sprawl that allegedly spreads from New York City to Washington. In 1950 its population of 49,508 placed it twentieth among counties, trailed only by Cape May. Forty years later the population had increased to only 65,294—meaning that fewer than 500 new people per year came to the county. Salem now is behind Cape May, solidly last in population among counties.

The only area that shows any major growth is the region immediately surrounding the east end of the Delaware Memorial Bridge. In that corner, too, the New Jersey Turnpike and Interstate Route 29 begin (or end, depending on the viewpoint). Outward stretches Salem County, the most rural, the least changed of counties. Anyone seeking to know New Jersey as it "used to be," is advised to look at Salem. Scattered throughout the county are at least 150 old brick houses predating the Revolution. Many of them are the so-called "pattern brick" houses, in which dates and initials of the builders and patterns are made vivid by colored, glazed bricks. Salem city's venerable streets are lined with enough handsome old houses to bring joy to an antiquarian. The ancient oak in the Quaker cemetery makes believable the declaration by humorist Robert Burdette that the tree is "four years older than the Atlantic Ocean." (The oak really is four to five hundred years old.)

Even the towns commemorate the names of original settlers: Pedricktown, Pilesgrove, Quinton, Hancock's Bridge, Woodstown, to name just a few. Out in the marshes surrounding Hancock's Bridge, dozens of muskrat trappers still supplement their earnings with a continuation of three hundred years of trapping in the swamplands. Above all, Salem still seems truly to mean peace. Since the beginning most people have found relative tranquillity here, even if the man who named it Salem never found on earth the peace he so much craved.

Gloucester County's courthouse, a striking brownstone, harmonizes completely with Woodbury's main street. A deteriorated earlier courthouse forced a new building in 1884; the county paid $100 for a new plan (and sold the old building for $225). Costs rose, from $40,000 to $50,000, creating ill will that was aggravated by false rumors that the foundation was unstable. Strained feelings were forgotten when the building opened in 1887.

GLOUCESTER

SUMMIT OF THE WORLD

Lyndon B. Johnson, President of the United States, was in Washington, D.C., on June 22, 1967. That day, Aleksei Kosygin, premier of the Soviet Union, was in New York City attending meetings at the United Nations. They agreed to meet the next day: if the President would come a little north, the premier would come a little south.

Diplomats frantically sought a place for this hastily arranged "Summit Meeting." It had to be midway between New York and Washington. There had to be ample room for conferences, for staff meetings, and for the regiment of newspapermen certain to fly in from all the world. If possible, the setting should be quiet, with the townspeople gracious and orderly.

The decision was quickly made. The Summit would be Glassboro State College, where the classic Victorian home of the college president met the needs of space and quiet. Suddenly Glassboro, in Gloucester County, New Jersey, became the nerve center of the world. Swarms of telephone men poured into town through the night to install special equipment for television and press needs. Workmen air-conditioned the house before morning. Security guards took over the roads.

To understand the magnitude of the meeting, it must be remembered that the United States and the U.S.S.R. were declared enemies, locked in a "cold war" with world-threatening nuclear weapons on the ready. Even a slight thaw brought hope. This meeting would warm the world.

President Johnson and Premier Kosygin talked for three days in Glassboro, occasionally interrupting secret sessions to appear before TV cameras or to wave to the thousands of spectators who jammed the area outside the historic house. The big black limousines roared out of town on Sunday afternoon, followed by swarms of reporters, TV workers, and sightseers. Glassboro would never be the same as it had been on the rainy June 22 afternoon when someone jabbed a finger at a map and said, "That is Glassboro. That is where we will meet."

More than 325 years of recorded Gloucester County history preceded June 22, 1967, but nearly everything before and since would be measured against the three days when Glassboro became a place of hope and The Summit of the World.

If anyone had cared even to think about Gloucester County's past, on those history-making days of June 1967, they could have been excused for assuming that this was an old English colony, matured with passing time.

Possibly the most "English" of all New Jersey county names is Gloucester, yet the South Jersey agricultural county might better be Stockholm or something equally

On June 24, 1967, President Johnson and Premier Kosygin met the press outside Hollybush on the Glassboro State (now Rowan) College campus. (*Irving Tuttle*)

Scandinavian. Long before English Quakers came to take over, Swedes and Finns had occupied the county creekbanks, but the name Gloucester clearly indicates what happened. The English moved in and moved ahead; the amiable Scandinavians moved over. They came to a "summit" meeting of minds long before it became necessary to subject such things to the glare of world publicity.

Except for Swedesboro on Raccoon Creek, the overt Swedish story is gone from Gloucester, but it lives on in the strong influence that the Swedes had in making the county an area of relatively small farms. Today only a handful of the county's hundreds of farms is more than fifty acres in size. Swedes led the way to intensive cultivation of the soil that as early as 1870 earned Gloucester a still-meaningful nickname—"Philadelphia's Garden Patch."

"New Sweden" began in 1638 on the west bank of the Delaware River near what is today Wilmington, in a region also claimed by the Dutch. Exploring Swedes came across the river to settle in what is now New Jersey. Some may have stayed at the mouth of Raccoon Creek in that first year of Swedish occupation. The Dutch and Swedes vied quietly for the territory until the Dutch gained the upper hand in 1655. Eventually both lost, because in 1664 England accepted the Dutch surrender of the Delaware River valley. Neither the Dutch nor the English paid the slightest attention to Swedish claims.

Not that the Swedes in the area had much allegiance to Sweden by that time. Rocky soil near Wilmington resisted their husbandry, so they had drifted across to the New Jersey side of the Delaware—as individuals, not in colonies—to break the rich soil. Many of them were indentured servants who had left their masters, and they worried little about who ruled the land, as long as they farmed it.

Swedish centers arose, particularly along Raccoon Creek, although as a historian has pointed out, Swedish settlements usually were merely scattered farms, "held together by the gossiping propensities of Swedish matrons." Cordiality between Swedes and English Quakers existed from the time the first English colonists arrived in 1677. Swedes acted as interpreters when the Quakers bought land from the Indians, between Timber and Oldman's creeks. No one remembered or cared that the enterprising Indians had long before sold the same land to the first Swedes to arrive.

One of the early Quakers, William Penn, showed great interest in this English colonization. In 1681 he seriously considered the present site of Paulsboro as the place where he might build the center of his vast Quaker holdings. He decided the land was too low. A year later Penn turned to the higher west bank of the Delaware River to found Philadelphia.

All of West New Jersey then revolved around Burlington, but soon the Swedes and Quakers resented the long trip to the West New Jersey provincial capital. Accordingly, on May 28, 1686, representatives met at Arwames (now Gloucester city) and organized Gloucester County. Some historians maintain that the representatives formed the county themselves, without action or permission of the provincial legislature, thus making Gloucester the only county in New Jersey deriving existence from the direct action of its people. Others know that the legislature had to give at least tacit approval to the new county.

"Old" Gloucester sprawled from the Delaware River to the Atlantic Ocean. It embodied all of present Cam-

den, Atlantic, and Gloucester counties—nearly twelve hundred square miles, or about one-sixth of New Jersey. Atlantic's secession in 1837 took away 613 square miles and Camden's breakaway in 1844 took away another 225 square miles, leaving only 330 square miles of the original Gloucester County area.

Repaupo and Mullica Hill became centers of Swedish life until the completion of the King's Highway to Raccoon (Swedesboro) shifted influence there in 1702. Quaker life centered in Woodbury, founded in 1683 by Henry Wood from Bury, England. Slowly the Quakers came to dominate county affairs.

Old-time Swedes fought to keep themselves and their children "Swedish." Establishment of the Swedish Lutheran Church in Raccoon in 1703 helped, even though the first minister, Lars Tollstadius, possessed such dubious character that in 1706 he was "bound over" to Burlington Court for getting Ole Persson's daughter into difficulties. A Repaupo school set up in 1715 perpetuated old-country language and customs for many years, but "Swedishness" couldn't last.

Young Englishmen found young Swedes attractive, and vice versa, and nature took it from there. In 1750 the assimilation was so complete that few people complained when the Swedish town name of Raccoon was anglicized to Swedesboro. The following year the Lutheran minister agreed to keep records in English rather than Swedish. So New Sweden expired.

Gloucester County assumed a twofold importance during the American Revolution: its "garden patches" attracted food seekers from both armies and its strategic position just below Philadelphia made it an obvious place for river-dominating fortifications.

Continental land agents bought a large plot of land at Billingsport at the mouth of Mantua Creek on July 5, 1776—the first property purchased by the just-born "Thirteen United Colonies." The infant government built rough fortifications at Billingsport, having them ready when George Washington stopped by to inspect the area on August 1, 1777. In the fall of 1777, when Philadelphia's fall to the British seemed imminent, the American army strengthened both Billingsport and Fort Mercer, on the bluff at Red Bank, directly across the river from South Philadelphia.

British troops struck first at Billingsport, sending more than five hundred men ashore early in October 1777 to drive Colonel William Bradford and his 100 regulars and 150 militiamen out of the fort. Bradford burned the barracks, bakehouse, and other buildings and destroyed ammunition and cannons before fleeing. The British then turned their attention to Fort Mercer.

Four hundred ragged and despairing Rhode Island soldiers waited behind Fort Mercer's log walls for the attack they knew must come after the fall of Billingsport. Finally, on October 22, 1777, twenty-two hundred Hessians struck under cover of a river barrage from the sixty-four-gun *Augusta* and the eighteen-gun *Merlin*. Colonel Christopher Greene cautioned his American troops to hold their fire until the Hessians reached the walls.

A hail of musketfire and grapeshot viciously cut down the first line of Hessians. They withdrew, then charged again, only to become panicky in the face of the murderous fire. Their disorderly flight toward Haddonfield left nearly four hundred dead and wounded under the walls, including their mortally wounded commander, Colonel Carl Emil Von Donop.

Meanwhile, American guns mounted on barges sank

Ann Cooper Whitall sat spinning in this house while the Battle of Fort Mercer raged on October 7, 1777. A cannonball ripped through the room and forced her to continue spinning in the basement. (*Walter Choroszewski*)

both the *Augusta* and the *Merlin*, but not before shot from the British vessels peppered the side of James Whitall's farmhouse near Fort Mercer. Inside the house, Mrs. Anne Cooper Whitall sat calmly spinning while the battle raged outside. She worked stubbornly until a cannonball blasted through the side of the house and hurtled past her into the far wall. The imperturbable Quaker lady picked up her wheel, went into the cellar, and continued to spin until the guns were silent. Later, as Mrs. Whitall bound up the wounds of the Hessians, she scolded them for coming to America to fight the colonists.

American troops had to abandon Fort Mercer on November 20, burning the fortification to make it useless to the British. The invaders held full sway over the lower Delaware, enabling Lord Cornwallis's foraging parties to exploit Gloucester's gardens whenever Mad Anthony Wayne and his hard-hitting raiders did not beat him to the harvests. Cornwallis stayed in Woodbury briefly, November 21–24, in a home seized from patriot John Cooper, brother of Anne Cooper Whitall.

Woodbury's emergence as Gloucester's county seat and leading town began in 1786, when the decrepit old county buildings in Gloucester town burned and courts were moved to Woodbury. A cornerstone for a new courthouse was laid in Woodbury, and county government moved into the new home on March 23, 1787.

The village at the head of navigation on Woodbury Creek prospered as the nineteenth century neared. It took justifiable pride in its progressiveness: in its Free School, started by the Quakers in 1773; in its famed Woodbury Academy, opened in 1791; and in its Gloucester County Abolition Society, one of the nation's first such groups, founded in 1793.

America's first airborne trip came to an end in a field near Woodbury on January 8, 1793, when Jean Pierre François Blanchard stepped from a balloon after a leisurely one-hour trip from Philadelphia. The smiling Frenchman bore a letter from Washington, asking that he "be extended every courtesy." Farmers courteously carried the hot air balloon to Cooper's Ferry (Camden) and helped Blanchard load it aboard a ferry.

Blanchard was diverting, if a bit frightening, but far more vital to Gloucester County's growth were the Stan-

As troops fought for Fort Mercer, land-based American cannon blasted British ships beneath Red Bank's bluff.

gers (or Stingers), seven German brothers who left Casper Wistar's Salem County glassworks in 1775 and four years later started the glass industry that boomed in many parts of Gloucester County for more than a century.

Settling down in the dense pine forest at what is now Glassboro, the seven Stangers built their successful "Glass Works in the Woods." During the war, they accepted as much Continental money as they could get. When Congress announced in 1780 that forty Continental dollars equaled only one gold or silver dollar, the Stangers learned the sad meaning of "not worth a Continental." They went to debtors' prison in 1781 and their glassworks passed into the control of Colonel Thomas Heston.

Eventually the Stangers won freedom, some of them to work for Heston and some to begin other plants. The Stanger success prompted other glass ventures: at first in Malaga, Williamstown, and Clayton, and later in Woodbury in the 1880s. All disappeared because of

Founded on an endowment of $500,000 in 1923, when this administrative center was built, Glassboro State College became Rowan College in 1992 to honor the $100 million-dollar gift from Henry M. and Betty L. Rowan. (*Walter Choroszewski*)

cheaper competition elsewhere, but while they lasted their owners prospered, in large measure because they owned almost everything in their glass villages and took back in trade what they paid out in wages.

Gloucester County's pre–Civil War social life centered in the many taverns scattered over the area, such as Clarksboro's Death of the Fox Inn, where sportsmen gathered to chase the elusive reynard; the White Horse Tavern, which gave Five Points the name "Hell Town"; George Sheat's hotel in Bridgeport, where men gathered to down grog before watching the horse races in the village streets; and the Williamsport Tavern, where boastful hunters met.

Tavern talk inevitably got around to Jonas Cattell, a Gloucester County figure whose life spanned almost a century, from 1758 to 1854. Cattell is a part of history, although some of his remembered feats seem more legendary than factual.

When he was fifty years old, Jonas outran an Indian in a foot race from Mount Holly to Woodbury. Once he walked eighty miles to Cape May, delivered a letter, and returned with an answer the next day. He loved fox hunting, but he always traveled on foot, right up there with the pack; the horses, riders, hounds, and foxes were always more tired than Jonas. Those tales rested on fact, but such old fishermen's yarns as his wrestling a fifteen-foot sturgeon in the Delaware prompted disbelievers to declare that Jonas's imagination and his tongue were as lively as his legs were swift.

Woodbury attracted hundreds of men from surrounding farms on Saturday afternoons in the 1820s. They frequented the county seat to drink a little "Boston Peculiar" (New England rum), to wrestle and pitch quoits and to watch the militia drill, armed with everything from 1776 flintlocks to cornstalks. Gaiety took a back seat in 1825, however, to serious talk when Camden challenged Woodbury's right to retain the county seat. Bitter wrangling engulfed the county that year before Woodbury won a victory at the polls and probably precipitated Camden County's eventual secession in 1844.

Firmly established as the county seat, Woodbury rejoiced even more in 1831 when the seventy-five-year-old dam across Woodbury Creek below the town was broken. The dam long had hamstrung the village at the head of navigation. So when two sloops sailed through the broken dam, crowds cheered and cannon roared a welcome. An orator enthusiastically pointed out that the tide which "ran out seventy-five years ago finally has run back."

Seven years after the dam break, a railroad rolled down from Camden to strengthen Woodbury's ties with Philadelphia. The first train from Camden reached Woodbury on January 20, 1838, and five trains ran daily.

Nevertheless, Gloucester County grew slowly, mainly because of poor roads. The county's first turnpike was not built until 1848, at a time when the turnpike movement was nearly a half-century old and beginning to die elsewhere in New Jersey. By then, both Atlantic and Camden counties had taken their leave of old Gloucester, mainly because of the transportation distances to the courthouse in Woodbury.

A strong temperance movement swept over Gloucester in the two decades before the Civil War. Paradoxically, a whiskey bottle made in Glassboro for the 1840 presidential campaign of William Henry Harrison helped to bring the word "booze" into common use. Shaped like log cabins, supposedly symbolic of Harrison's humble beginnings, the bottles were filled by a Philadelphia distiller named E. C. Booz. Soon these became known as "Booz" bottles, popularizing the word "booze," which had been used in this country as early as 1812 by Parson Weems, and even earlier in England.

Bolstered by the long-time Quaker opposition to slavery, Gloucester stood solidly behind the Union cause in the Civil War. Mullica Hill even sent an all-Quaker company into active service.

Immediately after the war a pressing religious fervor swept Gloucester, resulting in the establishment during the 1870s of huge camp meeting grounds at Pitman and Malaga, both of which still exist. A camp meeting gave Pitman its name. When the first meeting began on August 1, 1871, Methodist sponsors named the site Pitman's Grove in honor of Charles Pitman, a Methodist divine. Religion was not Pitman's only lure. Alcyon Park, opened in the town in 1891, quickly attracted outsiders to its picnics, band concerts, and vaudeville acts. Intoxicating liquors were not allowed, but promoters advertised "plenty of good drinking water."

Two centuries of complete agricultural dominance passed before two men—one a home-town boy and the other from across the river—gave the county large-scale industrial impetus.

George G. Green, son of a county patent-medicine maker, thought big when he returned to Woodbury on Thanksgiving Day, 1872, with a new bride. A Civil War veteran, he had been away several years, serving as a traveling salesman, and a druggist. Now he returned to buy and run his father's small medicine business.

The Green medicines long had been known locally. "Green's August Flower" cured dyspepsia (and so on) and "Boschee's German Syrup" cured illnesses of the chest (and so on). George G. Green scoffed at cure-alls and "modestly placed his medicines before the public." He gave away 10 million free samples of "Boschee's" and 2.4 million, four hundred thousand samples of "August Flower." Five million almanacs went forth from Green's each year to advertise the products. So much mail went in and out of the plant that Woodbury became seventh in New Jersey postal revenues.

Hundreds of Woodbury residents secured work in the spreading Green enterprises. George prospered greatly. He built a huge hotel in Pasadena, California, and a big summer home at Lake Hopatcong. George G. Green became one of South Jersey's biggest men; in Woodbury he was all. The town's most remembered night took place annually when Green's nineteen salesmen came home to a sales meeting, wearing high silk hats and swallowtail coats. Each year, before the Greens left for Pasadena, the family's private "palace car" stood on a siding and all townsfolk were invited to go through at their convenience.

Green's medicine worked wonders for Woodbury's economy. The Woodbury Glass Works opened in 1881 to supply the glass bottles and vials that Green needed. A box factory thrived on making packing cases for the wondrous medicines brewed in Green's laboratories. The patent medicine business declined; today several smaller concerns occupy the big Green factory and only a handful of employees work for the Green company.

Out on the Delaware River, where shad fishing had brought some wealth and good health to scores of fishermen, big business also sprouted. Lammot du Pont of the noted Wilmington du Ponts bought a farm in Gibbstown in 1880 and built the largest dynamite plant in the world.

Lammot and his cousin William, construction boss, each day rowed themselves across the wide Delaware to watch the progress of the new plant rising amid the cornfields. Du Pont initiated features at Gibbstown that, with only minor changes, are standard practice in the explosives field today. Ironically, Lammot du Pont died on March 29, 1884, in an explosion at the plant.

Some years later, in 1902, the du Pont company opened its Eastern Laboratory at Gibbstown, the beginning of the company's research program and probably the first industrial research laboratory in the country. Among hundreds of other developments, the first commercial production of TNT was initiated at Eastern Laboratory.

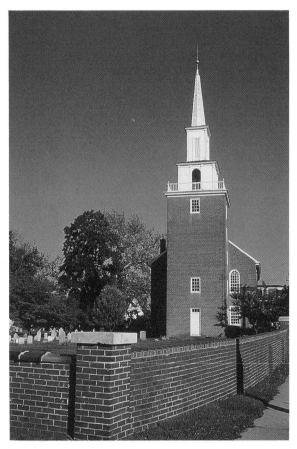

Built in 1784 by a Swedish congregation, Swedesboro's Trinity Church has been Episcopalian since 1789. (*Walter Choroszewski*)

The last half of the nineteenth century saw agriculture reach maturity, particularly in the eastern section of Gloucester where liberal uses of varied fertilizers turned sandy soil into rich farmlands. Many of the farms were spread over acres of former pine woodland, which the defunct glass industry had cleared to obtain timber for use as charcoal in its plants. Elsewhere in the Pine Barrens, the glass and bog iron industries were blamed for ruining the land; in Gloucester, farmers made the clearings blossom.

Farmers used the rivers to ship produce to market until about 1880, when railroad lines took over most of the vegetable and fruit trade. Glassboro edged into the peach forefront before 1900. Sweet potatoes, harvested as early as 1835 in the county, were big business by 1890. Asparagus was a major crop before 1910. Gloucester was not about to lose its self-designated title: "Garden Spot of the Garden State."

Gloucester's growing pains, including a new $75,000 courthouse started in 1885 and a new $10,000 span built to replace the covered bridge over Woodbury Creek in 1891, resulted in a minor revolt in 1890. Angered by the extravagance of the freeholders in boosting the county tax collector's annual salary from $250 to $500, the people elected a majority of Democrats to the Board of Freeholders in 1890, the only Democratic board in Gloucester's history.

How Gloucester grew, yet remained rural, appears in these headline-making items from 1890 through World War I: 1891, John Blake, owner of the Pole Tavern, killed his 1,157-pound hog after a weight-guessing contest that excited all of South Jersey; 1892, Swedesboro got the first mile of stone road in New Jersey under a new state law; 1893, bitter fighting delayed construction of the trolley line from Camden to Woodbury—opponents said it was really meant to benefit Billy Thompson's racetrack in Camden County; 1900, Postmaster Jessup was soundly denounced by merchants because he suggested free home mail delivery (that would mean the end of afternoon window-shopping, merchants said); 1900, Dr. Buzby sold his three horses in Swedesboro and bought an automobile; 1911, New Jersey had only twenty miles of old turnpike road left, seventeen of them in Gloucester; 1915, the county bought the seven-mile Woodbury-to-Mullica Hill toll road for $25,000; 1920, Gloucester County built its first paved road.

Gloucester County veers slowly away from the rural traditions of three centuries. The New Jersey Turnpike and Route 205 and the postwar bridge from Bridgeport to Chester, Pennsylvania, opened the western section of the county to new residents. Population rose briskly between 1950 and 1970, jumping from 135,910 to 323,132—nearly 200,000 in twenty years. By 1990 the total stood at 395,000. The growth has not overwhelmed any area. Monroe and Deptford townships have seen the greatest growth, yet both have populations of about twenty-five thousand, scarcely more than large towns. Life in Woodbury and surrounding towns is geared to commuters who travel daily to Philadelphia or who work for DuPont.

A population jump to nearly 400,000 necessarily is partner to a steady decline in farmland. Home developments, industrial parks, and malls have replaced one-time vegetable fields. Asparagus and sweet potatoes, once of major farm significance in Gloucester County, are no longer important. The most visible and profitable farm evidence is in the peach and apple orchards, mag-

nificent in spring blossoms, splendid in late summer and autumn harvests. Gloucester leads all counties in apple and peach production.

If the summit meeting of President Johnson and Premier Kosygin in 1967 is arbitrarily conceded to be Gloucester's most important historic event, the second might well also be centered on the Glassboro campus, where the name Glassboro State College has disappeared. In July of 1992, Henry M. and Betty L. Rowan of Rancocas donated $100 million to the college, the largest cash donation ever given to a public college or university anywhere. The gift was doubly amazing: neither of the Rowans had attended Glassboro State College. On September 1, the college became Rowan College of New Jersey, rich in tradition, in educational heritage, and now truly rich in endowment. The future can only be imagined.

If industry and home developments ever crowd out agriculture, Gloucester County will be sadly different. Ever since the Swedes and Finns first poked up Raccoon Creek nearly four hundred years ago, this land seemed destined for a plow, reserved, in a way, as a garden patch, for the age when cities elsewhere expanded—and ate what Gloucester's fields produced.

After Mount Holly was voted the permanent Burlington County seat in 1795, work began on this remarkable courthouse. Opened in 1796, the two-story yellow brick building is believed to be the oldest courthouse in the United States that is still used by county courts. Recognized as one of the nation's finest examples of Georgian colonial design, the courthouse has been kept as close as possible to its original appearance.

BURLINGTON

JERSEY'S LARGEST

Map changers, county founders, and land schemers have been envious of Burlington County's vast acres for more than three centuries. Repeated cuts at its boundaries have reduced Burlington to less than half its original size, but the intensive surgery has not mortally wounded the old territory. Burlington is easily New Jersey's largest county, big enough to stretch from the Delaware River to the Atlantic Ocean.

Burlington was the first county in New Jersey to have a court system, the core of county government, and thus can claim to be the state's first county. Its territory stretched from the tip of Long Beach Island to High Point, including today's Hunterdon, Morris, Sussex, and Warren counties, and parts of Mercer and Ocean counties. That loosely defined county included nearly half of New Jersey.

The first severance from Burlington's original borders was Hunterdon County in 1713. Since Hunterdon then included all of present-day Morris, Sussex, and Warren counties, that was a cruel slice. A bit more was cut off in 1838 to help form Mercer County. Then, in 1891, a large section on the Atlantic Ocean side was lopped off and added to Ocean County.

Those geographical cuts took away about 1,750 square miles of old Burlington but the county still re-tained 808 square miles—an area that could include all of modern Bergen, Hudson, Essex, Passaic, and Union counties, plus another 115,000 acres left over for a state park. Burlington really doesn't need another state park: nearly one-fifth of the county land is in state parks or forests. Additionally, federally-owned Fort Dix Reservation and McGuire Air Force Base are in the county (and off the local tax rolls).

Burlington's riverfront has come startlingly alive since World War II, thanks to new highways and the flight from nearby cities. Population has soared, possibly giving rise to thoughts that the county is close to filling up. Nothing could be further from fact.

Out to the east, the great "Pine Barrens" still stretch, untamed and awesome. Burlington is the heart of the "Barrens." The pine woodlands are far from barren; the name lingers from colonial days when land was judged barren if it could not sustain traditional crops. In this "barrens," wild orchids grow along with scores of other plants, some of them very rare. The Pine Barrens also stretch into parts of Monmouth, Ocean, Atlantic, and Gloucester counties, but Burlington has by far the biggest share.

Place names in the Pine Barrens are simple, often recalling the first people to pass by: Sooy Place, Ong's

Hat, Sim's Place, Mary Ann, Bulltown, Jenkins, Harrisville. Settlement in this land was simple, although never easy.

The first to arrive learned that. They were the hardy Quakers on the *Shield of Stockton*. On a frigid December night in 1678 they fastened their ship's rope to a giant sycamore tree on the Delaware at what is now Burlington. According to tradition, the ship's company walked ashore on the ice the next morning to join other Quakers who had laid out the village in 1677, and made their homes in rude lean-tos for the rest of the winter.

Quakers from Yorkshire and London joined in founding the first village, dividing properties along a street running south from the Delaware River. The Yorkshiremen chose to live east of the street (now High Street); the Londoners to the west. Pleased with their work, they called the town Burlington in deference to Yorkshire ascendancy; Burlington was an old Yorkshire village in England.

Many new settlers followed within the next four years, attracted both by the fertile ground and by the very liberal rights granted in the *Concessions and Agreements* of the West New Jersey Proprietors. Traffic with Pennsylvania began almost immediately, via the ferry established by Samuel Clift in 1680. A year later, the first Quaker Assembly convened in town, making Burlington the capital of West New Jersey. A jail went up in 1682, followed in 1683 by the courthouse, evidence that thoughts of punishment preceded thoughts of government.

Settlers pushed outward from the first town. Thomas Farnsworth went eight miles up the Delaware River in 1682 and founded Farnsworth's Landing (now Bordentown) on a breeze-swept bluff. Rancocas Creek was an invitation to the interior; Quakers went up its placid waters soon after 1700 and founded Bridgetown (now Mount Holly) on the flats beneath a holly-covered hill. John Wills, son of Burlington's first physician, started a famous gristmill on the Rancocas in the 1690s. Until Andrews's mill was opened at Tuckerton in 1704, customers on horseback toted grain all the way across the province from Little Egg Harbor to Wills's Mill. The cross-state visitors brought news of scattered bands of solitude-loving settlers working their way from the At-

lantic Ocean up the Mullica, Wading, and Bass rivers to sink roots in the pine woodlands, Burlington's eastern edge.

Burlington County's destiny was linked to Philadelphia's. The county's harvests of fruits and vegetables were welcomed by the city. Quantities of shingles, logs, boat planks, and fence posts went downriver from the pinelands to the city of Brotherly Love. The county's future was set along a straight line between New York and Philadelphia, through the towns of Bordentown and Burlington. New Jersey might be slated to be "like a barrel tapped on both ends," but Burlington County leaders had no intention of being overwhelmed by the drainage.

Crude roads twisted across New Jersey around the northern edge of the Pine Barrens, joining Burlington and Bordentown with Perth Amboy, the capital of East New Jersey. River packets from Philadelphia to Burlington or Bordentown soon appeared. By the 1730s boat-stagecoach trips between Philadelphia and New York were firmly established, although advertisements of their punctuality, their speed, and their comfort were far superior to the service.

Travelers included many a noted individual, but a penniless teenager who crossed the county in 1723 seemed more a beggar than someone headed for greatness. The seventeen-year-old boy stayed one night at Dr. Joseph Brown's inn in Bordentown, apparently beguiling his host into giving him a free night's lodging. The next day he strode through Burlington, and according to local tradition purchased gingerbread from a lady in the Revell House. Years later the teenager, grown to manhood, told of the Burlington County adventures in his *Autobiography*. He was Benjamin Franklin, who among other things in his remarkable life set up a print shop in Burlington in 1728 to print paper money for New Jersey.

Bordentown was still called Farnsworth's Landing in 1723. Wealthy Joseph Borden had been buying up land for a half dozen years by then, but the first mention that he had been honored with a town named for him came in 1739. Minutes of a Quaker meeting that year tell of permission given to local people to erect stocks at "Bordings Town" to chastise boisterous, hard-drinking river bargemen. Borden established his own cross-state stage route in 1750, promising to cut forty-eight hours off New York-to-Philadelphia transit time.

Burlington County's widespread area and its Quaker liberality could embrace varied people. Episcopalians founded St. Mary's Church in Burlington in 1702 and a year later built there the first Episcopal church in New Jersey. Many former Quakers became members.

More unusual was the establishment of an Indian reservation at Edge Pillock (now Indian Mills) in 1758. About two hundred Lenape Indians settled as the last sad remnant of a once great tribe. Even that remnant failed to survive. All but a few moved to New Stockbridge, New York, in 1802 and eventually shifted westward to Green Bay, Wisconsin.

The Revolutionary War found Bordentown and Burlington prosperous. Both towns had their share of leaders who argued that all this good life stemmed from the King. William Franklin, son of Benjamin Franklin and governor of New Jersey, was forced from his aristocratic Green Bank estate in Burlington and lost his royal governorship rather than agree with the revolutionaries. The Reverend Jonathan Odell, rector of St. Mary's Church, wrote fierce satires against an independent America. Both Franklin and Odell remained dedicated Tories and both ended their days in foreign countries.

Despite such opposition, Burlington people welcomed the Provincial Congress of New Jersey to the town from June 10 to July 4, 1776. That Congress sent off to Philadelphia the five New Jersey delegates who signed the Declaration of Independence. The five included keen-witted and sharp-tongued thirty-eight-year-old Francis Hopkinson of Bordentown. A young lawyer, Hopkinson had excellent connections; his wife was Ann Borden, daughter of the powerful Colonel Joseph Borden.

Hopkinson predicted the Revolution in a 1774 essay titled, "A Prophesy." By 1776 he was in full swing as a revolutionist writer, jabbing mercilessly at the furious British. Later he designed the Great Seal of the United States and aided in the design of the Stars and Stripes. During his life Hopkinson mingled with the nation's foremost citizens and won acclaim for his musical com-

Elaborate ironwork on the Joseph Borden house at Bordentown. (*N.J.D.C.E.D.*)

positions. Some of Hopkinson's lasting fame rests on his twenty-two merry verses satirizing "The Battle of the Kegs."

The kegs, filled with gunpowder, were launched by the Americans on the Delaware River's ebbing tide in January 1778. The hope was that the floating mines would strike British ships anchored at Philadelphia, creating havoc when they detonated. Only one of the kegs found a mark, killing four men, but the floating mines created panic in the fleet. Flint-happy redcoats for days fired at everything in the river. Hopkinson's tongue-in-cheek jingle extolled such "bravery." His poem ended:

> *Such feats did they perform that day,*
> *Against those wicked kegs, sir,*
> *That, years to come, if they get home,*
> *They'll make their boasts and brags, sir.*

Despite its strategic location, Burlington County suffered no major Revolutionary War episodes, although foraging parties and minor skirmishes kept the county embroiled throughout the war. A band of four hundred Hessians invaded Burlington city in December

The Chesterfield Friends Meeting House, erected in 1773, and the old oak tree, seventeen feet in circumference, are landmarks of Crosswicks.

1776, and a punitive naval expedition was sent against Bordentown in May 1778 (in retaliation, it is said, for Hopkinson's unappreciated poetry). The ships returning to Philadelphia from Bordentown fired on Burlington, first taking the precaution to warn small boys off the bank!

Mount Holly was the scene of a clash in June 1778, when the ironworks and other properties were destroyed, and English soldiers slaughtered a steer in the town's old Friends Meeting House. At Crosswicks a sharp engagement took place when Continental volunteers and Hes-

sians fought at the bridge on June 23, 1778. Three cannonballs struck the Quaker meetinghouse beneath the giant Crosswicks oak.

Thomas Paine, who fired colonial imaginations and lagging patriotism with his "times that try men's souls" writings in 1776, found peace in Bordentown from 1783 until he traveled to Europe to become embroiled in the French Revolution in 1789. He wrote longingly of Bordentown while in France, but when he returned he found that few of his old friends cared to see him. His "Age of Reason," a highly literate pamphlet written in

France, failed to touch the hearts of one-time revolutionists who had grown conservative with age. He was run out of town by a mob of jeering pursuers.

Adjacent houses in Burlington city, so close that they seemed (and still seem) to be one, welcomed to-be-famous sons in the 1780s. James Lawrence was born at 459 High Street in 1781, and James Fenimore Cooper was born at 457 High in 1789. James Lawrence, who went into the navy, won immortality for his plea, "Don't give up the ship!" as he lay dying after a sea battle with the British in the War of 1812. The Coopers moved away to Cooperstown, New York, when James Fenimore was a year old, but Burlington can claim a modest reflected glory from that great early American novelist.

At the war's end, Burlington farmers eagerly turned back to the soil. One of them, Charles Newbold, decided something better than the crude old methods of tilling was imperative. He patented the nation's first cast-iron plow in 1797, but overcame only with difficulty the prejudices of farmers who feared Newbold's invention would poison the soil.

The county had grown so by 1796 that the county seat was moved from Burlington to Mount Holly—a splendid choice. The new county seat boasted a rich heritage, even by 1796. It pointed with quiet pride to John Woolman, the intense local Quaker who fought slavery with brilliant prose and ready tongue. It discussed with satisfaction the famed Indian missionary John Brainerd, who preached in Mount Holly from 1767 to 1775 and spoke courageously against the British in 1776. One of Brainerd's joys was the Indian reservation at Indian Mills. He taught school there among the Indians he loved before accepting the call to Mount Holly.

Just east of Mount Holly the great pinelands began. They stretched far, covering two-thirds of Burlington County as well as parts of adjacent counties. Charles Read penetrated the forest in 1766 to set up an ironworks on the Mullica River at Batsto, but it was General Washington's good friend Colonel William Richards who made those Burlington County works productive during the Revolution. Iron forges and furnaces prospered elsewhere at the dawn of the nineteenth century, combining the bog iron dug from the swamps with seemingly unlimited supplies of charcoal timber to turn out quantities

of iron pipe, firebacks, Dutch ovens, and other iron goods. Burlington County at one time had more than a dozen ironworks within its borders.

Out along the Delaware, Bordentown experienced a burst of excitement in 1816 when Joseph Bonaparte, exiled king of Spain and brother of Napoleon, bought fifteen hundred acres of land at Point Breeze. A special act of the legislature was required to sell him the land, and the passage of the act earned New Jersey the sobriquet of "New Spain."

Joseph developed an elaborate estate, and he liked Bordentown so well that in 1820 he unhesitatingly turned down a delegation from Mexico that offered him that country's throne. For their part, Bordentown residents liked the foreign nobleman in their midst, calling him "the *good* Mr. Bonaparte." Joseph returned to France in 1832, came back to Point Breeze in 1837, and

Joseph Bonaparte, brother of Napoleon, who came to live in Bordentown in 1816 and soon earned the respect of his Quaker neighbors.

left for good in 1839. His nephew, tall, handsome Prince Napoleon François Lucien Charles Murat, caused local some sighs of despair when he eloped with Caroline Fraser, the belle of Bordentown.

Bordentown's river quaintness changed forever in the 1830s. First, Isaac Dripps assembled on the town dock the English-built locomotive "John Bull" in 1831 and prepared the steam engine for travel across the state to South Amboy on the Camden & Amboy Railroad. In 1834 the Delaware & Raritan Canal was completed between Bordentown and New Brunswick by way of Trenton. The railroad established big shops in the city, and the canal terminal required lodging places for somewhat ungenteel canal mule drivers and their mules. Many of the aristocrats refused to compromise with this nineteenth-century progress. They moved out of town.

Culture continued vital. The Quakers had established a school in Burlington as early as 1782, and a library opened in that town in 1758 under charter from King George II. Mount Holly's little brick schoolhouse on Brainerd Street was opened in 1759. St. Mary's School, founded by Episcopal Bishop George Washington Doane in Burlington in 1837, grew into a famed girls' school before the Civil War. Many of its students came from Southern states.

Burlington County's cultural pride also reached out to Clara Barton, a quietly determined woman who reached Bordentown in 1851. Aroused by the lack of schooling for the poor, she established one of America's first free schools in a one-room brick building. When townspeople insisted that she be supervised by a male principal, Miss Barton resigned and went elsewhere, eventually to found the American Red Cross.

Not exactly another humanitarian, but certainly fascinating, was Hezekiah B. Smith, who emigrated from New England in 1865 to convert an abandoned thread mill on Rancocas Creek into a thriving machine manufacturing center. Modestly he renamed the village Smithville.

Smith, simple and proud of his humble beginnings, affected a Quaker hat and shawl. That was a cloak, for he lived the life of an industrial prince, maintaining a gambling casino in town and a well-filled liquor cellar.

Smith manufactured the high-wheeled Star bicycle, among other things. He took out more than forty patents and was at times experimenting with models of flying machines and steam wagons.

Hezekiah created a sensation with the trained bull moose that he imported to pull his carriage when he campaigned for Congress, using his Smithville Brass band to stir the crowds. Smithville mourned with Hezekiah in 1881 when his young wife died. His own death in 1887 brought Smithville up short, however, because at will-reading time another wife and five children suddenly appeared from Woodstock, Vermont, where Hezekiah allegedly had deserted them. Thus, Smithville learned for the first time that Hezekiah, for all his glittering, was not pure gold.

Such diversions as Hezekiah B. Smith could not erase concern over the economic collapse of the pinelands. The bog iron mining industry was ruined in the 1850s by the development of railroads and canals elsewhere. These carried coal to upstate ironworks, making the smelting of bog iron economically unfeasible. Glassworks deep in the woods prospered for a time at such places as Lebanon and Herman, but they were gone by 1870. A paper mill started at Harrisville reached its peak in the 1880s, only to fold in 1892. The crumbling ruins of furnaces and mills began to dot the forest.

Lumbermen and charcoal burners found livings of varying sorts in the Pines, but they conducted their businesses with a wanton disregard for the facts of forest life. They cut and burned without recognition that their actions and the horrendous forest fires that raged freely and frequently were dooming the fine white cedars as well as less desirable pines. The advent of cinder-throwing railroad locomotives in the 1850s caused many fires and quickened the ruin of the woodlands. Soon the cedars were scarce and the straggling pine and scrub oak growth that replaced them could not sustain any sizable lumbering enterprise.

Nature lent a hand at this point by beckoning entrepreneurs to cultivate and to expand the wild cranberry bogs in the forests. By the middle 1880s the Pines were producing half the nation's crop; today only Massachusetts and Wisconsin produce more cranberries than South Jersey's pine bogs.

The many vanished industries in the Pine Barrens are recalled by these ruins of a paper mill at Harrisville. (*N.J.D.C.E.D.*)

Miss Elizabeth C. White, daughter of one of Burlington's earliest cranberry growers, recognized another fruit with potential greatness. Miss White enlisted natives to locate prime wild blueberry bushes, then cultivated these into noted blueberry varieties. New Jersey now leads all states in production of cultivated blueberries, thanks to Miss White.

Population declined steadily in the Pines between 1860 and 1920. Dr. John W. Harshberger in his *Vegetation of the New Jersey Pine Barrens* in 1916 called the area "one of the wildest, most desolate portions of the United States." He told of traveling as far as ten miles without seeing even a house, much less a human being. He wrote that the sparse population had contributed to the county some of the nation's most personalized local names, such as Mount Misery, Hog Wallow, Mary Ann Forge, Bozarthtown, Martha Forge, Apple Pie Hill, School Hollow, and Beehive, all suggestive of the people who had passed through or had stopped and had been remembered in a crossroads settlement. Dr. Harshberger definitively called attention to the unique and diversified flowers, trees, and plants thriving in the so-called Barrens.

Just before World War 1, Miss Elizabeth C. Kite, a

Started a century ago, cranberry farming has become a substantial income producer for many farmers in Burlington County. (*U.S.D.A.*)

social worker from the Vineland Training School, startled the state with a vivid report of sordid conditions among residents of the woodlands. She told of illiterates living in squalor and of people like "The Squire," who elected himself "the law" and for a flat fee of fifty cents "gave writin's" ranging from a marriage license to a "divorce writin'." The social worker claimed that the worst conditions were in Burlington County, and a direct result of her work was the establishment in 1916 at New Lisbon of Four Mile Colony for the mentally retarded.

Miss Kite traced the origins of the "Pineys" (a name given to withdrawn pineland inhabitants) back to the "Pine Robbers" and Tory refugees of Revolutionary War times. These were joined through the years by Hessian deserters, by people who sought religious freedom, or many who desired just plain independence. A few were disreputable, of course, but mainly the Pineys wished merely to be left alone. Unfortunately that desire, not harmful in itself, also manifested a lack of responsibility toward others. That meant that schools were not built, roads were not maintained, and people were a law unto themselves.

Arguments about the merits and faults of the Pineys have raged throughout the years ever since Miss Kite's report. Visiting journalists often perpetuate wild and false tales of lawlessness and treachery. The people of the Pines are, and always have been, shy and reticent rather than mean.

Many of the Pineys were drawn from the forests to help construct Fort Dix in World War I and to rebuild it for World War II. Many of them found work on the state highways cutting through the forests. They work as guides or as skilled forest hands in the state forests at Lebanon, Green Bank, Wharton, and Bass River, and

as workers in the cranberry bogs. Significantly, during World War II Selective Service found few shirkers among the Pineys, and if ever there was a spot in which to dodge the draft, it is the Pines. There is still much evidence of free spirit, but very little crime.

Humans have slowly cut away at the pines. The United States army bought nearly six thousand five hundred acres near Wrightstown in the summer of 1917 and hastily threw up Camp Dix to receive drafted civilians. At its peak in 1918, the camp had about 55,000 men

Batsto, dominated by a handsomely preserved village, owes its origin to the now-defunct bog iron industry. (*N.I.D.C.E.D.*)

Nearly one-fourth of New Jersey is covered by the mysterious Pine Barrens, most of which are in Burlington County. (*N.J.D.C.E.D.*)

housed in barracks or tents. Renamed Fort Dix, the camp came to life again in 1940. The government bought another 17,000 acres and acquired "trespass right" to another 70,000 acres. Title searchers uncovered original deeds tracing back more than two centuries. Camp personnel sent hundreds of thousands of men off to duty and returned them to civilian life. Altogether, 1,182,118 World War II veterans were separated from service at Dix.

Fort Dix remained operational continuously and supplied troops for both the Korean War and the Viet Nam struggle. By 1985 the installation included 32,605 federally-owned acres. The base became non-operational in 1992 when the "cold war" with the Soviet Union disappeared. The Fort Dix Army Air Field, started in 1941, renamed McGuire Air Force Base, remains a fully operational government jetport.

Settling even an army base or a military jetport in the Pine Barrens has not been a problem. The State of New Jersey has located about 105,000 acres of state forests or parks elsewhere in Burlington County. These include all or parts of six state facilities: Penn, Green Bank, Bass

River, and Lebanon state forests; Mount Laurel Park, and 71,000 acres of the state-owned Wharton Tract. The latter, spread over 97,000 acres in three counties (Burlington, Atlantic, and Gloucester), was purchased in 1954 for $3 million, mainly to conserve underground water reserves. It has become as well a popular recreational area and the old iron village of Batsto—a one-time "ghost town"—has been restored.

Since World War II worried conservationists have battled to save as much of the Pine Barrens as possible. One major concern is the estimated 17 trillion gallons of pure water in its underground acquifers. The region is dotted with rare flora and fauna. A major protective step in 1980 was establishment of the New Jersey Pinelands Commission to monitor the region; its headquarters is at New Lisbon, fittingly in Burlington County. In 1977, the United States Congress made the Pine Barrens the nation's first National Reserve.

Wide-open spaces in the Pine Barrens give a misleading picture of what has happened in Burlington County since 1950. Population jumped 290,000 between 1950 and 1990 (when the county had 395,066). Even that is misleading, because most of the surge came between 1950 and 1970—and nearly all of it took place between the Delaware River and a line about fifteen miles to the east. Within that region are three major bridges crossing the Delaware to Pennsylvania, the New Jersey Turnpike, Interstate 295, and several other four-lane highways.

Willingboro, now the largest in population, has seen a rise bordering on meteoric. In 1950 it was a farm village of 582 people, not vital enough even to be a wide pavement on Route 130. Then, in the late 1950s, the Levitt Corporation of Long Island brought its astounding building techniques to the township. Houses rose by the thousands, very good houses, despite traditionalist criticism. Local officials gratefully forsook the township's old name that dated to 1688 and called the place Levittown. Good sense returned in 1963, and historic Willingboro again became the name. By any name, population soared close to 40,000—seventy times the pre-Levitt figure.

Much of "Old Burlington" remains despite the industrial and residential developments near the river. Burlington city is filled with eighteenth-century buildings. Mount Holly's 1796 courthouse and 1759 school are gems of preservation. In Bordentown, Clara Barton's little red schoolhouse commemorates her stay and delicate ironwork decorates many town structures. Major horse-breeding farms are seen nearby the highways, particularly near Moorestown and Jobstown. Moorestown's quiet, old Quaker dignity lands distinction. Quantities of vegetables, particularly sweet corn and tomatoes, come from the fields. Blueberries and cranberries brighten the pine woodlands.

For those who know Burlington County well, it comes as no surprise that Batsto in the Pines is well preserved. It seems natural that the West New Jersey Proprietors convene at high noon every April 10 in Burlington to conduct business, just as they have since 1687. It is fitting that Mount Holly's Fire Department, 200 years old in 1952, is the oldest in the United States. Tradition lives on—in place names, in Quaker meetinghouses, in lasting memories.

More than anything, there are those beckoning pines, that land of mystery, of intrigue, of broken dreams. The Pine Barrens wait human decisions, for better or for worse. In them is most of Burlington County's future— and much of concern for all New Jersey.

THE JERSEY SHORE

Scores of millions of people know the Jersey Shore . . .

They know of ocean-washed sands, of suntan lotions, of beach umbrellas, of boardwalks, of souvenirs. They know of traffic jams, of Miss America, of casinos and the unceasing quest for pleasure. True, that *is* the Jersey Shore.

This, too, is the Jersey Shore . . .

Where Southern aristocrats rocked on Cape May verandas until the Civil War sent them home; where Diamond Jim Brady and others of like mind made Long Branch prosperous and happy. Where Presidents and governors bathed in the dashing surf, a wave away from the commoners who came down in wagons. Where a railroad from Camden turned the sandy wasteland of Absegami Island into glittering Atlantic City.

This is the Jersey Shore . . .

Where winter turns vacationland into ghost towns, with boardwalk stands silently braving the icy brunt of January storms. Where sailing ships once beached and broke up on the desolate sands, where the federally supported lifesaving service was born, and where summer's welcoming waves turn into winter's savage surf.

This, then, is the Jersey Shore, all things to all people of all ages: a land of magic, of wistfulness, of excitement, of changing moods. This is a place where today erases yesterday and anticipates tomorrow—whether that tomorrow brings a fall hurricane or more glossy casinos beside Atlantic City's boardwalk.

This is the Jersey Shore . . .

Monmouth County's four-story courthouse on Court Street, Freehold, was a break with history when dedicated in October 1955. Four previous courthouses, dating back to the earliest colonial days, had all been on Main Street. The "new" courthosue is brick, with limestone facing. Its chief features are the four solid Indiana limestone pillars at the front entrances. Each weighs 100 tons and is 72 feet tall.

MONMOUTH

SURF AND SOIL

Robert Juet, an officer aboard Henry Hudson's *Half Moon*, gazed intently shoreward on September 2, 1609, as the ship sailed north along the Atlantic coast. He wrote in his journal of the "high hills," then penned an accolade that ever since has served all Jersey Shore publicists well: "This is a very good land to fall with, and a pleasant land to see."

Juet's "high hills" probably were the Navesink Highlands of today's Monmouth County, for the *Half Moon's* anchor was dropped inside Sandy Hook Bay the next day. Hudson's crew set out in small boats to explore the bay and to seek fresh water in the hills. Indians greeted the newcomers and exchanged "greene tobacco" for knives and beads. Monmouth County's recorded history had begun.

A few Dutch settlers drifted over from New Amsterdam before 1660, only to be edged into the background when English colonists from Gravesend, Long Island, bought the Highlands from the Indians in March 1664. Other Englishmen quickly moved in, establishing widespread plantations in what they called Middletown and Shrewsbury. Baptists settled extensively in Middletown, while the Quakers chose Shrewsbury.

Indians harassed the newcomers. Richard Hartshorne, one of the original big landowners, complained in 1677 of Indians who threatened to "kill my cattle and burn my hay." Hartshorne paid thirteen shillings on August 8, 1678, to extinguish forever all Indian rights to pick beach plums or to hunt and fish on the Englishman's land. It was a sizable concession by the Indians: Hartshorne's holdings included all of Sandy Hook.

Middletown and Shrewsbury had prominence enough in 1675 to warrant being established as the "County of Nevysink" with indefinite borders. By then Colonel Lewis Morris had acquired control of New Jersey's first ironworks, started in 1674 on the "Falls of Shrewsbury" by James Grover. Morris bought 3,540 acres on the Shrewsbury River "to dig, delve, and carry all such mines for iron as they shall find." He called his plantation Tintern Manor, which local usage corrupted to Tinton and then Tinton Falls.

Influence in high places was the privilege of a powerful ironmaster, so when Monmouth became one of East New Jersey's first four counties in 1682, Morris asked that it be named Monmouth after his native Monmouthshire in Wales. East New Jersey Proprietors looked very fondly on Monmouth; in the 1680s it was the wealthiest county in the province of East New Jersey and consequently paid the most taxes. Monmouth already had a reputation as "a great resort for industrious and reputable farmers."

A boatload of Scotsmen stranded on the Jersey coast

Sandy Hook Light, oldest operating lighthouse in the United States, has guided ships since "41 oil blazes" were lit in June 1764. A fixed, electrically powered light is now visible for nineteen miles out to sea. (*Walter Choroszewski*)

bought land where county fathers had decided the new courthouse would be. Generously he sold a plot to the county for a mere thirty shillings, thereby proving his political acumen. Construction of the first courthouse in 1715 made his own holdings increase tremendously in value, proving he had good business sense as well.

Bordered on the north by Raritan Bay and on the east by the Atlantic Ocean, Monmouth County looked to the waters for its main transportation arteries. Such exceptionally broad and well-protected streams as the Shrewsbury, Navesink, Shark, and Manasquan rivers brought oceanborne commerce.

Streams of vessels passing Sandy Hook made a lighthouse imperative on the long, dangerous peninsula. Work started in 1762 on the beacon, and the light flashed seaward for the first time on June ll, 1764. Ships passing through Sandy Hook channel paid threepence per ton to defray lighthouse expenses. The tall white structure still operates as the oldest continuously lit lighthouse in the United States.

Downcounty in what oddly enough was called "Upper" Freehold, gristmills hummed busily on Doctor's Creek at Allentown and Imlaystown and on Crosswicks Creek at Waln's Mills, long before the Revolution. Scows laden with flour went down the Crosswicks to Philadelphia, since lower Monmouth (Upper Freehold) looked westward for its trade. Transportation to Philadelphia was far easier than an arduous trip to New York.

In the first decade of the eighteenth century a wandering New Englander named Mordecai Lincoln stopped in Upper Freehold Township, where he married Hannah Salter, daughter of wealthy landowner Richard Salter. The couple set up housekeeping near Mordecai's blacksmith shop at Filmore and started a family before drifting westward. One of their sons, John, was the great-grandfather of President Abraham Lincoln.

Historians who recorded the vital discovery of marl on Peter Schenck's farm near Freehold in 1768 neglected to get the name of the discoverer. Listed simply as "an Irishman," the anonymous benefactor of early agriculture recognized the greensand marl from having used it in "the old country." Tried on nearby fields on the Irish-

made their way inland to near Freehold in 1685, some Dutch traveled across Raritan Bay from New York to take up land in the 1690s, and French Huguenots settled in the county in 1700. Simultaneously, a few settlers pushed westward to found Allentown and Imlaystown. Settlements were widespread enough by 1713 to warrant the choice that year of a centralized county seat at Monmouth Court House (Freehold).

A few weeks later one John Reid, who ranks high among Monmouth's most enterprising residents,

man's say-so, the marl produced "extraordinary results." Quickly its usage enriched surrounding farms and gave the region its name, Marlboro.

Monmouth suffered cruelly during the Revolution, both from small bands of raiding British troops who slipped in from the sea and from Tories who congregated on Sandy Hook or hid in the forests. Further woes came from the "Pine Robbers," who could strike at either side as it suited their fancy. Jacob Fagan and Lewis Fenton gained notoriety as bandit leaders, while General David (Black David) Forman hunted the raiders down mercilessly and "hung them without waiting for superfluous ceremony."

That strictly local pattern of guerrilla warfare exploded into major battle on the extremely hot day of June 28, 1778, when General Washington's pursuing army finally caught up with General Clinton's British troops in the fields west of Monmouth Court House after a chase across New Jersey. Washington held a slight advantage in numbers of troops, but Clinton had superior position in the thick woods and extensive marshlands.

The chance of a full American victory vanished at the outset when General Charles Lee failed to carry out Washington's orders to attack. Washington faced the sulky Lee on the battlefield and in his anger was said to have "swore 'til the leaves shook in the trees." What motivated Lee is not likely ever to be known, but he was court-martialed and dismissed from service for his dilatory actions. Washington rallied Lee's troops and the battle raged all day without decision before Clinton slipped off and escaped over the Highlands. The Americans could not claim victory, but the battle proved their ability to fight the British on an open battlefield.

Both sides suffered severe losses in the indecisive action, from the deadly June heat as well as from enemy fire. An estimated total of five hundred men died at Monmouth, three-fifths of the casualties being British. Wounded soldiers were taken to Tennent Church or to St. Peter's Church in Freehold.

Monmouth's heat brought to the fore an American heroine of legendary proportions—red-haired, freckle-faced Molly Hays, who had followed her soldier husband John to the battlefield from Carlisle, Pennsyl-

vania. Under the hot June sun Molly carried pitchers of water from a nearby creek to the parched soldiers, earning the nickname of "Molly with the pitcher," or "Molly Pitcher." According to tradition, an enemy bullet wounded John, whereupon Molly took his place at the cannon and kept the weapon in action.

One shocking war episode remained for Monmouth as the war neared its end. Captain Joshua Huddy of Colt's Neck, captured at Toms River in March 1782, faced British charges that he had killed Tory Philip White. Evidence proved Huddy had been in a British prison when White was shot, but an enemy company executed him on the gallows at the foot of Navesink Hills. Huddy's senseless death outraged and stunned even British leaders.

Wartime bitterness subsided quickly in Monmouth, however, possibly because of the remarkably deep roots of the county's churches. Shrewsbury, for example, had New Jersey's first Quaker meetinghouse, built in 1682. The state's first Baptist congregation was organized at Middletown in 1668. Christ Church, Middletown, and Christ Church, Shrewsbury, were both organized in October 1702, while St. Peter's Church, Freehold, traced its beginnings back to 1695. Old Tennent Church was built in 1751, and Bethesda Methodist Church at Adelphia, founded in 1780, was the state's oldest regularly constituted Methodist Church.

A few wealthy seaside enthusiasts came to Monmouth's shore and built summer homes after the Revolution, the most noted being U.S. Senator William Bingham of Philadelphia, who entertained lavishly at his Rumson Neck home. Bringham's guests comprised an exclusive circle; it remained for an unidentified old lady to open the shore for summer "renters." The elderly lady was in charge of a Long Branch mansion when Elliston Perot of Philadelphia successfully coaxed her to rent him the building in 1788, on condition of his providing the beds and the food.

Other Philadelphians begged the privilege of sharing the big old house with the Perots, and this demand sparked the business imagination of one Lewis McKnight. He bought the mansion for £700, invited down the best families of Philadelphia (no rabble, mind you), and

Harper's Magazine for June, 1878, depicted Molly Pitcher in action at the Battle of Monmouth. (*Newark Library*)

cleared $40,000 on his investment before his death. Another accommodation, conducted by Messrs. Herbert and Chandler, advertised in 1792 "a good stock of liquors and everything necessary for the entertainment of ladies and gentlemen." When this place was bought by Joshua Bennett in 1806, Long Branch was so popular with visitors that Bennett enlarged the house to take care of 250 guests.

Long Branch in those days vied with Cape May for the favor of Philadelphians, some of whom made the long trek across the state in wagons that were returning to the shore after their owners had sold loads of fish in Philadelphia or Trenton. Farmers along the Monmouth coast opened their homes to paying guests, aware that cultivating summer visitors offered far better prospects than digging their thin beachfront soil.

Long Branch gained wide attention for its discreet bathing regulations. When a white flag went up only ladies bathed; when a red flag went up only gentlemen tested the surf. Strangers often went on the beach at the wrong times (through ignorance, of course), and one day in 1819 a wag hoisted both flags together, "which created some awful squinting and no little confusion."

Inland from the sea, untroubled by such trivia as red or white flags, farmers spread marl over land once considered worthless. Nature responded bountifully. Monmouth fields by 1840 were "under the highest state of cultivation." Many farmers began growing Irish potatoes in the 1840s, with yields so great that the invention of a mechanical potato digger by Thomas Stout of Keyport in 1853 met a pressing need.

All Monmouth throbbed with transportation hopes and plans in the two decades preceding the Civil War. Steamers had provided the logical link with New York from the late 1820s on, with vessels touching at Sandy Hook, Keyport, Matawan, Oceanport, Red Bank, Eatontown Landing, and Long Branch. Some of them brought in summer visitors, but farm trade provided necessary stability for the steamers in the months when visitors stayed home.

Oceanport's steamers also relied on products made in James P. Allaire's Iron Works in Howell Township between 1822 and 1846. Allaire, a New York builder of marine engines, bought the Howell Township works after a series of proprietors had struggled with it in the early part of the nineteenth century. The works prospered under the new ownership for two decades and its products enjoyed wide distribution until Allaire & Company abandoned the property in 1846. The land stayed in the Allaire family and slowly became a "lost village." The State of New Jersey began acquiring the area in 1941 to develop Allaire State Park, centered now on the restored village.

Red Bank and Keyport both grew rapidly after steamers started tying up at their docks in the 1830s. Red Bank, called in 1840 "the most rapidly increasing village in the state except for Keyport," carried on a brisk trade in vegetables, wood, and oysters. Keyport, established in 1830, hoped for great importance when promoters began to build a cross-state plank road from Keyport to Florence in 1852. Only short stretches were built before the impracticability of wooden highways became apparent.

Farmers led the way in encouraging railroad ventures, getting behind the Freehold & Jamesburg Railroad in 1853 and the Raritan & Delaware Bay Railroad in 1854. Branch railroads pushed out to the big marl beds at Squankum and Marlboro. A short line carried farm produce from Freehold to Keyport piers. Finally, the building of the New York & Long Branch Railroad in the late 1860s and early 1870s ended traditional dependence on steamboats to take out vegetables or to bring in summer visitors.

The N.Y. & L.B. Railroad, rolling down over the sandy wastes, changed Monmouth County's character from an off-the-beaten-track place for a select few to an area open to nearly all people. However, with the excep-

tion of Long Branch, the North Jersey shore was little frequented before 1870, except by the rare few who could afford to stay all summer.

Take, as prime examples, Ocean Grove and Asbury Park. Only one family lived permanently at Ocean Grove in July 1869, when twenty people pitched their tents on six acres of desolate land that had been purchased for $50.00. They were the first "camp meeting" worshipers. The following year twenty-six members of

Christ Episcopal Church, Shrewsbury, erected in 1769, is topped by an iron British crown on the weathervane. (*N.J.D.C.E.D.*)

the Ocean Grove Camp Meeting Association each put up $25.00 to buy more land. The Association offered this land at an auction of one hundred lots on June 1, 1870, and sold thirty lots for a total of $1,500.

The notion of a religious seaside resort "free from the dissipations and follies of fashionable watering places" caught on with a rush. Sixty cottages were built in Ocean Grove by the end of 871; by 1875 lots purchased for $50.00 at the 1870 auction were selling for $1,500. A

Beehive stack is all that remains of the iron furnace at Allaire, although the state-owned village itself is well preserved. (*N.I.D.C.E.D.*)

covered auditorium seating 3,000 people was opened in 1880.

James A. Bradley, a New York City brush manufacturer, bought the first lot auctioned at Ocean Grove in 1870, but his thoughts dwelt mainly on the briarcovered acres across to the north of Wesley Lake. Not a soul lived on that stretch of beach in 1870. The asking price of $90,000 for 500 acres seemed ridiculously high. Bradley bought, nevertheless, and named his wilderness Asbury Park after the great Methodist bishop Francis Asbury. The first hotel was built in 1873; eight large hotels and hundreds of smaller boardinghouses covered the one-time "Bradley's Folly" in 1878.

Ocean Grove and Asbury Park did not get railroad service until August 28, 1875, when three trains arrived during the day at the depot shared by the towns. Statistics for the station in 1883 proved the transition from wilderness to resort in less than thirteen years. As many as 103 trains ran daily, bringing in 8,000 people in one peak day and a total of 600,000 people between June and September. The record is even more remarkable in view of the fact that trains were not permitted to stop on Sundays in either place until November 1911.

Summer resorts of widely varying natures sprang up in the county. Several of them in the region of the Highlands and the Navesink and Shrewsbury rivers became highly exclusive. Until the late nineteenth century, however, farmers made Wreck Pond near Sea Girt their destination on the second Saturday in August in celebration of "Beach Day." The bucolic visitors traveled many miles in wagons, wearing their bathing suits under their overalls and pinafores going and coming. Sea Girt lost its picnickers' appeal after New Jersey's governor and his staff began visiting the resort every August to review National Guard troops.

Guardsmen held rifle practice on the north side of Manasquan Inlet as early as the summer of 1884, but it was not until 1890 that a large Sea Girt tract was set aside by the state as a National Guard reservation. Men trained there for three wars, although New Jersey Guardsmen also were sent to other camps during World Wars I and II. The Sea Girt camp was employed for the training of army specialists in the twentieth-century wars.

Gustav Kobbé's 1889 guidebook, *The New Jersey Coast and Pines*, had this comment on other Monmouth shore resorts: Spring Lake, "a resort conspicuous for elegance"; Elberon, "laid out with much taste"; Monmouth Beach, "its great charms are privacy and refinement"; Rumson Neck, "on all sides there is evidence that it is controlled by people of wealth and taste"; Sea Bright (where foreign cricket teams and great tennis players always visited), "one of the gayest resorts on the coast."

Long Branch boomed spectacularly after President Ulysses S. Grant made the resort the nation's summer capital with frequent visits after 1868. Presidents Rutherford B. Hayes and Benjamin Harrison stayed at Long Branch's Elberon Hotel, and President James A. Garfield came to die in Elberon after he was shot in Washington in the summer of 1881. Presidents Woodrow Wilson, Chester A. Arthur, and William McKinley also stayed in Long Branch in later years. (The seven presidents are "together" in St. James Chapel in Long Branch in a museum called the Church of the Presidents. Brass plaques on the wall recall the days when all seven worshiped at the church at one time or another.)

The tone of Long Branch changed considerably in the 1890s, as flamboyant characters made "the Branch" their playground. Quite obviously, the red and white bathing flags had long since vanished; males and females now frolicked as they pleased. Phil Daly ran his gambling house even on Sundays, and such Broadway personages as Lillie Langtry, Diamond Jim Brady, and Lillian Russell found the resort to their fancy. The sporting set thought Long Branch wonderful, but Kobbé's guidebook guessed that the place probably repelled as many as it attracted. Kobbé's opinion to the contrary, Long Branch remained one of America's most noted resorts throughout the nineteenth century.

Monmouth Park, in nearby Eatontown, lured the Long Branch betting crowd after racing started in 1870. The racetrack had rocky days until 1878, when a new group took control, increasing the racing season from four days in 1878 to twenty-five days in 1888. Purses jumped in those years from $12,600 to $210,850. As the size of purses went up, the quality of racing fans went down. Indignation against New Jersey racetracks in the

This 1872 engraving from *Leslie's Weekly* shows Long Branch at the height of its glory. (*Newark Library*)

1890s closed them all. A new Monmouth Park, this one opened at Oceanport after World War II, now draws the faithful.

Monmouth County's reputation for fine horses dated to colonial days. As far back as 1840 the Lairds of Colt's Neck trained horses, with the little mare Fashion becoming nationally famous. Joe Laird, who rode Fashion, became known as the "best jockey of the North." Noted stud farms took root in the Eatontown-Tinton Falls-Scobeyville-Holmdel region, where many splendid horse farms still thrive.

The southern part of the Monmouth coast grew slowly during the nineteenth century. Indians long had come to the "Manatasquawhan" River, their name meaning "Stream of the Island for Squaws." English settlers called the river Manasquan for short and Squan Village rose on its banks. Boatbuilder William Brown started operations in 1808, and by 1834 *Gordon's Gazetteer* said Squan's boardinghouses were "much frequented for sea bathing."

Up the coast a bit, Commodore Robert Stockton of Princeton, a U.S. navy hero, built an oceanfront mansion at Sea Girt in 1852. Stockton's mansion was shaped like a ship, to give the illusion of being at sea. The commodore had a farm and a three-quarter-mile racetrack on the property to help him wile away his annual six

Few persons were more esteemed along the Monmouth County beachfront than fishermen, vigorously displayed in this engraving from the 1880s. (*Library of Congress*)

weeks at Sea Girt. Stockton sold his holdings to developers before his death in 1863, just as the area began to grow. Ocean Grove summer residents founded Belmar in 1873, two years before the New York & Long Branch Railroad tracks reached Sea Girt. James Bradley, founder of Asbury Park, established Bradley Beach at the same time.

Colonel L. U. Maltby deserves remembrance in Sea Girt and Spring Lake. The colonel owned the Beach House at Sea Girt and two-thirds of the Monmouth House at Spring Lake in the 1880s when he approached the railroad with a proposition. If the railroad would promise service from Jersey City to Sea Girt in ninety minutes, he would guarantee 150 Wall Street brokers to ride it daily. The railroad compromised at two hours. Maltby made good his promise, and should get major credit for the influx of commuters to Monmouth County.

Ailing author Robert Louis Stevenson visited Manasquan for six weeks in 1888. While there he wrote part of *The Master of Ballantrae* in the old Union House. Artists and writers came often to the wild seaside near Manasquan to walk the sands and watch the fishing boats returning from the sea through Manasquan Inlet.

Few of New Jersey's counties had their characters so firmly set at the turn of the century as Monmouth. By then farming had become the predominant year-round economic base, although marl had largely given way to more balanced fertilizers. Potato raising grew rapidly; Monmouth County was far out in front of all New Jersey potato-raising areas up through the 1940s. Monmouth also had become a year-round place for commuters.

Throughout Monmouth's long life the sea has been the background for most of the action, bringing pirates, colonists, enemy troops, vacationists, and commuters (more or less in that order). Sandy Hook lighthouse and

Navesink's twin lighthouses blinked security to vessels on the Atlantic's swelling surf. Still, through the years ships have smashed upon Monmouth's shores—such as the *New Era*, which broke up in December 1854 off Deal Beach, with a loss of five hundred lives, and the *Morro Castle*, whose burning hulk drifted to rest at Asbury Park in September 1934.

Bootleggers came by sea in the Thirsty Twenties. Atop the Highlands, in a home formerly owned by Oscar Hammerstein, illicit liquor salesmen erected one of the nation's most powerful radio stations. They supplied customers from Maine to Florida before a 1929 raid broke up the ring (or, more truthfully, moved it elsewhere).

Manasquan Inlet also had its visitations by bootleggers during the Prohibition period, when a speedy dash into the inlet foiled government pursuers. However, that wide waterline dividing Monmouth and Ocean counties became better known as a haven for private and public fishing boats and as the start of the important Inland Waterway stretching all the way to Florida.

Sandy Hook's exposed position made it a logical spot for military emplacements. A fort was started at the tip of the hook before the Civil War, but by the 1890s it had not been finished. Then the Hook reverberated to the sound of a proving range when smokeless powder developed by Hudson Maxim at Farmingdale was tested on Sandy Hook in 1893. The Hook's Fort Hancock served the nation in World Wars I and II.

If an anonymous Irish marl digger and an unnamed elderly lady boardinghousekeeper can get credit for the early pattern of Monmouth County development, look at two twentieth-century happenings that profoundly shaped the county's more recent transformation from a farming-seaside county into part of the metropolis surrounding New York. These two are Fort Monmouth and the Garden State Parkway.

Fort Monmouth started in 1917 as a small Signal Corps development center, at a time when military communications was not far removed from the days of wigwag flags, carrier pigeons, and battlefront telegraph keys. Gradually the army consolidated its electronics research at Fort Monmouth. It has contributed mightily to radio, radar, satellites, and many other electronics miracles.

Today Fort Monmouth is headquarters of the Communications Electronics Command (CECOM). More than six thousand people work in various CECOM projects in Monmouth County, with more than 80 percent of them civilian personnel. Equally vital to the local economy, some forty electronics firms of varying sizes flourish in Monmouth County as a result of Fort Monmouth's rapid spin-off of electronics ideas.

Chief of all the electronics "babies" spawned by Fort Monmouth is the Bell Telephone Laboratories, handsomely housed in a six-story glass tower in Holmdel. Work on the $34-million facility began in 1959 and was finished in 1966. More than four thousand people work in the glass castle.

Fort Monmouth's importance to Momouth County's well-being received dramatic underscoring in 1993 when the federal government considered it as one of the bases to be closed in a nationwide economy move. The threat created near-panic in the area, but fortunately for the county, Fort Monmouth was spared the fatal blow.

The broad fields west of Red Bank are host to a thriving number of thoroughbred farms.

Just as Fort Monmouth's prominence set a solid base for the county economy, completion of the Garden State Parkway in 1954 set in motion a string of opportunities for lumberyards, plumbing shops, builders, carpenters and other artisans, banks, and perhaps most of all, real estate offices.

Swarms of people streamed into the county seeking homes as close to the Jersey Shore as possible, grateful that the Parkway enabled them to commute by automobile to Newark or New York City. Potato fields, pasturelands, and hillsides fell before the onslaught of home developers. Property values soared.

Population statistics told the story. Between 1954 and 1960, more than 100,000 new people moved into the county. Another 130,000 newcomers occupied development homes between 1960 and 1970. By 1990, Monmouth's population of 553,124 placed it fourth among the state's counties, albeit by a mere twenty-five people ahead of Hudson County. Before the population explosion erupted in 1954, Monmouth ranked ninth.

Despite the boom, only seven of the county's fifty-seven municipalities had major growth. Of the seven, old Middletown Township, one of the oldest settled areas in the county, had the most startling rise, from 16,203 in 1950 to nearly 70,000 forty years later. Howell Township, with 6,696 residents in 1950, had a population just under 40,000 in 1990. Raritan Township expanded its population eleven times between 1950 and 1976 and in the process changed its name to Hazlet.

Year-round population in the string of shore towns from Atlantic Highlands through such resorts as Sea Bright, Monmouth Beach, Deal, Allenhurst, Belmar, and Manasquan has had surprisingly little increase in the decades since World War II. Their year-round populations were small then; they are small now. The two largest shore towns, Asbury Park and Long Branch, also have remained stable in population, averaging about 17,000 for Asbury Park, about 25,000 to 28,000 for Long Branch.

All of the coastal towns come vividly alive during

Fort Monmouth's five-sided "Little Pentagon," center of U.S. Army research and development on electronics, is an outgrowth of a small Signal Corps center opened in World War I.

July and August, swelled by renters, guests, and the day-trippers who still pour down on the Garden State Parkway to beaches nearest to crowded northern New Jersey.

Monmouth County has absorbed all of the permanent newcomers and continues to host the summertime crowds. Despite the swelled population the county continues to have pleasant, wide-open land. Old Tennent Church is graceful and serene. Churches and historic homes in Middletown, Freehold, and Shrewsbury are well preserved. Estate country abounds in the Lincroft-Holmdel-Scobeyville region. Horse farms are extensive west of Red Bank. The Monmouth Battleground has been preserved to remember that day in June 1778. Allaire State Park is a mixture of history and rich, green country. Sandy Hook, a beckoning peninsula of mystery, is saved, part as a state park, the rest in the federal Gateway National Recreation Area. Nearby, the Highlands of the Navesink are wooded and exciting.

Gone are the days when families came by train with a myriad of trunks and suitcases to spend the summer. The "day-tripper" speeds in and out of seaside towns, coming in the morning and going home on the Garden State Parkway. Monmouth is well on its way to being much more than a place for a long vacation. It has become, instead, a wonderful place in which to live a pleasant life.

Built in 1751, Old Tennent Church overlooks the site where the Battle of Monmouth took place in blazing heat on June 28, 1778. Several of the battle's victims are buried nearby. (*Walter Choroszewski*)

The inhabitants of southern Monmouth County who split away in 1850 to form Ocean County were a frugal lot. Thus their grandiose decision to model their courthouse after Hudson County's had to be modified by the proviso that it be "smaller and less ornate." That original brick courthouse remains in Toms River as the core of a county building complex greatly expanded in 1950.

OCEAN

EBB AND FLOW

County founders wasted little time in naming Ocean County after its separation from Monmouth on February 18, 1850. Simply and directly they titled their land in recognition of their dependence on the sea, and if in their hearts they also meant to recognize the alternate savagery and lure of the surf, so much the better.

There was no casting about to pay tribute to some English nobleman or a remembered English shire town. So many diversified nationalities had drifted in and out of Ocean County by 1850 that an "English" title would not have been logical. Besides, with a coastline of 50 miles and 150 years of sea-linked memories, why anything but Ocean? All the county's rich past—and hope for the future—went into that simple name.

Henry Hudson took a faraway look at Ocean County's beachfront in 1609 as his *Half Moon* sailed off the coast. He did not stop, but his ship's log left an easily recognizable description of Barnegat Bay and Inlet: "We came to a great lake of water, as we could judge it to be. . . . The mouth of that lake hath many shoals, and the sea breaketh on them as it is cast out of the mouth of it."

Captain Jacobsen Mey, a much-traveled Dutchman, took a closer look on a voyage from New Amsterdam in 1614. He bestowed two names which have nearly withstood the anglicizing tides of time—Barende-gat (Bar-

negat or "Inlet of Breakers") and Eyre Haven ("Egg Harbor").

Nomadic fishermen and whalers put in to Barnegat and Egg Harbor bays soon after Mey's visit and mingled with the Lenape Indians who frequented the shore in summertime looking for sea food and shells for wampum. Occasionally a ship flying the Jolly Roger dropped anchor off the coast. The pirates came to bury treasure, the excitable say. More likely, they came seeking fresh water. Other ships foundered on the shoals and cast their passengers upon the sands. The coming of people to this area was by way of the ocean, willingly or otherwise.

Some of the early arrivers stayed without the formality of buying the land, possibly reflecting to themselves that English noblemen had no more right to split up land sight unseen than they had to settle, sight seen. Captain William Tom, English official from Newcastle, Delaware, looked into the area in about 1673, and for his looking had Toms River—creek and town—named after him.

However, Henry Jacobs Falkinburg of Schleswig-Holstein became the first legitimate settler. He bought eight hundred acres from the East New Jersey Proprietors in 1698 near what is now Tuckerton. At about the same time Mordecai and Edward Andrews, Quaker brothers from Oyster Bay, Long Island, bought land nearby. Edward Andrews built the first gristmill on the New Jersey coast in 1704, powering his millstones with water from a pond created by energetic South Jersey beavers.

Others who came before 1720 represented varying nationalities and creeds. Most of them were squatters and admitted it. They wished merely to be left alone and they did not bother others. A minister who toured the coast seeking souls wrote this about settlers along that lonely oceanfront in 1750: "Some are decent people, who have lived in better places; but those who were born and bred here have neither religion nor manners." His writings also revealed his rather meager success in conversions, which undoubtedly colored his interpretations of human actions.

Two noted Quaker missionaries from Tuckerton—Ann Gauntt and her niece Ann Willet—attained far greater fame than that bitter itinerant preacher while they intermittently toured North Atlantic states from 1728 until the Revolution, quietly spreading the word.

Rogerine Baptists came to Waretown in 1737. Members of a sect founded in New England by John Rogers, the Rogerines refused to observe Sunday as a special day, believing that all days were equally holy. They refused medicine, prayed silently, and worked at such things as sewing or making axe handles during services. A small band of them met in a Waretown schoolhouse from 1737 to 1748, only to find no peace. They went to Morris County, hoping in vain for a better world.

More successful was the founding in 1766 of the first Universalist Church in America. Thomas Potter erected his own church building at Good Luck in 1766, then waited patiently for a preacher to arrive who would reflect his own liberal views of a universal God. Four years later, John Murray, stranded when an English sloop went aground nearby, came to Potter's house seeking food. Murray and Potter talked, learning that each believed in a just and loving God, in a time when most religious leaders looked upon God as stern and harsh. Murray agreed to stay and preach in Potter's church. The Universalist Church in America grew from that little spot named Good Luck near the barren New Jersey coast.

Sawmills dotted the county's numerous creeks before 1760. Dozens of sailing vessels set out for distant markets from Toms River or Tuckerton before the Revolution. Steady streams of fish-laden wagons left the coast to trundle through the Pine Barrens, headed for Mount Holly and Philadelphia, where their fish was prized.

The nature of their occupations and their personal characteristics made these coastwise people willing to undertake war with England or with anyone else who threatened the independence that they had declared long before July 4, 1776. Privateering became a way of life; the chance of fat profits helped induce sailing men to undertake risks in the name of patriotism. Privateers easily slipped out of Barnegat Bay and Little Egg Harbor to attack the King's shipping, then deftly slipped back in to sell their captured cargoes in Toms River or Tuckerton. Many of the supplies were taken to Philadelphia. No one asked any questions.

Privateers sailed into and out of the Atlantic Ocean through Cranberry Inlet, directly east of Toms River. The fifteen-foot-deep channel allowed two- and three-masted schooners to maneuver into the upper Barnegat Bay area until a violent storm in 1812 closed the inlet. It was a boon to the Revolutionists while it lasted.

The most valuable captured vessel was the *Love and Unity*, brought through Cranberry Inlet to Toms River. She carried several thousand bottles of London porter and Bristol beer; eighty hogsheads of loaf sugar; quantities of salt, flour, and cheese as well as fine china and glassware. Soon after, four British ships lay in wait outside the inlet and recaptured the vessel as she set sail under her new colors to seek more booty.

Toms River gained unique Revolutionary importance as the site of salt works established by the Continental Congress and the State of Pennsylvania. Congress spent £6,000 (about $30,000) to set up its works, while Pennsylvania expended £400. Later, many other private salt works flourished along the coast, since the flavoring and preservation of many kinds of food depended on salt. The installations at Toms River were the largest and most important.

A windmill pumped salt water from Barnegat Bay to vats near Toms River, where evaporation under the hot sun turned the saltwater into brine. This in turn was

Evidences of Ocean County's continuing dependence on the sea are the commercial and sport fishing docks at Point Pleasant and elsewhere along the coast.

boiled down into salt worth $15.00 a bushel in Toms River and $35.00 a bushel in Morristown, where it was used in making gunpowder. The British considered the salt manufactories vital, too, and in 1778 sent an expedition of 135 men to destroy all of the salt works along the coast, with special attention to the operations at Toms River.

Only about two thousand people lived in present-day Ocean County at the end of the Revolution. Ocean-going trade revived quickly (if, indeed, it ever stopped). Oysters became a chief export from Barnegat Bay, where a provincial law enacted in 1719 forbade gathering the shellfish from May 10 to September 1. This pioneering effort to save the oyster beds kept the trade alive for nearly two centuries.

President Washington signed papers during his first term to make Tuckerton the port of entry for thirty miles of coast from Barnegat Inlet south to Brigantine Inlet. Tuckerton's harbor business spurted and its shipbuilders assumed leadership. An 1823 visitor reported the harbor full of ships and the place "rich in money," with taverns and boardinghouses full and hundreds of men cutting timber for the shipbuilders.

One of Tuckerton's shipbuilding families, the Shrouds, built the *Lorainer*, said to be the first brig (or brigantine) made. The two-masted, square-rigged vessel won lasting attention as one of the most popular sailing types ever built.

Elsewhere, at Waretown, Toms River, Barnegat, and Forked River, shipbuilders fashioned whaleboats, oyster boats, and smaller craft for coastwise commerce, leaving the larger vessels to Tuckerton. Ocean County masters sailed the world and the little boy who didn't dream of growing up to follow the sea was rare. To be a "captain" was to be a king in one's own sight, although most of the captains' vessels were far smaller than ships of the line.

Another important early part of the county's economic welfare started modestly in 1789, when David Wright lit the first fire in his iron furnace near what is now Lakehurst. An extensive works followed at Staffordsville in 1797 and by 1812 other forges hummed near Laurelton (Butcher's Forge), near Lakewood (Washington Furnace), on Bamber Lake (Ferrago Furnace), and on the headwaters of Cedar Creek (Dover Forge).

At first the ironworks depended on local bog ore, but later ships brought in iron ore from the Fishkill region on the Hudson River. Butcher's Forge made water pipe for New York City and mule teams hauled quantities of iron across the state from Dover Forge to Philadelphia. Ferrago Furnace turned out bar iron in what authorities called "one of the best planned and built forges in New Jersey."

Ocean's ironworks all had disappeared by the Civil War. Possibly the most lasting contribution of the forges was the fact that William Torrey, Sr., and Joseph W. Brick both came to seek fortunes in iron and stayed to bring new life to the Pines through other ventures.

Torrey bought 27,500 acres of woodland surrounding the old Wright Forge (at what is now Lakehurst) in 1841 to make charcoal on a large scale. He built a railroad to Toms River, using wooden rails and mule-drawn charcoal-carrying cars. Fifteen years later Torrey and his sons, William and John, stood up to the powerful Camden & Amboy Railroad monopoly and demanded a charter for a railroad across South Jersey between Raritan Bay and the lower Delaware River, passing through the western part of Ocean County. The Torreys won the right to start their Raritan & Delaware Bay Railroad in

1854. Completion of the railroad in 1860 opened the pinelands to outside interests for the first time.

Joseph Brick, meanwhile, rebuilt the old Washington Furnace in 1833 and saw it thrive before his death in 1847. His family carried on and the area became known as Bricksburg (now Lakewood) in his honor. In addition, the pretty lake that powered Brick's works was given the name of Carasaljo—combining the first syllables of the names of Joseph W. Brick's three daughters, Caroline, Sally, and Josephine.

Elsewhere in the Pines, John Webb—best known as "Old Peg-Leg John"—drained a swamp near Cassville in 1845 and grew cultivated cranberries, which netted him high sums in Philadelphia, whose sailing masters thought cranberries prevented scurvy on long voyages. Webb's success prompted neighbors to engage in modest cranberry plantings of their own.

Despite the quickened activities in the Pines, most life centered on the coast, where fear of the sea haunted coastal folk as much as love of it lured them. The treacherous shoals of Barnegat pounded ships to pieces and flung their cargoes and their dead and dying passengers on the sands. Hulks of ships destroyed by the moody ocean littered the outer islands. The coast from Point Pleasant to Little Egg Harbor truly merited its reputation as the most dreaded shoals north of Cape Hatteras.

Congress took official notice in 1834 by building the original Barnegat lighthouse at a cost of $6,000. The angry ocean fought back, licking away at the sands until the beacon toppled into Barnegat Inlet in 1856. Congress immediately appropriated $60,000 for a new 168-foot-tall light, built in 1857 and 1858 under the direction of Lieutenant George Gordon Meade, the U.S. army engineer who five years later commanded Union forces at the Battle of Gettysburg. F. Hopkinson Smith, author and playwright, worked on the lighthouse as an engineer, and in his spare time started to write his seaside classic, *The Tides of Barnegat*.

The cruelty of the ocean struck young Dr. William A. Newell with full force during a visit to Long Beach Island in August 1839. Out on the beach at the height of a summer storm, young Dr. Newell watched the Austrian brig *Count Perasto* break up on a sand bar only three hundred yards from shore. His horror mounted as, one by one, the captain and his crew of twelve drowned in the surf, with watchers powerless to help.

As Dr. Newell mourned the dead he conceived the idea of tossing a line to stricken ships by means of a shortened blunderbuss. Elected to Congress in 1846, Dr. Newell offered a resolution in 1848 which laid the foundation of the United States Lifesaving Service, forerunner of the present U.S. Coast Guard rescue stations. The sum of $10,000 was appropriated to provide surfboats and rope-tossing equipment along the Jersey coast. Appropriately, the country's first two nationally supported lifesaving stations were built in Ocean County.

At about the same time, Joseph Francis of Toms River, noted boatbuilder, also sought a means to snatch victims from the sea. In 1843 he built the first corrugated metal lifeboat and a year later invented an unsinkable life car. The life car and Newell's idea of a rope fired from a gun were merged on January 12, 1850, at Chadwick's on Squan Beach, where the Scottish barque *Ayrshire* struck a sandbar after she foundered in a blinding snowstorm.

Newell's system was used to fire a lifeline over the *Ayrshire*, and Francis's life car brought all 201 passengers safely ashore. John Maxen, who that night became the first man ever to throw a lifeline over a helpless vessel, received a gold medal for his feat and Congress honored Francis by striking a medal in his honor, said to be the "most massive gold medal" ever awarded by that body.

So, with thoughts of gallantry at sea fresh in their minds, the county's founding fathers really had no choice but Ocean as the name for their land after it split from Monmouth County in 1850. The booming pinewood and charcoal trade, as well as the prosperous shipyards, made people in the ocean-oriented region increasingly aware that Monmouth County government at Freehold overlooked their special problems.

The new county started with about 550 square miles of former Monmouth County land, stretching nearly forty miles along the shore from Manasquan River to the southern tip of Long Beach Island. Its western line, the divider from Burlington, followed the East–West Jersey line drawn by surveyor George Keith in 1687.

County decisions came painfully. For example,

Shipwrecks, an awesome fact of life along the shore, prompted William Newell of Ocean County to start lifesaving service.

economy-minded freeholders coldly rejected the first budget of $2,000, then settled on $1,800 as sufficient for Ocean County's 10,032 inhabitants. A courthouse commission chose Hudson County's splendid court as a model, but agreed that the Ocean structure must be "smaller and less ornate." Completion of the red-brick building on June 13, 1851, satisfied most, although some grumbled that $9,956 was far too much money to spend on any courthouse.

Despite the sparse population and the absence of even one lawyer in the entire county, Ocean saw one of its sons, Dr. George F. Fort of New Egypt, elected governor in 1850. Three years later another Ocean gubernatorial

Barnegat Light, known to millions of summer visitors as "Old Barney," is probably the best-known landmark along the entire Jersey Shore. (*N.J.D.C.E.D.*)

candidate, the Reverend Joel Haywood, lost by only 3,782 votes, and William A. Newell's election as the state's first Republican governor in 1856 brought joy to Ocean County, which felt that Newell's lifesaving activities on Long Beach Island made him at least an adopted son.

A cranberry craze swept the county in 1863. Everyone who had money or could borrow it started growing cranberries. Swampland became priceless and even pine barrens brought a hundred dollars an acre. The craze killed itself; as soon as the vastly expanded bogs bore fruit, cranberry prices collapsed. When cranberry growing settled down to a sane existence, growers formed one of the state's first farmer cooperatives at Bricksburg. Cranberries became a solid income producer.

Scores of families bought lots in 1866 when the Bricksburg Land & Improvement Company assured them that the soil could grow fruit trees in profusion. Two New York Stock Exchange brokers bought nineteen thousand acres of land at Bricksburg in 1879, built the Laurel House, changed the town's name to Lakewood—and wisely decided to capitalize on the pine trees rather than the apple trees.

Men of wealth followed the trail to the Ocean County Pine Barrens in search of the healthful pine air; Lakewood became one of the nation's earliest winter health resorts. Estates also flowered in Lakewood's pines, the most noteworthy being those of George Jay Gould and John D. Rockefeller. Both of these still exist, the Gould estate now being occupied by Georgian Court College and the Rockefeller estate being one of the largest county parks in New Jersey.

Out along the coast, shipping by boat gave way to shipping by rail in the 1870s. Fishing, clamming, and oystering zoomed in economic stature, and for years a standing joke in the state legislature was to call any bill dealing with oysters or clams an "Ocean County bill," a tacit recognition of the importance of oystering and clamming to the county before the pollution of Barnegat Bay.

Seaside resorts sprang up beside the railroads in the 1870s. Point Pleasant Land Company started selling lots in 1870, the same year that a group of Philadelphia

St. Vladimir's Church at Cassville is a copy of a sixteenth century Russian chapel. (*O.C.P.B.*)

Quakers founded Beach Haven. Seaside Park began as a Baptist religious resort in 1876, and a Methodist camp meeting came to Island Heights in 1878. Bay Head, started in 1883, became very fashionable, luring bathers from as far away as Washington. A railroad built on Long Beach Island in 1885 provided the potential for resorts strung along that long, narrow strand.

Ocean County was fully resort-minded by 1900. Seaside towns broke away from larger townships to ensure use of local taxes to build up their resort facilities. Barnegat Bay became a prime hunting and fishing ground for sportsmen, with Forked River, Waretown, and Barnegat all vying for the trade of gentleman gunners and anglers.

Staunchly Republican Ocean County received a left-handed gift from the Democrat-controlled state legislature in 1891. The Democrats wrote off Ocean County as impossible to convert to their cause, but reckoned they had a chance in Burlington. Accordingly, they cut Little Egg Harbor Township (and its Republican votes) away from Burlington and added the township to Ocean.

World War I brought a chemical warfare proving ground to Lakehurst to train troops in handling poison gas. The camp became a navy lighter-than-air craft base

Forked River's marina has been a haven for privately owned yachts and other pleasure boats for more than sixty years. (*Walter Choroszewski*)

Island Beach, whose long dunes are among the finest in the East. (*N.J.D.C.E.D.*)

after the war, and the first American-built dirigible, the *Shenandoah*, made her maiden flight from Lakehurst in 1923. After a series of accidents to American dirigibles, the ill-fated airships fell into total disfavor on May 6, 1937, when the German airship *Hindenburg* burned in midair at Lakehurst with a loss of thirty-six lives. The navy still uses Lakehurst, but even the blimp program was abandoned in the early 1960s.

Varied groups of immigrants started to arrive in Ocean County after World War I, notably the White Russians, who settled near Cassville, and Scandinavians, who found work in the county's offshore fisheries. An Ocean County journalist pointed out in 1923 that the county's "old Anglo-Saxon flavor is disappearing." Then, during the 1930s, refugees from Adolf Hitler's savage slaughter of Jews began to arrive. Many of them became chicken farmers.

Agriculture, which had been confined to the cran-

One of the nation's foremost natural seaside areas is Island Beach State Park, purchased by New Jersey in 1952. (*Walter Choroszewski*)

it that a person could sit beside two-lane Route 9 at Forked River after Labor Day and "see only a dozen cars all morning." Then the Garden State Parkway came in 1954, paralleling the oceanfront about three or four miles west of Barnegat Bay and eight to ten miles from the sands of Long Beach Island or the several resorts between Point Pleasant and Seaside Park.

By 1960, only six years after the Parkway's arrival, Ocean County population had nearly doubled. Thirty years later, the county population of 433,203 placed it ninth among counties. The density soared to 676 people per square mile.

About 75 percent of the growth has come within about ten miles of the Parkway, mainly to the west in former Pine Barrens wilderness. Dover Township (including Toms River) straddles the Parkway. Its population of 76,371 placed it tenth among New Jersey municipalities in 1990. If a local Rip Van Winkle came back to Toms River he could not fathom the miles of gasoline stations, fast food outlets, and restaurants ranged along roads leading to the ocean.

Settlements on the western shore of Barnegat Bay are centered on artificial lagoons. Many of the houses here have large boats docked beside them. In these lagoons and in the nearby pinelands, nearly all of the homes are for year-round living, in marked contrast with pre-Parkway days when Ocean County's economy thrived largely on the vacation months of July and August.

Many of the homes built during the boom have been well-planned, small, and for the most part well-built homes for retired people, eager for a less expensive life amid the reputed healthfulness of the pine woodlands of Lakewood and Jackson townships. Many areas are inhabited entirely by retirees in "villages" complete with recreation areas and medical facilities. Ocean County has one of the nation's fastest growing concentrations of older persons.

The oceanfront remains the magic ingredient, nevertheless, both for the year-round people and for the scores of thousands who flock every summer to Seaside Heights, Point Pleasant, Bay Head, Mantoloking, Normandy Beach, Ocean Beach, Lavalette, and the several towns on Long Beach Island. The latter is linked to the mainland by a high-level causeway, much to the delight

berry bogs and the blueberry patches—plus a small dairy and fruit area surrounding New Egypt—moved rapidly ahead in the 1920s. By 1925 the Toms River district had become known as one of the nation's most progressive poultry centers. Poultry products meant $14 million annual income to Ocean County in the 1950s. Then, as the nation began blaming cholesterol on eggs, sales plummeted. Nearly all of the poultry farms disappeared.

Startling transformations have taken place in Ocean County since 1950, when only 56,622 people lived in the county's 641 square miles. A county saying then had

of Long Beach Island's merchants and real estate agents, but considerably to the concern of those who fear that the island's beauty is steadily being bulldozed for housing developments, lagoons, and malls.

Rapid development will not overtake all of the seafront, fortunately. The State of New Jersey after World War I talked on and off for thirty years of buying Island Beach. When a real estate company began to move in on the property in 1952, the state acted promptly and bought the ten-mile-long peninsula for $2.75 million. It was a magnificent bargain, since the area had been in private hands for decades. Only a few homes were scattered among the trees and ground cover. Island Beach was, and is, a magnet for naturalists. The state has constructed both houses and parking lots on a portion of the property, but most of the strip remains in a natural state for surf fishing, birdwalks, and beach plums. Island Beach is one of New Jersey's ecological showcases.

Despite its population gain, Ocean County is far from crowded. At least 60 percent of its land is open. Schemers have proposed everything from giant jetports to big planned cities to fill up the beckoning spaces.

Meanwhile, the pine woodlands stretch wide and free west of Lakewood and Toms River. Cranberry bogs and blueberry plantations break the landscape in spots, but very few houses appear beside the roads.

Proof of available open space is Jackson Township, with an area of 101 square miles—more than twice the size of Hudson County (46 square miles). Great Adventure, one of the nation's most unusual combinations of wild animals (*real* wild animals, such as lions, tigers, elephants, and monkeys) and an amusement park, opened in 1974. Great Adventure sprawls across the landscape, yet the facility takes up less than 3 percent of Jackson land. The township has acquired people, too, growing from about six thousand in 1960 to more than thirty-three thousand now. Most of Jackson's new people came via Interstate Route 195, which links Trenton and the Garden State Parkway at Brick Town.

Ocean County still looks to the Atlantic, whence it took its name in 1850. Today's fortunes still follow the sea, and the fact is that renting or selling houses is far more rewarding (in dollars, certainly) than going down to the sea in ships ever was. Ocean it is: Ocean forever.

The first Atlantic County court proceedings took place on July 25, 1837, five months after the county was split from Gloucester. The proceedings were in a Mays Landing tavern, but within a year a red-brick courthouse had been built nearby—fifteen years before Atlantic City was founded. The renovated courthouse still stands in a grove of old oak trees, the center of an enlarging complex of Atlantic County offices.

ATLANTIC

QUEEN OF THE COAST

Atlantic County comes startlingly together for anyone striding across the widespread marshes of the Forsthye National Wildlife Refuge near Brigantine on an early evening in October. Disturbed migrating birds soar upward in the dusk, the fluttering of their wings and their raucous protests breaking the deep silence. Southeastward, six miles across Reed's Bay, the brightly-lit towers of Atlantic City rise to symbolize casino town, the gathering place for humans frantic to meet Lady Luck.

That in capsule is Atlantic County, known best only for Atlantic City, the cluster of towns along Route 9 and the Garden State Parkway, and the few settled spots beside the White Horse Pike (Route 30), which begins in Atlantic City and stretches westward across the United States. Outward from those relatively small areas stretches wide-open, sparsely settled Atlantic County.

The marshes have been there for thousands of years. Atlantic City dates back only to 1854, but for every person who visits the wildlife refuge, an estimated fifty thousand flock to the slot machines and blackjack tables. It's a safe bet that none of the fortune-seekers ever heard of (or cared to hear of) Dr. Jonathan Pitney, who might well be their patron saint.

Just out of medical school in New York City, young Pitney arrived in the mainland village of Absecon in May 1820, reining his horse to a stop at Hannah Holmes's Tavern. He had ridden from Mendham in far-off Morris County and he told loungers on the tavern steps that he aimed to stay. The welcome was spontaneous; if there was one thing this sandy stretch at the edge of the Pine Barrens needed it was a doctor. Absecon was glad he aimed to stay—and he did, for forty-nine busy years.

Pitney soon realized something that the oyster fishermen at Leed's Point and the saltmakers on nearby Absegami Island failed to grasp: that here on the edge of the rolling Atlantic Ocean was an earthly paradise waiting for humans. Here among the unpopulated sand dunes was health and here was wealth. No one begrudged Doc Pitney that odd notion in 1820, so forty years later when many called him "The Father of Atlantic City" no one begrudged him the title, either.

Dr. Pitney's coming overland from the mountainland to the north excited wonder and curiosity along the beach. Few visitors arrived by way of the sandy roads, for through the years the Atlantic Ocean had been the means to bring strangers to the coast. The Mullica, Great Egg Harbor, and Tuckahoe rivers had been the thoroughfares leading inland through the dense, forbidding pine forest.

Early in the 1600s bold adventurers had come to hunt whales off the coast. Eric Mullica, a venturesome

Separating Atlantic and Burlington counties, the slow-moving Mullica River is cherished by boating enthusiasts, conservationists, and lovers of flora and fauna. (*N.I.D.C.E.D.*)

Swede, explored in the 1640s the river that bears his name. Eric Mullica had come to stay. Considerably less interested in colonization were pirates like Blackbeard and his ilk, who tradition says found the countless bays and coves to the west of Absegami Island made to order for anyone seeking to elude pursuers.

Deep in the pine forest back from the coast, Philadelphia entrepreneurs exploited the easily worked bog iron they found in the riverbeds. One of the earliest of the ironmen was Charles Read of Burlington, who established a series of forges in Burlington and Atlantic counties during the 1760s. He built ironworks at Batsto in 1766, utilizing both the iron in the streams and the

plentiful nearby timber for fuel. Lumbermen and fishermen, as well as pineland squatters, willingly accepted his offers of employment.

Enterprising George May sailed up the deep Great Egg Harbor River in 1760 to open a store that supplied vessels putting in for timber at the head of the tide. Soon he also exchanged timber and bog iron for salt, rice, and indigo from the Carolinas. By the time of the Revolutionary War, May's Landing prospered, and a humming shipbuilding business added to its vitality as a trading center.

Batsto's ironmen helped Continental troops with products from their forge, but the embryonic Atlantic

County's greatest roles in the Revolution were played by its sailors. The same bays which had so nobly served whalers and pirates also proved splendid ports of call for privateers, who slipped out into the ocean to maul British shipping. The privateers did much for the cause, and well enough for themselves, too, with sales of cargoes from captured royal vessels. The British labeled the Mullica River area a "nest of rebel pirates."

Lieutenant General Sir Henry Clinton decided upon punitive action. He sent four hundred British troops ashore at Chestnut Neck on October 6, 1778, with orders to "seize, pillage, burn and destroy that place!" The invaders, covered by gunfire from an offshore fleet, swarmed over the thin breastworks of the village defenders. The routed colonial forces retreated up the Mullica River to make another stand, certain that the British would try to destroy the inland ironworks at Batsto. Chestnut Neck fell to the British torch but the triumphant redcoats refused to chase into the woods after the fleeing Americans.

After destroying ten vessels anchored off Chestnut Neck, the redcoats returned to their ships. They waited more than a week, then sent 250 men across the salt marsh to attack a picket post commanded by Lieutenant Colonel Baron Bose. The attackers struck hard, killing Bose and forty-four of his men. Americans led by Count Casimir Pulaski hastened to help Bose, but they arrived too late. The home troops had one consolation: as the British fleet sailed away, their mighty new flagship, the *Zebra*, ran aground. Rather than risk capture by the Americans, the British fired the ship and scuttled her.

Life went on in the forests, marred at times by the exploits of renegade Tory refugees, led by handsome Joe Mulliner, a man with a liking for wine, women, and song. It was said that Mulliner never let pass an opportunity to steal from the rich, but there is ample evidence that he would steal from anyone. As if to excuse Joe—a good talker and a good mixer—some said he was "a regular Robin Hood, stealing from them as had, and giving to them as didn't." Mainly, he gave to himself.

Mulliner was captured in a tavern near Pleasant Mills in the summer of 1781. Reporting his death by hanging on August 8, 1781, the *New Jersey Gazette* said, "This fellow had become the terror of the country. He had made a practice of burning houses, robbing and plundering all who fell in his way, so that when he came to trial it appeared that the whole country, both Whigs and Tories, were his enemies."

Long after, in 1855, Charles Peterson used the Mulliner story and Revolutionary War life near the iron furnace as the basis for the first truly New Jersey novel, *Kate Aylesford, or The Life of the Refugees*. Today an old house in Sweetwater is known as "The Aylesford Mansion" after Peterson's fictional heroine.

Inland bog iron establishments reached their peak in about 1820. William Richards acquired the Batsto works in 1784 and rebuilt them. He also started the Gloucester Furnace in Landing Creek in 1785–86, on a huge tract of timberland that abutted Batsto Furnace property. The major Atlantic County iron operation was at Weymouth (Batsto was across the Mullica River in Burlington, although its influence was widely felt on both sides of the river).

Charles Shoemaker, George Ashbridge, Morris Robeson, John Paul, and Joseph Paul established Weymouth Furnace in 1801 on an immense tract of 78,060 acres. By 1802, Ashbridge, the manager, was advertising for a "full set of forgemen to work a new forge, now erected and in complete order."

The Weymouth enterprise became uncommonly large. Eight large wagonloads of charcoal were fed into the maw of the thirty-foot-high furnace each day. Two men at the top of the furnace dumped six baskets of charcoal every few minutes over the iron that was melting below. Huge bellows driven by water power kept the blast hot enough to maintain a stream of molten metal running out the bottom of the furnace. The melted iron ran into molds to cast stove parts, iron pipes, and hitching posts. Philadelphia's first water pipes came from Weymouth in 1801, and many a hitching post in that city bore the big "W" of the woodland iron empire. Iron markers often were cast for graves and enough of these still remain in Atlantic County graveyards to confirm the boast that bog iron was "nonrusting."

Other industrialists joined ironmasters in seeking fortunes in the forests. William Coffin and Jonathan Haines built a glassworks in 1817 on a tract that Coffin named Hammond Town (Hammonton) for his son,

John Hammond Coffin. William Lippincott built a cotton textile factory at Sweetwater in about 1825 and named it Pleasant Mills. John H. Scott built a glass factory at Estellville in 1825 to make window glass and bottles. The Pine Barrens gave the region what little economic strength it had.

Pitney and others kept alive a long-smoldering agitation to separate from Gloucester County. Residents near the shore had asked for separation as early as 1785 and 1786, but the state legislature refused to act. By 1835 even the Gloucester County Board of Freeholders (which would lose land) resolved that a division would "greatly promote the convenience and the interest of all sections of the county."

Prolonged debate preceded the separation, but on February 7, 1837, it was agreed that two new counties, Passaic and Atlantic, could be created. Atlantic took 613 of Gloucester's original square miles and Gloucester allowed the seceders $6,947.75 as their share of the Gloucester County buildings. Pitney became first director of the Atlantic County Board of Freeholders.

The thinly settled county had only about eighty-five hundred residents within its borders. Few debated the choice of centrally located May's Landing as county seat. It was scarcely a major town, with three taverns, four stores, one Methodist Church, and twenty-five or thirty houses. The start of construction of the county's red-brick courthouse in 1838 stirred the little village into awareness that at last it had a future.

Mays Landing as it appeared in an 1842 woodcut already was busy, although Atlantic County was only five years old. (*Barber and Howe*)

Possibly the least appealing spot in all of the new Atlantic County was the coast, particularly the long off-shore Absecon Island, which had been the haven of pirates and squatters until Jeremiah Leeds acquired legitimate title to land and moved there early in the nineteenth century. Only one hand was needed to count the houses on the island when Pitney first visited the lonely windswept beach in 1820.

Hardy sportsmen occasionally found their way to the beach, where bird life was so plentiful that Jeremiah Leeds told of killing forty-eight "squawks" with one blast of his mighty gun. Most of the hunters stayed at the rough boardinghouse that Jeremiah's widowed aunt Millie opened in 1838.

The mainland younger set went to "Uncle" Ryan Adams's place for their beach parties. They came in boats, and as they rounded Rum Point in the inlet, they hoisted flags to their mastheads. That was enough to move Uncle Ryan. "Aunt Judith," he would call, "folks a-comin'. Set some food on."

The guests undressed among the dunes (until Uncle Ryan built them crude—and airy—bathhouses out of brush) and "down to the beach they danced to strains of Fisher's hornpipe, discoursed by a single fiddle." One of the dancers later recalled the dances as "a regular jump-up-and-down, cross-over, Jonathan," with "none of your mincing and smirking." At high tide the fun-seekers bathed, and "the hilarity of the occasion culminated when the young men carried the blushing and screaming maidens to the tops of steep sand hills and, tying their feet together, rolled them down to the water's edge."

Anyone who wanted to frequent the Atlantic County coast seriously went to Somers Point, described in 1844 as "quite a good place of resort for the Summer, with boarding houses for the accommodation of strangers."

No one ever visited Somers Point without learning of gallant Master Commandant Richard Somers of the United States Navy, a local boy who rose to become the brilliant twenty-five-year-old commander of the *Intrepid*, a vessel loaded with explosives and assigned to help destroy the Barbary pirate fleet at Tripoli in August 1804. Young Somers sailed the *Intrepid* close to the pirate fleet when suddenly his vessel exploded with a mighty roar, killing Somers and twelve others. It will never be known what caused the blast, but generally it was said Somers lit a match to the powder magazine to avoid capture by the pirates.

Pitney went often to the beach in the pursuit of his professional duties. He constantly admired its rugged beauty and its healthful air. He loved to walk along the sandy beach, and one day in 1845 as he stood on a hill watching the rolling green ocean with his Absecon friend, General Enoch Doughty, he turned and exclaimed: "This should become the El Dorado of the Atlantic Coast, Enoch!"

By 1852 Pitney and Doughty enlisted the enthusiasm of Richard B. Osborne, a railroad engineer, and young Samuel Richards, described as having "pleasing manners and tireless energy," qualities that have marked Atlantic City promoters ever since. They applied for a railroad charter and had it granted in March 1852, mainly because the powerful Camden & Amboy Railroad dynasty never dreamed that a railroad to the Jersey Shore could be successful. The promoters saw profits accruing immediately from the glassworks and iron furnaces of the interior, but their eyes also rested on the seashore potential.

Absegami Island received the name which now has meaning throughout the world on a day in the middle of January 1853, when a group of men sat around a table to discuss mapping a "Bathing Village" on the island. They decided first to choose a name for the coming seaside resort.

Such uninspired designations as "Surf," "Seabeach," and "Strand" were offered. Richard Osborne listened quietly, then suggested the board get on with his plan for the city. He unrolled his "great and well-finished map" and across the top the board saw "in large letters of gold, stretching over the waves that were delineated thereon as breaking on Absecon Beach, the words: 'ATLANTIC CITY.'"

Thus, for the ages and for the as yet unborn vacationists and souvenir labelers, the city was named. It became official on March 3, 1854, at the signing of the incorporation papers.

Adult males in the scattered houses along the beach quickly organized. Only eighteen of the twenty-one vo-

ters eligible on May 1, 1854, dropped ballots through the slit in a cigarbox fastened with yellow tape to ensure the inviolability of the ballot. Everyone who desired an office was elected, with Chalkley S. Leeds becoming the first mayor of Atlantic City.

The officials got down to business, passing regulations governing bathing and real estate taxes. Then they passed two ordinances, into which perhaps may be read lasting significance: the first was to control liquor licenses; the second, to authorize the building of a jail. That cleared the way for such things as schools.

The first Camden & Atlantic Railroad train rolled over the flat country from Camden in two and a half hours on July 1, 1854, carrying six hundred dignitaries and the press. The bridge was not finished over Beach Thoroughfare, but undaunted passengers cheerfully waited to be rowed across, then carried by train to the unfinished United States Hotel. Despite great rejoicing, the guests happily fled back to the comforts of Philadelphia the same evening. Three days later, on July 4, the C. & A. opened the route to the public.

Dr. Pitney's dream of seaside magnificence emerged slowly at first, hampered both by lack of accommodations for visitors and by the elements. The first excursionists amused themselves plodding through the sand among grass-covered dunes, gathering seashells or clambering over the hulks of wrecked ships. Nature played a cruel hand in 1857, when the coldest winter that the coast ever experienced froze ice six feet deep in the bays. A January nor'easter cast chunks of ice into twenty-foot heaps on the beach and stopped railroad travel for many weeks.

Even worse was the fly and mosquito plague of 1858, when greenhead flies, gnats, and mosquitoes threatened to wrest the island away from humans. Horses covered with blood wandered through the streets; cattle waded into the ocean to escape the torture. Excursionists begged train crews to leave for Philadelphia far ahead of scheduled departure times. Hotel guests threatened owners with bodily harm unless screens were put up.

The Camden & Atlantic Railroad sought earnestly to improve the beach, both because of the benefits it would bring to its railroad and also because most of its promoters were in the land company that had bought property on the beach for $17.50 an acre, in the hopes they might sell it someday for "as high as $500."

In 1870, Jacob Keim, tired of the sand being tracked through the rugs in his Chester House hotel, discussed the matter with Alex Boardman, conductor on the railroad. The two agreed the solution was a boardwalk on the beach. Boardman's bosses thought so much of the idea that they gave the conductor a leave of absence to promote it. The first walk (called "Boardman's Walk," some say) opened on June 26, 1870. It was eight feet wide and laid directly on the sands. The present permanent walk, the fifth in direct line of succession, was built in 1939.

The first of Atlantic City's famous ocean piers opened

Casino gambling has brought new life to Atlantic City, but on Easter Sunday in 1953, the Boardwalk, ocean, and hotels were enough. (*Atlantic City Press Bulletin*)

Atlantic City's skyline, impressive in pre-casino days, has added glitter since 1976, when state voters approved gambling on the Boardwalk. (*Walter Choroszewski*)

in 1882, and others followed when promoters saw the advantages of having all that ocean space to augment limited boardwalk frontage. Before the turn of the century, amusement piers were both numerous and lasting.

As business boomed in the resort city, other railroads saw the light. In 1878 the pressure for a second railroad brought the "Narrow Gauge," so-called because its tracks were spaced only three and a half feet apart, from Camden to Atlantic City in the phenomenally short time of ninety-eight days. The "Narrow Gauge Line" quickly cut fares and moved in on the booming passenger business.

The railroads brought benefits elsewhere in the county. Hammonton and Egg Harbor City, both beside the tracks, emerged as well-established communities.

New ways of making money had to be found in the Pines; the railroads that nurtured Atlantic City ruined bog iron dynasties, chiefly because ore in North Jersey became far more accessible with the advent of railroads. Forges in Morris, Sussex, and Warren counties used Pennsylvania anthracite in their fires. Bog iron operators could not compete.

The Gloucester Farm and Town Association, organized in 1854, coincided with the building of the C. & A. Railroad. The association bought thirty-six thousand acres and split them up into thirty-acre divisions in the new city of Egg Harbor. The association's start also coincided with the wave of "America for Americans" feeling that swept the country in the 1850s under auspices of the Know-Nothing Party.

The Egg Harbor land promoters welcomed immigrants; hundreds of Germans flocked to settle on Farm and Town Association streets. Egg Harbor's Germans were mostly cultured people who, according to an early chronicler, "abhorred whiskey but liked wine." They were delighted when John Wild found in 1858 that the surrounding soil was excellent for the growing of grapes. H. T. Dewey and Sons opened a commercial winery in 1867, but oddly in that very German section a Frenchman founded the greatest winery.

He was Louis N. Renault, stranded in this country by the Franco-Prussian War in 1870 while serving as an emissary for the Duc de Montebello. Seeking to establish himself, Renault started the Egg Harbor winery that grew into nationwide prominence.

Out on the western strip of the county one of South Jersey's greatest promoters, Charles K. Landis, interested Judge Richard J. Byrnes in 1858 in the possibility of a city rising in the Hammonton area where William Coffin's glassworks once prospered. Master publicist Landis flooded the country with vivid word pictures of the glories of Hammonton.

Scores of New Englanders, lured by Landis's laudatory prose, headed for Hammonton. Years later most of them still remembered the shock when their train stopped at Hammonton and they stepped down. There was no station—the only marker was a lime hogshead on which "Hammonton" was crudely lettered.

Yet they stayed. They found the soil ideal for fruits and berries and they found the Landis-Byrnes idea of small lots for people of limited means highly attractive. By 1868 they shipped seven carloads of strawberries daily to Philadelphia. Landis simultaneously moved into Cumberland County to found Vineland, then went abroad to Italy to tell Italians of both Hammonton and Vineland.

The first Italians stayed on the edges of Hammonton, making the soil yield vegetables and fruits that astounded the New Englanders. By 1876 the Italians had started their annual July 16 celebration of the Feast of Our Lady of Mount Carmel. That feast, with its colorful parade, still draws worshippers to Hammonton each summer.

Just west of Atlantic City, Pleasantville grew on the mainland, attracting many residents to the region that William Lake, a one-time Long Island whaler, had first settled in 1702. Two of William's descendants are still remembered in aptly named Pleasantville: Simon Lake, inventor of the Lake Submarine, and Jesse Lake, inventor of the self-track-laying car. All countries now use Simon Lake's patents in their submarines. Jesse Lake's self-track machine helped build the first highway between the mainland and Atlantic City in the 1860s. The self-track car carried sand and gravel and other materials across the soft meadows and tiny streams. Today the principle is used on farm tractors and on lethal army tanks. Pleasantville was incorporated as a borough in 1888 and adopted the city form of government in 1914. Within the very shadow of the world's greatest amusement area, it is now home to more than sixteen thousand people.

Nearly all of Atlantic County has been resort-conscious for three-quarters of a century. Ever since 1921, county inhabitants have basked in the reflected luster of the Miss America pageants. Ever since the 1890s they have been reading and believing what the public relations men have to say about the "salubrious air." But some also remember what happened during the Depression to the city that had all its economic eggs in only a recreation basket.

Atlantic City had reached its prosperous peak when Wall Street collapsed. The tremendous Convention Hall opened on May 31, 1929, to celebrate the city's seventy-fifth birthday. Hotel building went on apace. Money rolled in. Then came the Crash and Atlantic City collapsed. Twenty-eight banks closed their doors in the city. Business fell flat as the city languished during the hard times.

World War II brought a resurgence. Hundreds of thousands of soldiers arrived to take over the hotels, first as barracks and then as hospitals. Naturally Atlantic City found lush times in America's postwar yearning for rest and relaxation. In 1952, for the first time since 1929, new buildings started rising on the boardwalk.

Atlantic City hoped for new prosperity in the early 1960s, spurred by a wave of new motels that in most cases replaced rickety old wooden hotels. Motels built between 1958 and 1966 represented $100 million in

Lucy the elephant, sixty-five feet tall with twenty-two-foot tusks, was built on the sands of Margate in 1881. (*Walter Choroszewski*)

new investment in the city. The grand old hotel palaces along the boardwalk remained, some of them old enough to be considered landmarks, no matter how archaic the comforts.

In 1966 the city's publicity bureau trumpeted that twelve to fifteen million visitors came annually to enjoy the beach and the boardwalk. Two years later, a survey of hotel and motel owners claimed that 389,750 delegates attended conventions in Atlantic City, spending more than $50 million annually in the resort city, a tidy sum considering that a full-sized new automobile cost about $2,500 (compared with about $20,000 to $25,000 in the early 1990s).

Despite the outward prosperity, the city declined. Little money went to upgrade homes for the vast majority of city residents who worked in the hotels, motels, and restaurants. Major organizations, including large New Jersey groups, began spending convention funds in such pleasure-oriented and expensive havens as Hawaii or the Bahamas. The Queen of Resorts became shabby and old. Fickle winter visitors began flying off to Miami or Las Vegas.

City politicians and hotel-motel owners saw only one possible answer: casino gambling. State voters in 1964 roundly defeated a constitutional amendment to permit casinos, not mentioning Atlantic City specifically. Two years later an amendment to permit casino gambling only in Atlantic City won approval, savoring the promise that state revenues from the gambling would benefit "senior citizens and disabled residents of the state" and assurances that racketeers would have no share of the receipts.

The city and much of the surrounding area rejoiced. Casino owners promised to refurbish the fading city. New jobs would become available to build the high-rise casinos and to staff them on completion. Housing starts would jump, in the city and on the mainland. The business section would rebound. Atlantic County would hit the jackpot.

Ruins of the Weymouth Iron Works, founded in 1800, demonstrate the vivid contrasts found in Atlantic County. (*Walter Choroszewski*)

The rush by out-of-city investors to acquire boardwalk frontage reminded historians and Monopoly game players of how costly it can be to build on the Boardwalk, in real life as in game fantasies. Sale prices reached stratospheric heights and a few historians recalled when the original builders hoped someday to get $500 an acre for property that had cost them $17.50 an acre.

Even the staunchest admirers of the casinos can't say that life for most city residents has improved since 1978, when the first slot machines began clicking in Resorts International. True, about forty thousand new jobs have been created, but a large portion of those have gone to nonresidents. The implicit promise to rebuild Atlantic City outward from the casino hotels has been slow in fulfillment. Gamblers streaming in and out of the city in limousines, private cars, and buses are not routed through rundown areas. Behind her gleaming new face along the boardwalk, the "Queen" still needs much help.

It is estimated that more than thirty million visitors come to Atlantic City each year every day, almost around the clock. Few of those visitors know, or care, that Atlantic County stretches thirty miles westward into a largely unsettled interior. Municipalities out there are particularly interested in letting the world know that thousands of their acres are not developed—and perhaps never will be.

The unpopulated nature of Atlantic County is plain to anyone coming from the north by way of the Garden State Parkway or from the west on the Atlantic City Expressway. The Parkway slices through widespread marshlands and crosses high above the broad Mullica River. The Expressway cuts through silent pine woodlands, rising above meandering waterways with such names as Pennypot Creek, John's Brook, and Makepeace Stream. But peripheral vision has no place in the lives of those speeding to (or from) the casino towers on the ocean. Atlantic City and Atlantic County are for them synonymous.

The county reveals what the visitor seeks. If permanent residents are the object, most of them are as close to the beaches as they can cluster. About 50 percent of the county's total population resides within about five miles of the Atlantic Ocean, taking up not more than 15 percent of available land. There is no questioning the lure of the rolling waves.

Virtually all of the county lies west of the Garden State Parkway—a land that surprises anyone who thinks that Atlantic County is only an ocean bounded by casinos willing to take anyone's first (or last) dollar. West of the Parkway are the orchards, blueberry fields, and vegetable gardens, thriving so well that Atlantic is the only county in New Jersey where agriculture is holding its own, in both acreage and income. There, too, are the unconquered pine woodlands.

In the Pine Barrens the boardwalk seems much farther away than mere miles. Place names tell part of the story of isolation: Head of River, on the Tuckahoe River; English Creek Landing, on Great Egg Harbor River; Dorothy, midway between Rissole and Doughty's, neither of which can be considered anywhere; Pleasant Mills, with memories rather than substance.

Then there are the outlying "cities." There is Corbin City, three or four streets surrounded by the marshlands of the Tuckahoe River—a "city" where about four hundred people dwell. There is McKee City, consisting of a traffic circle, the Atlantic City Race Track, and assorted motels and restaurants that know the pleasant jingle of cash only when the ponies run. And there is Port Republic City, at the head of Nacote Creek, and by no known standard either a "port" or a "city."

Such "cities" are mementoes of grandiose land schemes that rose and fell between 1900 and 1930. A glance at an Atlantic County map shows scores of neat street layouts west of the Garden State Parkway. This might signify suburban living, but on-the-scene examination often shows the "streets" are vacant and the dream towns vanished except perhaps for few concrete "gateposts" crumbling into the pine woodland.

The casinos have had almost no impact on the county's population. In 1975, when gambling parlors were yet a dream, there were 189,182 people in the county; in 1990 the total had inched upward to 224,327—about 35,000 in fifteen years. Atlantic City in the glory days of 1950 had more than 60,000 residents; today it has fewer than 38,000.

Only Egg Harbor and Galloway townships have experienced major growth (by Atlantic County standards). Egg Harbor went from about 15,000 residents to 25,000 in the "casino era." Galloway went from 13,000 to 23,000. Pleasantville (16,000), Ventnor (11,000), and Somers Point (11,000) are the only other towns with more than 10,000 inhabitants.

Industry is not Atlantic City's strong point, unless casino gambling can be considered an industry. Lenox makes its famed china in Pomona and boat builders prosper along the Mullica River. The county's biggest employer outside of the boardwalk complexes is the National Aviation Facilities Experiment Station at Pomona, where more than three thousand employees research the mechanics and control of air flight.

Perhaps the wide open spaces won't last, but by 1990 the impact of the casinos had probably reached its highest level. More significant might be the Atlantic City Expressway and the high-speed rail line built in the 1980s to serve the casino interests. Both bring Philadelphia within about one hour of Atlantic County. Someday, perhaps even soon, Atlantic County may become a new haven for commuters, emulating Monmouth but with the focal point being Philadelphia.

Right now, Atlantic County retains several major natural assets—the beach, the sand, salt breezes, and the mild winter climate; the marshes, where herons far outnumber humans; the great stretches of pine woodland, and the heritage of a county that once considered the natural resources enough to attract visitors.

Cape May County knows where its courthouse is—in the town of Cape May Court House. Its greatest reason for pride in the nineteenth century was this two-story wooden structure built in 1850 for a total cost of $6,284, including a 333-pound bell cast for $99.33. County business is now conducted in an adjacent brick building, but for many this will always be the Cape May courthouse.

CAPE MAY

THE WATERING PLACE

Two firmly established Cape May County traditions quickly tell a stranger how deep are the roots of those who live on the Jersey cape. The first holds that there are more *Mayflower* descendants in Cape May County than in Plymouth County, Massachusetts; the second insists that once a person "gets sand in his shoes" he or she will never leave Cape May.

Walking down the shaded streets of Cape May Court House, where eighteenth- and nineteenth-century houses spread outward from the old white courthouse toward the malls and town shops, it is easy to understand why sand can get in a person's shoes. Down the Cape, meandering streets and a preponderance of well-kept Victorian homes and hotels in Cape May City bespeak the heritage of one of America's oldest "watering places." Cape May County is filled with the quiet pride of the Townsends and the Hands, the Leamings and the Ludlams, the Corsons and the Spicers—families whose ancestry can be traced, in most cases, back both to the *Mayflower* and to Cape May's earliest days.

New England roots are deep, but the county name derives from the ubiquitous Dutch captain, Cornelius Jacobsen Mey, who paid extensive attention to this coast as he maneuvered his ship *Glad Tidings* around the cape in 1620. Captain Mey found the climate charming— "like Holland" (which to a Hollander is the ultimate compliment)—and named the land for himself.

The Dutch made desultory attempts to colonize the land, and a few daring Long Island adventurers fished for whales in Delaware Bay as early as 1638, but it took determined colonists from New England (including *Mayflower* descendants) and Long Island to make Cape May whaling profitable.

Cape May's link with the *Mayflower* carried little early weight in this barren land. In fact, it went unheralded for more than two hundred years until Dr. Paul S. Howe, rector of the Church of the Advent, published his book *Mayflower Descendants in Cape May County* in 1921. He traced many residents back to the Pilgrims, particularly to John Howland, one of those on the famed ship. Dr. Howe estimated that one-third of Cape May City's people in 1920 had direct ties to the *Mayflower*.

The English whalers built thirteen houses on a high bluff overlooking Delaware Bay and called their village "Town Bank." They sallied into the bay in small boats to battle whales weighing up to 250 tons. Life was simple, if dangerous. If no whales were captured the one-industry town faced hard times. More personally, a harpooned whale had to be dispatched quickly in the elemental kill-or-be-killed struggle, since its lashing tail could bring death with a single flip to a boatload of whalers.

The whalers worked fast after they captured one of the ocean giants. They beached their quarry and stripped it, turning blubber and bones into salable products worth up to four thousand dollars a whale. William Penn wrote that Cape May's hunters "justly hope a considerable profit by a whalery." Gabriel Thomas in his *Account of Pennsylvania and West Jersey* told of "prodigious —nay, vast—quantities" of Cape May "oyle and whale-bone" taken every year.

Whaling understandably had a built-in imperma-nency about it, and even the tacit establishment in 1685 of Cape May County with vague northern boundaries failed to give the Cape solidity. Dr. Daniel Coxe of Lon-don must have seen a future, for in 1688 he purchased, sight unseen, ninety-five thousand Cape May acres. He never came to America, but his manorial ideas for the vast real estate holdings included two-story Coxe Hall, built in the whaling village by his agents and used for Quaker and Baptist services as well as the first county court convened in 1692.

Settlers could not readily obtain land titles until Dr. Coxe's holdings passed to the West New Jersey Society in 1692, the year that the county was officially set off. Shamgar Hand, first of a long Cape May line, bought one thousand acres at Rummey Marsh (now Cape May Court House) in 1690; Thomas Leaming, who came in 1692 at the age of eighteen to "go a-whaling," got sand in his shoes and stayed. John Townsend located land in the upper part of the county in 1690 and drove his team of oxen single file along the narrow forest path to his home-stead. Others bought land: Spicers, Schellengers, Hugheses, and Ludlams.

It was a difficult land to colonize. Just behind the beaches on the ocean side, marshlands up to three miles in width extended the length of the county. Out in the west and north nearly impenetrable cedar forests walled Cape May off from the rest of New Jersey. The building of the road between Egg Harbor and Cold Spring in 1706 helped immensely, but this region looked to the sea for movement. The first census in 1726 showed only 668 inhabitants spread over nearly three hundred square miles.

Pirates cruising off the coasts occasionally stopped for water from the Cape's cool springs, to repair their ves-sels, or (if the folklorists are right) to bury treasure. Cattle herders along the coast claimed they saw the buccaneers out where grassy meadows covered the ocean side of the county. There cattle roamed free, identifiable by un-usual Cape May "earmarks," such as that in Anthony Ludlam's 1737 will, describing his earmark as being "an El on yᵉ underside of left ear and a slit in yᵉ top of yᵉ right ear."

Farms back from the ocean and marshes replaced the whaling village early in the eighteenth century. Cape May people learned to stay inland, away from the ru-inous sea, whose furies toppled Town Bank into the waves and eradicated all traces of the whaling site. The inlanders chose Middletown for the county court in 1745. The county seat has been there ever since; passing time changed the name from Middletown to Cape May Court House. Fishermen, oystermen, and clam diggers eked out an uncertain living in the bays and ocean. Woodsmen began to convert the great cedar forests into eagerly bought timber.

Such was the land of Aaron Leaming II (born 1715) and Jacob Spicer II (born 1716), Cape May's most prom-inent early citizens. Sons of county founders, both were respected for their intelligent contributions as Cape May's representatives in the Assembly. They worked to-gether to produce in 1758 a noted compendium of New Jersey's early laws and concessions.

Spicer's statewide prestige diminished considerably among his own Cape May people in 1756, when he pur-chased from the West Jersey Society all unsold lands and privileges in the county. The purchase disturbed resi-dents of the Cape because it included all rights to "hawk-ing, fishing, hunting and fowling." An association had been formed in 1752 to buy the rights, but the associa-tion dallied while Spicer bought. The most bitter of the disappointed residents charged that Spicer's purchase price of £300 was set "at a time when the influence of the wine bottle usurped the place of reason." Spicer had the rights, no matter how.

Internal warring over "rights" faded in the common Revolution against the British, although the war mainly stayed out to sea as far as Cape May was concerned. Be-fore the actual fighting started, Cape May pilots refused to guide tea-laden British vessels up the Delaware River. John Hatton, British collector of the port of Salem and Cohansey, arrived in Cold Spring in November 1770 to put an end to coastal smuggling. Hatton's enthusiasm for his work and his "very unhappy, violent temper" caused him untold grief—and in no way stopped the smuggling.

Wartime found Cape May pilots striking at British coastwise shipping, while other residents stayed ashore to act as anti-British spies, relaying information by pony express riders who galloped to Philadelphia along the miserable sand roads in the pinelands.

Cape May's most important leap into vacation prominence may well have come on June 30, 1801, when Ellis Hughes, proprietor of the Hotel Atlantic, placed his now much-quoted advertisement in *The Philadelphia Daily Aurora*:

> The public are respectfully informed that the subscriber has prepared himself for entertaining company who use sea bathing, and he is accommodated with extensive houseroom, with fish, oysters, crabs and good liquors. Care will be taken of Gentlemen's horses.
>
> The situation is beautiful, just at the confluence of Delaware Bay with the ocean, in sight of the Lighthouse and affords a view of shipping which enters and leaves the Delaware; carriages may be driven along the margin of the ocean for miles, and the wheels will scarcely make an impression upon the sand; the slope of the shore is so regular that persons may wade a great distance. It is the most delightful spot the citizens can retire to in the hot season.

A stage left from Cooper's Ferry (Camden) every Thursday, Hughes said, and reached Cape Island the next day. The distance overland by way of Woodbury, Malaga, Port Elizabeth, and Dennis Creek totaled 102 miles. Those who preferred sailing "can find vessels almost any time."

Hughes was not the first to proclaim the virtues of Cape May as a "watering place." The Reverend Samuel Finley, pastor of the Cold Spring Presbyterian Church between 1740 and 1742, spoke often of the merits of

Eroding ocean currents have worn away all of this part of Cape May Point, where this original lighthouse stood until 1847. (*The Newark Library*)

Cape May bathing, even after he became president of Princeton College in 1761. Many physicians lauded the Cape's health-giving potentialities before Hughes. The difference was that Hughes aimed to be a paid host.

Others took in visitors, too, so that by 1812 local citizens regularly counted on summer dollars from Philadelphia guests. The Cape was far different from what the whalers had known; Town Bank had disappeared, washed away by the relentless sea, which by known measurement cut 169 feet from the Cape May beaches between 1804 and 1822.

The War of 1812 interrupted summer visitations. Residents at Cape May Point could see the British blockade fleet sailing offshore and British sailors came ashore occasionally to raid farms. When the enemy began using Lake Lily as a fresh water supply, residents laboriously dug a deep ditch through sixteen-foot dunes from the ocean to the lake. The saltwater flowed into the lake and ruined it temporarily.

Regular sloop service started between the island and Philadelphia in 1815, one year before Thomas H. Hughes, son of Ellis, built the original Congress Hall. People laughed at "Tommy's Folly," but big, hearty Tommy, the most popular man in town, replied: "The day will come when you'll have to cover every square inch here with a silver dollar to get enough land to put up a house!"

Steamboat service between Cape May and Philadelphia began in 1819, strengthening Tommy Hughes's prediction. Visitors began to arrive from Philadelphia, Baltimore, Washington, and the South—"as many as 3,000 in a single summer," according to an 1844 historian. In 1853, work began on the Mount Vernon, the largest hotel in the world at the time, according to contemporary accounts. Builder Philip Cain startled the resort by erecting Mount Vernon's front section 300 feet wide and four stories high, then added a wing 500 feet long and three stories high. That made 482 rooms available, each with a private bath—remarkable for the time. Proprietor Cain's dream of a third 500-foot wing and total accommodations for 2,100 guests vanished in a fire on September 5, 1855. Cain and four others died in the blaze.

Cape May town was the most famous resort in the na-

When *Ballou's* magazine published this woodcut in the late 1840s, Cape May was the nation's foremost seaside resort.

tion in the 1850s, local promoters said, ignoring the claims of Saratoga and Long Branch. Southern planters and the socially elite of the North exchanged discreet, genteel, and different opinions in the glittering hotels. Visiting plantation owners whiled away their time and whittled away their fortunes in such gambling houses as Henry Cleveland's Blue Pig. Town fathers passed a law forbidding nude bathing on the crowded beaches. Nationally known bands played for dancing in the hotels. Steamboats came and went every day.

Famous people came, too, such as President Franklin Pierce in 1855 and President James Buchanan in 1858. And an obscure Illinois politician slept in the Mansion House in 1849, signing in as "A. Lincoln and wife."

No visitor stirred Cape May as much as Henry Clay. Summer crowds had started to disappear from the Cape in August 1847, when "Harry of the West" asked for reservations at the Mansion House to spend a quiet week in mourning for his son killed in the Mexican War. Word leaked out, much to the satisfaction of the local hotelkeepers, and the outward-bound streamed back to greet Clay on his arrival from Philadelphia on August 16.

Golden-voiced Henry went swimming twice a day and possibly enjoyed it despite the vigorous ladies who chased him with scissors to clip off locks of his hair. "When he returned to Washington," said one writer, "his hair was short indeed!" A New York delegation waited on Clay with an invitation to visit there, but he refused in a moving declaration of grief for his son which made his until then griefless audience weep openly.

Inland, Cape May County grew, too, albeit slowly. The county had no physician until 1786, when Dr. John Dickinson moved down from Salem. Education came from itinerant tutors on horseback until 1830, when the first crude schoolhouses were built. Religious groups had solid foundations, the Baptists having been established at Cape May Court House in 1712, the Presbyterians at Cold Spring in 1714, and the Quakers at Seaville in the early 1700s.

Time slipped by. Cape May Court House rightfully took pride in the handsome new courthouse finished in 1850 at a cost of $6,284, including a 333-pound bell cast for $99.33. The ferry at Beasley's Point, established in 1692, flourished for two centuries. Nearby Tuckahoe had a busy shipbuilding trade. Out in the western cedar lands, Dennis Creek prospered from shipbuilding, timber cutting, and from cedar logs "mined" from the swamps, then cut into shingles, mainly for Philadelphia buildings. Dennis Creek could boast that its 1802 post office was the county's first, and that its shingles were used on the roof of Philadelphia's Independence Hall.

Only 7,130 people lived in all the county in 1860 when the fateful Presidential election neared. On the verandas in Cape May in the summer of 1860, discussion of the Breckinridge-Lincoln campaign provoked bitter arguments. Southerners returned to their plantations in August, and the wisest of both visitors and Cape May residents knew that an era had vanished. They were right. The assault on Fort Sumter shattered forever the veranda quietude.

Despite its position well below the Mason-Dixon line (if the line had not stopped at the Delaware River), and its annual seasonal injection of Southern blood, Cape May quickly supported the Union cause. Off to war went its young men, including Lieutenant Henry W. Sawyer, who became a rising star. On the morning of June 9, 1863, Sawyer went into battle at Brandy Station, Virginia, wearing his newly won captain's bars.

Rebel troops captured Sawyer that day and sent him to the infamous Libby Prison in Richmond. There, on July 6, he was called into the prison yard with other imprisoned Union captains and told that within a few days two of them must be hanged in retaliation for the execution of two Confederate captains within Union lines. Sawyer and Captain John M. Flynn of Indiana drew the unlucky tickets in a prison lottery and prepared to die.

Sawyer wrote his wife in Cape May. She sped to Washington, saw President Lincoln, and political wheels moved to save the Cape May captain. Secretary of War Stanton informed the South that if Sawyer and Flynn died, the North would execute General William Henry Fitzhugh ("Rooney") Lee, son of General Robert E. Lee, and another Confederate captain. The South readily exchanged the Union captains for the two Confederate officers.

Union veterans returned to a changed Cape May in 1865, eager to share in the progress that seemed sure to follow the coming of the railroad. Real estate values doubled in the summer after the war ended and more than fifty thousand visitors came in 1866. *The New York Herald* declared: "If they [vacationists] want a fast place, let them go to Saratoga. It is worse than even Baden Baden, and we guarantee that they will lose both health and money in it. People who 'are content to dwell in decencies forever' should go to Cape May, while those who like a spice of everything should patronize Long Branch."

New Stockton Hall opened in 1869, the year that President Grant visited Cape May. Mrs. Grant's presence set the ladies of the resort to sewing madly on red and blue flannel bathing suits in imitation of those that Mrs. Grant bought from a local tailor. President Grant shook hands, of course, but not nearly as many as the twenty-five hundred hands that President Arthur shook in a single evening during his 1883 stay.

Old Cape May town perished in the decade from 1869 to 1879. First, an 1869 fire ruined a quarter of the business section, including several old hotels. Then, on November 9, 1878, flames swept through thirty-five acres of buildings in the heart of the city, leveling most of the best hotels and private cottages. Many secretly expressed the belief that the fires were a blessing in horrible disguise, since they forced rebuilding with some planning for the future.

Varying industries sought to exploit Cape May's natural advantages in the years after the Civil War. The Porpoise Fishing Company opened a factory on Pond Creek in 1868 to make porpoise skins into leather, refine porpoise fat into oil, and make "dolphin steaks" from the flesh. Commercial fishing of all kinds reached such cutthroat proportions in the 1880s that nonfishing local residents protested violently at invasions of their areas, sometimes reinforcing their vocal protests by shooting at commercial vessels.

Upcounty at Rio Grande a group of Philadelphia promoters planted two thousand acres of sugar cane in 1881, their initiative strengthened by state bounties of a dollar a ton for all cane grown and a cent a pound for all sugar refined. The Rio Grande Sugar Company made seventy-six thousand pounds of sugar and eighty-seven thousand gallons of syrup in 1884, but termination of the state bounty in 1885 doomed the venture. Cape May's southern exposure also tempted various other agricultural experiments, ranging from licorice growing to mulberry tree culture and the use of sea lavender for honey, none of them successful.

More important was the increasing interest shown in the 1880s for the extensive pasturelands on the islands along the entire oceanfront, where the rolling summer surf on the best beaches in the state long had served only to cool herds of free-roaming cattle as they ate salt grass.

Ocean City grew from the strongly antiliquor Methodist summer island resort started on Peck's Beach in 1879 by three minister brothers, S. Wesley, Ezra B., and James Lake. Just to the south, Charles K. Landis, founder of Vineland and Hammonton, laid out Sea Isle City in 1881. A railroad spur reached Sea Isle in 1884, and by 1893 the town had thirty hotels and was widely known for its brilliant electric lighting.

Philip Pontius Baker of Vineland, state senator from Cumberland County, founded Wildwood in 1890 on Five Mile Beach, a spot known for its natural stands of wild hollies and other trees. Just back from Baker's beach, tremendously tall cedars cooled visitors. Gigantic wild grapevines and festoons of moss hanging from the trees delighted the eyes of explorers.

John Wanamaker, Philadelphia merchant, took such pride in Cape May Point, founded by Presbyterians in 1875 as Sea Grove, that he invited President and Mrs. Benjamin Harrison to visit him there. Friends built a ten-thousand-dollar cottage and presented it to the Harrisons when they arrived in 1890 for their second summer on the Cape.

Contrasting with down-Cape gaiety was establishment in 1891 of a Jewish colony at Woodbine, where sixty-two farms of thirty acres each were laid out for refugees who had fled Russian persecution. The new colonists bought farms, complete with a farmhouse, outbuildings, and stock, for $1,200 apiece. Woodbine had seven hundred inhabitants within a year of its founding.

A few miles south of Woodbine, young Eugene G. Grace left his birthplace in Goshen in June 1899 for a job with the Bethlehem Steel Corporation. Fourteen years later the village heard with pride that young Gene had been named president of the tremendous company.

Another young man of eventual fortune, Henry Ford, brought a racing car to the Cape in 1903 to enter

Living room furnishings of a restored Cape May house show that Victorian decor was far from gloomy. (*The Baltimore Sun*)

automobile races run on the flat, hard-packed beach. He tried to sell stock in his automobile company but most of the Cape's canny farmers refused to buy. Many years later James Couzens, who became a U.S. senator from Michigan, sold at tremendous profit the $5,000 in stock he had bought from Ford at Cape May.

Ford's poor stock sales came as no surprise. Visitors certainly preferred beach days to stock seminars and the Cape's few year-round residents put their money in such safe investments as fishing boats. Cape May in 1900 had 13,201 residents spread over the county's 263 square miles—almost exactly 50 persons per square mile. The attractive sands of summer stuck to very few shoes.

County leaders, meaning those prospering from vacationists, sought at the turn of the century to start a much-needed ferry to the State of Delaware. In 1900 a side-wheeler made several unsatisfactory runs across

Opened in 1964, the Cape May to Lewes, Delaware, ferry fulfilled a hope that had existed at the Cape for nearly a century. (*D.R.B.A.*)

Delaware Bay and in 1903 the two-hundred-foot steamer *Caroline* tried unsuccessfully to establish cross-bay service. Through the years several abortive attempts were made to link the states by ferry, featured by the 1926 effort which saw "Colonel" Jesse Rosenfeld of Baltimore sink an old concrete ship off Cape May Point as the anchor for a ferry terminal. The old ship still rests in the water, slowly eroding away.

Railroads did little more than bring in summer people, although by 1900 rails reached outward to all the series of long islands from Peck's Beach (Ocean City) on the north to Seven Mile Beach (Wildwood) on the south. Wildwood became a popular resort for one-day, one-dollar "fishing specials," which arrived in the village on Sundays so filled with Philadelphia fishermen that one account said the cars looked "like porcupines" because of the hundreds of fishing poles protruding from the windows.

By 1950, on the eve of the Garden State Parkway's arrival, Cape May County continued its Labor Day to Fourth of July hibernation. Railroads faded toward extinction. State Highway 9, the only highway link outward worthy of consideration, had all the vitality of a country road nine months of the year. Cape May was in every respect the end of the line.

The Parkway made a difference, intensified when the Atlantic City Expressway eased entrance for Pennsylvanians. Year-round population edged upward from

37,131 in 1950 to 59,544 in 1970 and 94,190 in the 1990 census. Many of the new permanent residents are retirees, who find homes definitely less expensive and winter temperatures at least a bit warmer than the climate of northern New Jersey.

The long-proposed ferry across Delaware Bay finally came into being in 1964 despite scoffing by critics who based skepticism on past failures. Service began with five large boats that had run on the Chesapeake Bay crossing between Cape Charles and Norfolk but had become surplus with the opening of the bridge-tunnel crossing of Chesapeake Bay. The ferry has outlived the doubters; the sixteen-mile trip across choppy Delaware Bay is reality.

Summer residents stream in, along with two-week renters and weekend guests. Getting into the county on a hot July or August Saturday between noon and 2 P.M. tests the fortitude and tempers of drivers in the long lines of steaming cars piled up far behind every toll booth or at the traffic lights that control entrance into Stone Harbor or Cape May Court House. Every resort town is crowded from June to September, with Wildwood's teeming boardwalk, big theaters, nightclubs, and scores of motels being the major magnet. Ocean City thrives, despite constant grumbling by some visitors against the continued ban on liquor. Between Ocean City and Cape May city are a half dozen or so seaside towns, all linked by the Ocean Drive, marked by "The Sign of the Gull."

Today Cape May County has as close a tie to the past as any county in New Jersey. Descendants of old families are numerous and proud of their heritage. Cape May's confusing street patterns date from the unplanned growth of the eighteenth century. Old houses, numerous and well kept, are the basis for the informal annual summer historical pilgrimages and the official Victorian days in October. The old Cape May Point lighthouse tells of the county's former dependence on the sea.

The past is most evident in Cape May city, where a federal urban renewal grant of $3.2 million in 1966 kept alive the lavender-and-old-lace flavor of Victorian days. Scores of houses and a few hotels are splendid examples of nineteenth-century days when carpenters lavished time and affection on "gingerbread" trim for their buildings. Cape May city has found its future by emphasizing its past.

Fishing, farming, and catering to visitors remain the Cape's principal occupations. Commercial fishermen frequent the off-Cape waters, particularly the fleets at Sea Isle City and Wildwood. Sport fishing is an important source of income, and several marinas are thriving stops for boats on the Inland Waterway. Farmlands extend all the way up the western edge of the county and through the northern part.

Cape May County remains a "watering place" of much dignity, particularly in such towns as Avalon, justly proud of its splendid dunes, and Stone Harbor, relying on its "small town" charm. Each year more than five hundred thousand visitors come to stay in the hotels, motels, and cottages scattered up and down the coast. The long, sloping beaches are crowded in spots, but visitors following the Ocean Highway are struck by

This row of Victorian houses in Cape May is only a part of the wealth of nineteenth century architecture in the town. (*The Baltimore Sun*)

No area of the Jersey Shore offers more excitement than the noted amusement park on the boardwalk at North Wildwood. (*Walter Choroszewski*)

the broad areas of as yet undeveloped land. The Cape's uninhabited stretches continue to attract birds (and bird watchers), as all of the Cape maintains its status as one of the country's most important bird havens.

Some of the summer visitors get sand in their shoes, and stay on. It is easy to do—and there is plenty of room.

But room for uneasiness was felt by 1976: so many new-comers had stayed that Cape May seemed destined soon to cease being New Jersey's least-settled county. Salem was nearly in line for the honor—and that came to pass in 1980. Cape May had risen to twentieth among New Jersey's twenty-one counties.

261

VARIETY
IS THE SECRET

There you have New Jersey—as small as its 7,836 square miles, as unbounded as the worldwide market it serves. It is as old as Henry Hudson's *Half Moon*, as new as research in hundreds of modern laboratories; as vibrant as its white sand beaches in the summer sun, as somber as the sooty Newark Meadows in winter's twilight.

Variety is the secret. In a small area that a Texan might consider merely an overgrown ranch, there are mountains, cities, farms, a vast pine woodland, and beaches—all of them well-defined and nationally known. Few states crowd such diversity into 166 airline miles: 166 miles—that's all—from High Point to Cape May.

Obviously New Jersey is progressive. A state forty-sixth in size can't rank high in the nation in research without being alert to twentieth-century demands and techniques. New Jersey is attuned to the twentieth century, but much of the state's fame derives from its exceptional role in the Revolutionary War.

New Jersey is scenic, too, although that is impossible to prove to the millions who each year see the state only from the window of a speeding train or through the windshield of an automobile tearing over a turnpike at speeds well beyond the legal fifty-five miles an hour. Even the Sistine Chapel would not look good at sixty-five miles an hour.

But that's fate: the very highways and railroads that speed through the scenically poor parts of the state also have brought to New Jersey its commercial might. New Jersey's manufacturing performance is fabulous, and that superlative is provable by statistics.

Possibly the most astounding thing about New Jersey urbanization is its concentration close to a relatively narrow corridor stretched between Philadelphia and New York. That accounts for figures that show New Jersey is still only about 30 percent urbanized with the remaining 70 percent in forestland or farmland.

That three-fourths is where New Jersey's future rests, and that future is closing in on the trees and the furrows everywhere.

In North Jersey, research laboratories and handsome new manufacturing plants grow on the hills west of Newark and Elizabeth. Housing developments have mushroomed everywhere since World War II on North Jersey land that since the beginning of colonization had been considered agriculture's domain.

South Jersey, blessed for three hundred years with a million acres of near-wilderness in the noted Pine Barrens, is stirring. Naturalists are busy in the Pines, seeking to document its value and striving to save most of it from blight. Scattered communities such as Lakewood, Hammonton, and Vineland have proved that the Pines offer opportunity that doesn't mean environmental ruin.

New Jersey's future may well rest in the Pine Barrens, scarcely known to millions of people who roll through the region each summer, bound from Wilmington or Philadelphia to the New Jersey Shore. Few of those sun-seekers understand or appreciate the area. Long ago the Pines buzzed with the activity and prosperity of dozens of ironworks and glass manufactories. Since those collapsed in the nineteenth century, the widespread woodland has waited—and waited—for people of character to use the land intelligently, with full allowance for its high natural values.

Down along the lower Delaware River valley, Burlington, Gloucester, and Salem counties are beginning to share in the industrial boom which has overtaken that valley since World War II. That part of New Jersey is in the thick of riverfront industrial development that is likely to alter forever its traditional agricultural tone.

So, New Jersey has a rich heritage, a pleasant today, and the possibility of an exciting, intelligently planned tomorrow. These are the elements that intrigue and please anyone who seeks to understand the state lodged between New York and Philadelphia.

Unfortunately, too many of New Jersey's own residents fail to open their eyes and ears and hearts to that which is close at hand, accepting that their state "is like a barrel, tapped at both ends." There is truth in that, of course, but the pity is that more don't stop to sample the brew still in the barrel.

"Jersey Lightning." It's heady stuff!

INDEX

ABOUT THE
AUTHOR

John T. Cunningham has been a lifelong resident of New Jersey and now lives in Florham Park, New Jersey. He is the author of thirty-three books, including *Newark* (distributed by Rutgers University Press) and over 1,500 magazine articles. Five times a winner of the Award of Merit from the American Association for State and Local History, Mr. Cunningham has served as chairman of the New Jersey Historical Commission, vice chairman of the New Jersey Bicentennial Commission, and president of the New Jersey Historical Society.